Literary
Translation
in
Russia

Literary Translation in Russia

A Cultural History

Maurice Friedberg

The Pennsylvania State University Press
University Park, Pennsylvania

Library of Congress Cataloging-in-Publication Data

Friedberg, Maurice, 1929–
    Literary translation in Russia : a cultural history / Maurice Friedberg.
        p.   cm.
    Includes bibliographical references and index.
    ISBN 978-0-271-02820-0
    1. Translating and interpreting—Russia—History. 2. Translating and interpreting—Soviet Union—History. 3. Literature, Modern —Translations into Russian—History and criticism. 4. Russia —Intellectual life. 5. Soviet Union—Intellectual life.   I. Title.
PN241.5.R8F75   1997
418.01'0947—dc20   96-6726
                                                                                                                       CIP

Copyright © 1997 The Pennsylvania State University
All rights reserved

It is the policy of The Pennsylvania State University Press to use acid-free paper for the first printing of all clothbound books. Publications on uncoated stock satisfy the minimum requirements of American National Standard for Information Sciences— Permanence of Paper for Printed Library Materials, ANSI Z39.48-1992.

Contents

	Acknowledgments	vii
	Introduction	1
1	Historical Background	19
2	Theoretical Controversies	69
3	Plying the Translator's Trade	109
4	Translators and the Literary Process	187
	Index	211

For Rachel the Sabra and Edna the Hoosier

Acknowledgments

This study was launched with the help of a fellowship from the John Simon Guggenheim Memorial Foundation and was completed during my tenure of a fellowship from the National Endowment for the Humanities. A grant from the Hoover Institution enabled me to examine its impressive holdings; and the International Research and Exchanges Board (IREX) made possible a research trip to the Soviet Union. The Research Board of the University of Illinois at Urbana-Champaign, as well as its Scholars' Travel Fund, aided this project at different stages, while the Center for Advanced Study provided some precious released time. I am greatly indebted to all of them.

I am also grateful to my colleagues Michael Shapiro, Karl-Heinz Schoeps, and Emile J. Talbot for their help with questions pertaining, respectively, to English, German, and French literature. It goes without saying that the responsibility for any errors that remain is mine alone.

Introduction

As I look back in time, I realize how many books of my Polish childhood were translations. The fairy tales of Perrault and Hans Christian Andersen were read to me in Polish by my mother. *Huckleberry Finn* was the first book I read all by myself. Then came Robert Louis Stevenson, James Fenimore Cooper, Jack London, and Jules Verne. I also read Karl May, the nineteenth-century German creator of the noble Indian warrior Winnetou, and his contemporary Mayne Reid, an Englishman captivated by the American frontier. Paradoxically, the latter two are quite unknown in the United States, though Mayne Reid's erstwhile fame can be guessed from his obituary in the London *Times* of October 22, 1883, which began, "Every schoolboy, and everyone who has ever been a schoolboy, will learn with sorrow of the death of Captain Mayne Reid." It is also attested by another oblique tribute, Chekhov's short story "The Boys" (1887), which portrays two very young Russians whose excessive devotion to Mayne Reid inspires them to plan a perilous journey to the Wild West, much as Don Quixote's fatal infatuation with courtly romances contributed to his downfall.

The reason for the heavy preponderance of translation in my juvenile reading diet was quite simple. Children's books in my native Polish are relatively scarce—which, as Chekhov demonstrates, is also true of Russian. Indeed, the scarcity continues to exist to this day, along with shortages of decent thrillers, to say nothing of erotic fiction and light entertainment generally. When Chekhov expressed his contempt for the imported "Offenbach confections" that inundated the Russian stage at the turn of the century, he apparently failed to realize that the fault lay with the failure of the Russian dramatists to create an analogous native repertory. In fact, translations are in part a normal market response to insufficient or unsatisfactory domestic literary production. They also benefit from natural curiosity about foreign life and customs (what Soviet sociologists call the "Columbus complex")—a major factor in countries as isolated from the rest of the world as Russia has traditionally been, especially in the Soviet period. These two considerations explain in part the comparatively modest place of translated writings (and also films!) in the high as well as the popular culture of the United States and Western Europe. More subtle reasons, such as the foreign literary work's superior aesthetic merit or intellectual depth, seriously influence only a relatively sophisticated public whose reading preferences tend to be more selective and eclectic.

Literature in the modern sense of the term, indeed secular writing generally, appears in Russia only in the eighteenth century, that is, hundreds of years after Dante, Shakespeare, Cervantes, and Rabelais. One can only wonder how within an astonishingly short time this culturally and otherwise backward nation could produce a body of writing generally recognized as equal to that of the much older and richer literary traditions. The beginnings were understandably hesitant. Two of the early Russian masterpieces, both published in 1833, made reference to the importance of foreign literature to the country's small educated reading public. In Pushkin's "Queen of Spades" the old countess, when offered a novel she might enjoy, inquires incredulously whether Russian novels really exist. They did, but they were not yet very good. In Griboedov's comedy *Woe from Wit* the wealthy bureaucrat Famusov, father of a marriageable daughter, observes that "French books are keeping her awake, while Russian ones put me to sleep." Obviously the aristocratic maiden was reading her French romances in the original, but it is likely that in the case of other languages she had to resort to translations. Some twenty years later the radical critic Nikolai Chernyshevsky confirmed this literary evidence from Pushkin and Griboedov. "Translated literature," he wrote in 1857, "is of enormous importance to us. Until Pushkin it was incomparably more important than original [Russian] writing. And even now it is by no means certain whether original [Russian] writing has become more important than translations."[1] Although some of the world's greatest literature has since been written in Russian, translations have remained important. Except for the xenophobic period of Stalin's rule, Western European and American fiction, poetry, and drama in translation have retained their accustomed place as part and parcel of the reading fare of virtually every Russian who loves books.

Decades of intensive translation of Western European writing refined the tastes of Russia's reading public, provided her writers with models for emulation, and also enriched the literary language, often through simply adopting foreign words, particularly in areas of the lexicon that were lacking in analogous concepts. In the absence of a native tradition of courtly love and chivalrous romance, translations from the French inspired the creation of calques like *liubovnik* from *amant* and *svidanie* from *rendez-vous*. Mikhail Lomonosov, the eighteenth-century scientist and Neoclassical poet, may have been overly hasty when, in an outburst of patriotic pride, he claimed for the Russian language extravagant virtues that it was only beginning to acquire. Russian, in Lomonosov's estimation, possessed "the splendor of Spanish, the liveliness of French, the power of German, the tenderness of Italian, and moreover the richness and exceedingly concise imagery of Greek and Latin. . . . Cicero's mightly eloquence, Virgil's resplendent majesty, and Ovid's agreeable rhetoric lose none of their virtues in the Russian tongue."[2]

The immediate impact on literature of the Communist coup d'état of November 7, 1917, was mixed, but translation fared better than most other areas of literary activity. It benefited because it was viewed as a cultural dimension of "proletarian internationalism." Indeed, translation provided, quite literally, the daily bread for thousands of unemployed and starving

---

1. Iu. D. Levin, *Russkie perevodchiki XIX veka i razvitie khudozhestvennogo perevoda* (Leningrad: Nauka, 1985), p. 4.

2. *Perevod—sredstvo vzaimnogo sblizheniia narodov: Khudozhestvennaia publitsistika* (Moscow: Progress, 1987), p. 402. Lomonosov's statement was inspired by the observation of Charles V, the Holy Roman Emperor, that it befits one to converse in Spanish with God, in French with friends, in German with enemies, and in Italian with the fair sex. This dictum appeared for many years as an epigraph on textbooks of Russian grammar. It was sometimes supplemented with a quotation from the Soviet poet Vladimir Maiakovskii, who provided a simpler reason for studying the language: "Were I even an aging Negro, I would sweep aside doubts and sloth, and learn Russian for the sole reason that this was the language Lenin spoke."

intellectuals. Symptomatic of the early revolutionary enthusiasm was the launching of what was probably the most ambitious single venture in the annals of literary translation within less than a year after the upheaval and with the Civil War still raging.[3] On September 10, 1918, the Soviet government's official newspaper *Izvestiia* announced the inauguration of a project called *Vsemirnaia literatura* (World [or Universal] Literature). This new undertaking was to publish, within a mere three years, 800 volumes and 2,000 pamphlets of translations of Western European and American writing. (The pamphlets, containing a single short story or two or several brief poems, were apparently intended for newly literate readers.) Within a year the scope of the undertaking was expanded to include Oriental literature, and the number of individual books was nearly doubled to 1,500. The guiding spirits of this enterprise were Commissar of Education Anatoly Lunacharsky, representing the Soviet government, and the novelist Maxim Gorky, who acted as spokesman for the authors and publishers. The two men further agreed to sponsor a library of 70,000 translated volumes and to establish a studio for the training of literary translators. Pending the availability of new graduates, *Vsemirnaia Literatura* employed vast numbers of men and women from among the *déclassé* old intelligentsia. The unlucky ones were paid in worthless paper money; the more fortunate, in grain and salted fish. However, the ranks of the translators (and above all, of the project's organizers) dwindled rapidly, mostly as a result of emigration. By 1924 *Vsemirnaia Literatura* had ceased to exist.

Literary translation in the USSR declined further in the 1930s, but underwent a major revival after Stalin's death. In 1979 *Babel,* the journal of translation, informed its readers matter-of-factly that "UNESCO has already affirmed that the Soviet Union is in the lead with respect to the number of translated books."[4] This statement was probably somewhat misleading, because for decades Soviet publishing statistics lumped together books and pamphlets and counted as separate titles reprints, individual volumes from multivolume sets, and translations from and into the scores of minority languages. Nevertheless, there is no question that the old USSR was one of the world's leading publishers of prose, poetry, and drama

---

3. The enterprise was described in an anonymous *samizdat* essay that reached the West in 1982. The essay (along with a parody of the project by Evgeny Zamiatin, the author of the anti-utopian classic *We*), appears in *Pamiat': Istoricheskii sbornik,* 5th ed. (Moscow, 1981; Paris, 1982), pp. 287–314.

4. *Babel,* no. 1 (1979): 3.

translated from foreign languages. In the early 1970s fully 70 percent of all titles printed in the Soviet Union were translations.[5]

By 1980, according to official Soviet statistics, the USSR had published 1,948 translations with an aggregate press run of 129 million copies. These figures included translations from and into the languages of the Soviet minorities. Between 1918 and 1980, more than two hundred foreign authors had been published in more than a million copies each.[6] However, no reliable figures are available for the Gorbachev years (1985–1991), owing to the decentralization of state-owned publishing (particularly in the non-Russian republics) and the emergence of quasi-private "cooperative" publishing. The cooperatives continue to be quite active, printing quite a few translated books, particularly such money-makers as Western European and American thrillers.

During the Soviet period, official pronouncements on the subject of translations often had a jingoistic and self-congratulatory flavor. To cite one fairly typical example:

> Our country firmly occupies the first place in the world in translation of books from all languages. The Soviet Russian school of translation is recognized unconditionally as the world's best. It has reached that status after an embittered struggle with soulless literalism, with affected fashionable Formalism, with the pitiful remnants of decadence, with the schemes and plots [to smuggle in] low-grade hack-work. Our translated book output is the world's best. Hardly anyone questions that.[7]

Unfortunately, private individuals sometimes made similarly propagandistic statements. Thus the respected novelist Chingiz Aitmatov, who wrote in both Kirgiz and Russian and for a time served as editor-in-chief of *Inostrannaia literatura*, the country's foremost journal for the publication of translated writing, stated flatly in 1980 that "nowhere else is literary translation on as high a professional level [as in the USSR]."[8] And the late Lev

---

5. A. Zhovits, "Poeziia, podstrochnik, perevod," *Prostor*, no. 4 (1972): 114. The author was a translator of Korean poetry from interlinear "ponies."

6. Boris Stukalin, then chairman of the State Committee on Publishing, in *Moskovskie novosti*, June 14, 1981.

7. Mirlan Karataev, "Postizhenie originala-uslovie uspekha perevoda," *Prostor* (Alma Ata), no. 8 (1977): 111.

8. Chingiz Aitmatov, *Voprosy literatury*, no. 12 (1980): 4.

Ginzburg, an otherwise subtle and erudite Soviet translator of German poetry, berated Western translators of verse for producing emasculated, lifeless renditions without rhythm or rhymes (a criticism that would invalidate nearly all French translations of poetry from Russian!). He went on to assert, with egregious inaccuracy: "So far, Western readers have no access to either Pushkin, Lermontov, or Blok"—this at a time when four recent renditions of Pushkin's *Eugene Onegin* and seven of Blok's *The Twelve* existed in English alone. One reads with further embarrassment Ginzburg's extravagant comment:

> In such circumstances the Soviet school of literary translation acquires truly global significance. Its healthy [*ozdorovliaiushchee*] impact is beginning to leave its mark on the world literary process. . . . The authority of our school of translation is unquestioned; it is universally recognized, and is acquiring ever more followers. One may state without exaggeration that the Soviet art of literary translation is no less unique, and no less a cause for pride in our culture than, say, the art of ballet.[9]

In reality, the quality of Soviet translation was quite variable, as even some Russians will confirm, at least privately. In the fall of 1990 I myself heard complaints on this score from several professional translators in Moscow. Unqualified amateurs, they said, produce horrid Russian renditions of English and French thrillers—just for the money. Curiously, a number of Soviet émigrés—many of whom had left the USSR owing to dissatisfaction with the regime—seemed to share the official view of Soviet cultural accomplishments. True, they lacked reliable information; but their somewhat idealized picture of Soviet literary translation may also have had a psychological foundation in a need to believe that their country of origin did have some redeeming qualities. Shortly after World War II the Harvard Interview Project established that even the most bitterly anti-Soviet émigrés appeared to take pride in at least one or two features of Soviet society—say, medical care or musical education. In matters cultural, what better candidate for this role than the ostensibly innocuous art of rendering Western writing into Russian, the more so since so many of its practitioners were victims of the regime?

---

9. Lev Ginzburg, *Nad strokoi perevoda: Stat'i raznykh let* (Moscow: Sovetskaia Rossiia, 1981), pp. 3–4.

As both prerevolutionary and Soviet scholars readily acknowledged, most translations in old Russia left much to be desired. The same Soviet scholars, however, seemed to detect no inconsistency in claiming that their school of translation—which continued prerevolutionary Russian traditions—was the world's very best. There may be several reasons for this paradox. The first and most obvious one is that until very recently the Soviet authorities encouraged such boasts. Second, literary translation—as opposed to original Soviet writing—was traditionally viewed as a nonpolitical activity. The tendency for prominent victims of Communist thought control to seek refuge in translation when they were no longer allowed to publish original work—foremost among them Boris Pasternak and Anna Akhmatova—served to strengthen this belief. Very few readers were aware that Soviet translations of Western writing were routinely censored, and that offending passages, mostly disrespectful references to Communism and the USSR as well as overly frank portrayals of sex, were suppressed. Victims of this censorship ranged from Hemingway to Le Carré and from Alan Sillitoe to Gore Vidal. Matters have vastly improved since the era of *glasnost'* in the late 1980s. Such anticommunist classics as George Orwell's *1984* and *Animal Farm* have been published, as has Henry Miller's *Tropic of Cancer*.[10]

Polemics about the feasibility of translation are probably as old as the art itself, and even serious philosophers have entered the discussion. John Locke (1632–1704) argued that translation is quite impossible in the final analysis because different cultures do not always possess the same concepts. Conversely, David Hume (1711–76) insisted that even languages far removed from one another possess terms to describe the same simple ideas, which demonstrated, in his opinion, that such ideas have a degree of universality. However, the writer and critic John B. Priestley (1894–1984) disputed this argument, maintaining that words in different languages do not have the same meaning when used metaphorically, that is, in a literary context.[11] Similarly the Italian philosopher Benedetto Croce (1866–1952)

---

10. See Maurice Friedberg, *A Decade of Euphoria: Western Literature in Post-Stalin Russia* (Bloomington: Indiana University Press, 1977), pp. 16–57, and *The Red Pencil: Artists, Scholars, and Censors in the USSR*, ed. Marianna Tax Choldin and Maurice Friedberg (Boston: Unwin Hyman, 1989), pp. 21–28. G. Egorov's Russian translation of Henry Miller's *Tropic of Cancer* (*Tropik raka*) was published in New York in 1964 by Grove Press. The same rendition, with particularly offensive obscenities softened, appeared in Russia a quarter of a century later in *Inostrannaia literatura*, nos. 7 and 8 (1990).

11. Stephen K. Land, "Universalism and Relativism: A Philosophical Problem in Translation in the Eighteenth Century," *Journal of the History of Ideas* 35 (October–December 1974): 597–600, 604–5.

held that translation is quite impossible because "that which has already acquired an aesthetic form cannot be reduced to another form that is equally aesthetic."[12]

Misgivings about the effectiveness of translation will probably never cease. Indeed, they are striking in their similarity. The quip attributed to Rabelais (c. 1490–1553), who held that a translation, like a woman, is unfaithful when beautiful and faithful when homely, resurfaced in our own time when Isaac Bashevis Singer, a Yiddish novelist who regularly collaborated in the translation of his own works, declared that "a translation, like a woman, can be true and faithful and still miserable."[13] The statement of Friedrich Schlegel (1772–1829) that "the best is what gets lost in your run-of-the-mill good or excellent translation" became better known in contemporary America as Robert Frost's alleged definition of poetry as "that which gets lost in translation."[14] Significantly, George Steiner's observation in 1975 to the effect that "whatever treatise on the art of translation we look at, the same dichotomy is stated: as between 'letter' and 'spirit,' 'word' and 'sense' "[15] applies even to distant antiquity. In 46 B.C. Cicero wrote: "I did not translate . . . as an interpreter but as an orator . . . not . . . word for word (*verbum pro verbo*); but I preserved the general style and force of the language."[16] More recently, "force of the language" was a favorite concept in Boris Pasternak's translating aesthetics!

The fact of the matter is that literary translation is but one kind of *interpretation* of the text, and as such it is necessarily *subjective,* even if the rendition from one language to another is as rigorously literalist as the grammar and usage of the target language will allow. Precisely for this reason, a translation is not viewed as "sacred" — even if the original text is so regarded. Thus the Bible is periodically retranslated into different languages. As one commentator remarked: "If the poet, in Valéry's concep-

---

12. In *Problèmes litteraires de la traduction: Textes des conferences presentées au cours d'un seminaire organisé pendant l'année academique 1973–74,* Bibliothèque de l'université de Louvain (Belgique) (Leiden [Pays-Bas]): E. J. Brill, 1975), p. 58.

13. *The World of Translation,* papers delivered at the Conference on Literary Translation, New York City, May 1970, under the auspices of P.E.N. American Center (New York, 1971), p. 111 (hereafter cited as *World of Translation*).

14. André Lefevere, *Translating Literature: The German Tradition from Luther to Rosenzweig* (Amsterdam: Van Gorcum, Assen, 1977), p. 59.

15. George Steiner, *After Babel: Aspects of Language and Translation* (New York and London: Oxford University Press, 1975), p. 262.

16. *Libellus de optimo genere oratorum* 4.14; in Reuben A. Brower, ed., *On Translation* (Cambridge: Harvard University Press, 1959), p. 274.

tion, translated ordinary discourse into the language of the gods, our critics translate the language of the gods back into ordinary discourse."[17] Levon Mkrtchian, a Soviet Armenian scholar, noted perceptively:

> Not even the most faithful of translations can be "absolutely exact" and coincide with the original in every respect. . . . [A] translation may be inferior to the original, at times even in some important respects. In practice, however, it serves as a substitute for the original. (It may, for example, contribute to the fame of the original, or stimulate new and unexpected interpretations.) *A translation is possible and necessary precisely because it differs from the original, because it is not the original.*[18]

Furthermore, literary tastes evolve. When people who are able to read a text in the original no longer find it attractive (for whatever reason) they simply cast it aside, often temporarily: the pendulum of taste may in time swing back again. But we all accept the original as in some sense *permanent*. Translation is another matter. It is "interpretation." When one interpretation no longer suits us, it can and should be supplanted with another. Similarly, texts written in an early form of a language occasionally need to be brought up-to-date, such as *Beowulf* rendered into modern English, or *The Lay of the Host of Igor* into contemporary Russian. (Several versions of the latter exist.) New translations become necessary when the gap between the language and cultural associations of the original text and those of the target language has become too wide. In my view, Allen Tate was right in suggesting that ideally each age needs to render the classics anew. Admittedly, not everyone sees the point of this. The Pakistani poet Zulfikar Ghose was puzzled by the idea of obsolescence in translation, saying: "I find it curious that Homer remains Homer all the time. But each of his translators is doomed to become out of date. And I find it very curious that we can still read Alexander Pope with great pleasure, but very few of us read his translations with any pleasure."[19]

---

17. Smith Palmer Bovie, in *The Craft and Context of Translation*, ed. William Arrowsmith and Roger Shattuck (Austin: The University of Texas Press, Humanities Research Center, 1961), p. 51.
18. Levon Mkrtchian, *Voprosy literatury*, no. 5 (1979): 18.
19. Allen Tate, *The Translation of Poetry* (Washington, D.C.: The Gertrude Clarke Whittall Poetry and Literature Fund, 1972), p. 17.

Without question the influence of translation on the literary process is enormous. Translation can expand manyfold the number of readers for authors writing in languages with comparatively few native speakers, such as Icelandic, Flemish, or Danish. Most of Milan Kundera's admirers do not read him in the original Czech, and hardly any devotees of Isaac Bashevis Singer know his work in Yiddish. Ibsen's plays are classics of world drama, as are Strindberg's, but only a minority of their performances are in Norwegian or Swedish. Literary translation can, in fact, bestow immortality on works written in languages no longer spoken. Homer and Virgil and Sophocles have outlived their original languages. Hardly any Christians read the Old Testament in Hebrew or the New Testament in Greek.

Surprisingly, translations are occasionally found useful even by persons well able to read the originals. This is because a competent translation is also a commentary that enables the reader to see the original in a new light. For example:

> Lev Nikolaevich Tolstoy wrote on one occasion that the magic perfection of Pushkin's dramatic poem "The Gypsies" became apparent to him only upon reading the poem in French. A comparison of the original with the translation unexpectedly unfolded to him hitherto unnoticed aesthetic qualities of an overly familiar Russian text. The translation became the mirror which enabled Tolstoy to see those features of the original which he was unable to notice earlier.[20]

In a similar vein, Lev Ginzburg reported:

> Russian-speaking Englishmen confess that after reading Samuil Marshak's [Russian] translations, they began to see Robert Burns in a new light: they got to like him for different reasons. Russian readers perceive [François] Villon's poetry more vividly and in a sharper focus than a Frenchman who reads him in the original. A modern translator of poetry enjoys a number of advantages over an author who lived two or three hundred years ago. He speaks in modern idiom, and is "technologically" better equipped. He is

---

20. Grigorii Lenkov, "Priblizhaias' k Pushkinu," *Inostrannaia literatura,* no. 12 (1977): 227.

backed by several generations of verse honed and grown more perfect over the centuries.[21]

Germans have long justly prided themselves on their renditions of Shakespeare. Thus the publisher Alois Brandl wrote: "In our classical translation [of Shakespeare] by Schlegel-Tieck the meaning is put forth so clearly that when I had to reprint it in a popular edition, there was sometimes not even one passage to be explained in a whole play—so perfectly had the Tudor words been recast in lucid and up-to-date German." Accordingly, Brandl could argue that a German reader or playgoer might understand Shakespeare better than "a Londoner, who has no other choice than to take him in the original."[22]

A more extreme case is that of Goethe, who wrote to Gérard de Nerval, the French translator of *Faust,* "Never before did I understand myself as well as I did while reading your translation."[23] In fact, he declared, "I no longer want to reread *Faust* in German, but in French everything impresses me again. It seems fresh, new, and timely."[24] And in 1825 Goethe told Eckermann that *Hermann and Dorothea* was almost the only one among his long poems that continued to bring him joy: "I like it especially in Latin translation. It appears nobler in Latin."[25]

Certain American writers also owe much of their fame to translation. Edgar Allan Poe is a case in point. In the view of critic Dudley Fitts, "Poe may not be much to begin with, but he takes on a real authority in a foreign tongue."[26] He does indeed. Poe has long been both popular and influential in Russia, like another American, author Jack London, who also "may not be much to begin with" in his homeland.[27] Yuri D. Levin, a leading Soviet specialist on literary translation, explained this phenomenon as follows:

> The foreign perception reflects a sense of distance and perspective. It enables us at times to see what one does not notice at close range.... [An example is] Sinclair Lewis, who upon reading an

21. Ginzburg, *Nad strokoi perevoda*, pp. 20–21.
22. Newton P. Stallknecht and Horst Frenz, eds., *Comparative Literature: Method and Perspective* (Carbondale: Southern Illinois University Press, 1961), p. 73.
23. Lenkov, "Priblizhaias' k Pushkinu," pp. 228–29.
24. Lev A. Anninskii, comp., *Khudozhestvennyi perevod: Problemy i suzhdeniia* (Moscow: Izvestiia, 1986), p. 367.
25. Ibid.
26. Brower, *On Translation*, p. 33.
27. For an informative account, see Joan Delaney Grossman, *E. A. Poe in Russia* (Wurzburg, 1973).

English translation of *Fathers and Sons,* discerned in Bazarov the "prototype of the innovator and radical of all time." We [Russians], on the other hand, could not see that. The universality of Bazarov was concealed from us by its concrete interpretation, which was influenced by the social conflicts in Russia during the 1860s. It was no accident that [the poet] Gumilev noted on one occasion, "To truly understand a poet, one should read all of his translations into foreign languages."[28]

Lev Ginzburg's unjustified implication that the Russian love for Western writing was not being reciprocated (and that this was grossly unfair) was symptomatic of the highly politicized atmosphere of Soviet literature. Interestingly, Fedor Dostoevsky had voiced very similar grievances over a century earlier, with much more justification, in *The Diary of a Writer.* Foreigners, he wrote in 1873, will never understand Gogol, Pushkin, or Turgenev; therefore "all our major authors may well remain completely unknown in Europe for many years. Indeed, the greatest and most original among them will remain unrecognized the longest." (He was proven wrong, of course, but that is another matter.) Dostoevsky considered his fellow Russians far superior to Westerners in their understanding of foreign cultures, stating:

> I am convinced, we understand Dickens in Russia almost as well as the English do, perhaps even with all the nuances. It may well be that we love him no less than his compatriots do. And yet, how original is Dickens, and how very English! What, then, must one conclude from that? Is this understanding of other nations a special gift that the Russians possess to a higher degree than [other] Europeans? A special gift this may well be. And if this gift does exist (just as the gift of speaking foreign languages, which they possess indeed in a higher degree than any [other] Europeans), then it is extraordinarily significant, and bodes much for the Russians.

While praising his countrymen's allegedly superior understanding, Dostoevsky also feared that their receptivity to foreign cultures was dangerous. Analogous cultural misgivings often haunted Russia's rulers and thinkers in the decades that followed. Seemingly these doubts have been a perma-

---

28. *Khudozhestvennyi perevod: Voprosy teorii i praktiki* (Erevan: Izdatel'stvo Erevanskogo universiteta, 1982), p. 30.

nent fixture of the country's intellectual landscape ever since the reforms of Peter the Great (r. 1689–1725). At issue was the dilemma of how to modernize Russia (including its culture) without eroding its fundamental values and beliefs. As cultural imports, translations inevitably were carriers of alien ideas and often were inimical to the attitudes the country's spiritual and political leaders wished to foster. This fear of foreign influence explains Imperial Russia's censorship of translated literary works as well as the infinitely more rigid Soviet censorship, which, until just a few years ago, prevented the publication of such ostensibly apolitical writers as Joyce, Proust, and Kafka, to say nothing of Camus, Huxley, and Orwell. Dostoevsky's own misgivings were probably not permanently resolved, although when he returned to the subject of translations in 1876, patriotic pride apparently overshadowed his doubts:

> I maintain, indeed I insist, that every [Western] European poet, thinker and lover of humanity will—except in his homeland—be best understood and most eagerly accepted in Russia. Always in Russia—more than anywhere else in the world. Shakespeare, Byron, Walter Scott, and Dickens are closer to Russians, and Russians understand them better than, say, the Germans [do]. And that in spite of the fact that we don't sell even a tenth of the number of copies of these writers' translations that are sold in book-rich Germany.

The French, Dostoevsky wrote, were entirely different in character. In 1793 they conferred honorary citizenship on Schiller, a noble gesture, to be sure. Yet though the German poet was officially designated *ami de l'humanité*, the only Frenchmen who knew his work were a few professors of literature, while in Russia, through Zhukovsky's translations, "he entered the Russian soul, left his imprint on it, and very nearly became a milestone in our [spiritual] history."[29]

Notwithstanding the importance of translation in the literary process and in the international cultural traffic, most writings on the subject are little more than chatty reminiscences and anecdotes. The light tone of these publications creates an impression that the study of translation is unworthy of serious scholarly attention. According to André Lefevere, the author of an important book on the subject: "[This attitude] has made the study of translation seem a 'slight' if not altogether disreputable pursuit, worthy

---

29. *Perevod—sredstvo vzaimnogo sblizheniia narodov*, pp. 68–70.

perhaps (and at this point the workings of the vicious circle become apparent) of an article in a more or less bantering vein, but certainly nothing else."[30] Presumably that same prejudice contributed to the situation described in 1963 by the late Czech scholar Jiří Levý, a specialist in translation studies: "Thus far not a single [national] literature has produced major studies of [literary] translation, even though no history of literature can be considered complete without a historical and literary analysis of this species of literary creation."[31]

As already suggested, the importance of literary translation in Russian culture can hardly be overestimated. To cite only a few telling figures, Goethe's "Mignon" was translated fifteen times between 1817 and 1978, not counting the two poems by Pushkin that merely use Goethe's motifs.[32] A 1958 Soviet bibliography listed 4,300 Russian renditions of 700 original texts of Heinrich Heine by 280 Russian translators.[33] A bibliography of Russian translations of American writing and of relevant Russian literary criticism, published on the bicentennial of American independence, lists 7,500 entries![34] Translators of Western writing include some of Russia's most famous authors. Soviet press runs of translations reached astronomical figures; and the impact of translations on the shaping of Russian literature has been immense. Translations have traditionally figured prominently among hard-to-obtain books.[35] All the same, the history of translation in Russia has been little studied. In 1968 one Soviet scholar referred to

30. André Lefevere, *Translating Poetry: Seven Strategies and a Blueprint* (Amsterdam: Van Gorcum, Assen, 1975), p. 2.
31. Irzhi Levyi [Jiří Levý], *Iskusstvo perevoda*, trans. Vl. Rossel'sa (Moscow: Progress, 1974), pp. 231–32. The Czech original appeared in 1963 and a German translation in 1969.
32. A list appears in J. Douglas Clayton, "The Russian *Mignons*: A Study in the Poetics of Translation," *Canadian Slavonic Papers* 23 (March 1981): 3–4.
33. A. G. Levinton, *G. Geine, Bibliografiia* (Moscow, 1958). The information is found in German Ritz, *150 Jahre russischer Heine-Übersetzung* (Bern, Frankfurt am Main, and Las Vegas: Peter Lang, 1981), p. 19. The very large number of renditions by different hands and over a long span of time enabled Ritz to examine them as a case study in an overall history of Russian literary translation. See *150 Jahre*, p. 17.
34. V. A. Libman, *Amerikanskaia literatura v russkikh perevodakh i kritike: Bibliografiia, 1776–1975* (Moscow: Nauka, 1977).
35. In 1974, Soviet citizens were allowed to exchange forty-four pounds of scrap paper for one copy of any one of nine hard-to-get books. Of the nine only three were Russian: the comic novel *The Twelve Chairs* by Il'f and Petrov, and two science fiction works with elements of social anti-utopia, Aleksei N. Tolstoy's *Aelita* and *Engineer Garin's Hyperboloid*. The other six were translations: two volumes of Hans Christian Andersen's fairy tales, *The Hound of the Baskervilles* by Arthur Conan Doyle, *The Woman in White* by Wilkie Collins, *The Maigret Stories* by Georges Simenon, and *Queen Margot* by Alexandre Dumas. See Friedberg, *A Decade of Euphoria*, pp. 58–81.

the whole field as "a researcher's virgin territory [*tselina*]."[36] Analogous sentiments were echoed a decade later by Mykola Bazhan, a leading Soviet Ukrainian author.[37] Yuri D. Levin, the chief Soviet authority on the subject, suggested in 1963 that the writing of the first history of translation in Russia would be impeded by the dearth of investigations into the evolution of translation theory.[38] The situation had scarcely changed more than twenty years later when he wrote: "There have been a number of attempts to relate, in its entirety, the history of translation in our country. . . . *Because of their brevity, however, these articles can only be viewed as preliminary outlines.*"[39]

Originally it was my intention to write a history of literary translation in Russia during the Soviet period alone, as a companion piece to my earlier books, *Russian Classics in Soviet Jackets* (1962) and *A Decade of Euphoria: Western Literature in Post-Stalin Russia* (1977). The resulting monograph was to include a study of the broader subject of non-Soviet literatures in Soviet society and of alien "bourgeois" culture in a "socialist" state. As my research progressed, it became increasingly apparent that the prerevolutionary roots of Soviet translation theory and practice had to be probed as well and compared with literary translation as it had evolved in the West. The "Russian" part of this study represents the first attempt to consider the subject in English, while the "Western" portion may prove of particular interest to Russian readers. Mine is thus in many ways a pioneering effort. Its shortcomings are the ones characteristic of such undertakings. As the Russians say, "Pervyi blin vsegda komom" [The first pancake always comes out lumpy]. Its usefulness, however, is ordinarily acknowledged.

The four chapters that follow emphasize the ideological dimension in Russia of a literary pursuit that is elsewhere not considered particularly susceptible to political pressures. Chapter 1 discusses the ambivalence of the country's officialdom as well as its opponents toward an activity that, however praiseworthy culturally and useful to the cause of modernization, presented some serious problems. Specifically, the publication of literary

36. A. Shor, "Iz istorii sovetskogo perevoda (Stefan Tsveig na russkom iazyke)," *Tetradi perevodchika*, no. 5 (1968): 53.
37. *Edinstvo: Sbornik statei o mnogonatsional'noi sovetskoi literature*, 3d ed. (Moscow: Khudozhestvennaia literatura, 1977), p. 52.
38. Iu. D. Levin, "Ob istoricheskoi evoliutsii printsipov perevoda (K istorii perevodcheskoi mysli v Rossii)," in *Mezhdunarodnye sviazi russkoi literatury*, ed. M. P. Alekseev (Moscow and Leningrad: Izdatel'stvo Akademiia Nauk SSSR, 1963), p. 6.
39. Levin, *Russkie perevodchiki*, pp. 4–5; emphasis added.

translations in an isolationist absolute monarchy (and, later, in an even more isolationist Communist dictatorship) resulted in the dissemination of books that were, inevitably, carriers of alien Western values. This ambivalence toward foreign cultures helps explain why translations in Soviet Russia were traditionally a reliable barometer of the country's political moods. They benefited from periods of relative ideological tolerance and suffered during years of xenophobia and political witch-hunts.

Chapter 2 reviews the debate between partisans of literal translation, who aimed at retaining maximal fidelity to the form and content of the original text, and their foes, who maintained that preservation of the original's "spirit" justified the sacrifice of its less important features. That such differences could even have theological implications was demonstrated as early as the Middle Ages, when Christian theologians accused the Jews of obstinacy for their insistence on word-for-word precision in translations of the Hebrew Bible. Accordingly, Jewish "literalism" allegedly concealed a refusal to recognize the legitimacy of christological speculation, which discerned in the Old Testament a prophecy of the advent of Christ. Theology aside, partisans of free renditions in Western Europe dominated translation during the ascendancy of Neoclassicism when standards of aristocratic decorum were imposed on texts of "barbarian" origin. (Voltaire's opinion of Shakespeare is a telling case in point. "Civilized" renditions of Homer are another.) By contrast, the Romantics showed greater curiosity about other times and customs and displayed less assurance about their own civilization—attitudes conducive to literalism. Finally, "free" translation benefited from the rapid growth of a superficially educated reading public in the latter part of the nineteenth century.

Russian debates on the subject of "free" versus "literal" translations generally followed Western European patterns, and the two approaches coexisted more or less peacefully until the eve of World War II. It was then that Soviet translators were informed that elitist literalism is but a manifestation of literary Formalism and, accordingly, outside the pale. One reason for the decree was no doubt the fact that "free" translation justified minor censorship of foreign literary texts. Disrespectful quips about the USSR or Communism by characters in foreign novels or plays could simply be omitted as "unessential." Curiously, the official approval of "free" translation was welcomed by such great poets as Boris Pasternak, who were then unable to publish original work and for whom translation served as sublimation for their creative impulse. Between the end of World War II and the advent of *glasnost'* and *perestroika* under Gorbachev in the late 1980s, no public defense of literalism was possible.

In contrast to Western Europe, where few major authors were translators, in Russia, as related in Chapter 3, nearly all important nineteenth-century poets and writers of prose did at least some translating. A few, like the poet Zhukovsky, were, indeed, leading translators; others, like Dostoevsky, began their literary careers by doing translations. Many prominent Russian translators were important government officials. Their conservative politics contrasted with the attitude of a significant number of professional translators of plebeian origin. The latter attempted to disseminate Western writing of iconoclastic bent, such as the poetry of Heinrich Heine. Obviously, no such personal predilections could be openly expressed during the Soviet period, when translation, as already suggested, became a refuge for major authors in disfavor. The profession thus attracted a disproportionate number of men and, especially, women with politically dubious backgrounds, such as Jews or former inmates of Soviet prisons. Conversely, few professional translators were Communist Party members.

Finally, Chapter 4 examines the impact of translations on the literary process. Translations were a boon to Russian authors in the eighteenth and early nineteenth century, serving as models for emulation to writers who were only beginning to create a secular Russian literature. To a lesser extent, translations continued to play that role in later periods by introducing new genres and poetic meters to Russian writing. They also facilitated the transplantation to Russian soil of Western aesthetics and, indeed, literary schools. Thus Russian Symbolism and Futurism owed much to translations, just as Neoclassicism and Romanticism had done earlier. The country's readers were profoundly affected by many of the values contained in translated Western writing. In the nineteenth century, these values frequently reinforced the message of Russian authors; the social compassion of Dickens and Hugo comes to mind. In the twentieth century, the message contained in Russian renditions of Western prose, drama, and verse often implicitly contradicted the values championed in Soviet literature. (The disclaimers of Soviet critical introductions, which insisted that the injustices denounced in these foreign books occured in capitalist conditions alone, were rarely very convincing.) Through translations Soviet readers were exposed to such concerns of twentieth-century authors as Remarque's and Hemingway's denunciations of war, Dreiser's exposés of economic injustice, or the refusal of the new generation of writers to accept the values by which its fathers had lived (for example: Salinger and Britain's Angry Young Men). It is my contention that the translation of such books (and, to a lesser degree, the staging of plays by Arthur Miller and Tennessee Williams or the showing of Italian and French films) contributed over the years to the erosion of Soviet pieties that ultimately led to the collapse of the USSR in 1991. During the Soviet period, Russian renditions of foreign writing also helped sustain men and women who were skeptical of official assurances that the social ills and psychological malaise depicted in these imported books had no relevance to their own grievances and aspirations. In a very real sense, these literary translations served as bridges to the West that transcended political barriers.

1

Historical Background

Translation is an ancient art. A very famous early translation project was the Greek rendition of the Hebrew Bible, undertaken between 285 and 244 B.C. and known as the Septuagint after the seventy men who labored on it. Additional religious texts undoubtedly were translated in the Jewish diaspora as a result of linguistic acculturation and assimilation. However, the world's earliest known *literary* translation was apparently Livius Andronicus's Latin verse rendition of Homer's *Odyssey,* completed about 250 B.C.[1] Somewhat later, the translation of Greek plays into Latin was partly responsible for introducing hexameter verse to Rome. Major Roman authors like Cicero and Catullus were frequent translators from Greek. Although many educated Romans knew Greek, in the time of the Roman empire many Greek works were translated into Latin and, less frequently, Latin works into Greek.[2]

---

1. Reuben A. Brower, ed., *On Translation* (Cambridge: Harvard University Press, 1959), p. 271.
2. Theodore Savory, *The Art of Translation* (London: Jonathan Cape, 1957), p. 37.

The beginnings of translation in Russia are more difficult to pinpoint. The acceptance of Christianity in Kievan Rus' in the late tenth century is rightly claimed as the defining event in the establishment of the three East Slavic nations: Russia, Ukraine, and Belarus. Their three distinct languages, however, emerged only gradually out of the unified Slavonic tongue spoken by the Eastern Slavs in the tenth century.* Translations into Old Slavonic certainly antedate the baptism of Vladimir (circa 988), the first Christian prince to rule Kiev.[3] The process began in the 860s with the mission of the Byzantine missionaries Cyril and Methodius, who developed an alphabet for Old Slavonic as it was then spoken by the bulk of the non-Greek population in the Balkan peninsula. Many religious works were translated from Greek into Slavonic in the tenth century under the Bulgarian empire of Tsar Simeon (r. 893–927). With the conversion to Christianity of Kievan Rus', these existing translations were copied for use among the Eastern Slavs, who spoke a dialect still close enough to that of the South Slavs to make these texts understandable.

While the spoken language evolved over the centuries, the written form of Old Slavonic survived as the liturgical language known as Old Church Slavonic. Translations and adaptations of Greek religious literature into Old Church Slavonic proliferated in Russia down to the seventeenth century. These included not only Byzantine hagiographical works, such as the popular lives of saints, but also romances and chivalrous literature and even religious writings belonging to non-Christian traditions, such as the life story of the Buddha and Flavius Josephus's *The Jewish War*. Greek-Slavonic dictionaries of sorts evidently were produced in medieval Russia as early as the eleventh century. However, all of this activity was haphazard, sporadic, and to use a modern locution, quite unprofessional. Even in the reign of Peter the Great in the early eighteenth century, many translations were produced by clerks from the Foreign Office because of their command of languages and (apparently) not overly onerous work load.[4]

Some of the nations that were eventually annexed to the Russian empire — in particular Georgia and Armenia — had much more venerable traditions of translation than the Slavs did. In fact, every October the Armenians still

---

*Old Slavonic was a spoken language, unlike Old Church Slavonic, which was and remains the written and liturgical language of the Eastern Orthodox Church in Slavic-speaking countries and in other places where Slavic populations have settled. The designations "Old Slavonic," "Old Church Slavonic," and "Old Bulgarian" are often used interchangeably.

3. M. I. Rizhskii, *Istoriia perevodov Biblii v Rosii* (Novosibirsk: Nauka, 1978), pp. 23–24.

4. M. P. Alekseev, "Problema khudozhestvennogo perevoda," in *Sbornik trudov Irkutskogo gosudarstvennogo universiteta*, vol. 18, no. 1 (Irkutsk: Izdanie Irkutskogo universiteta, 1931), pp. 172–73.

observe a Translator's Day—a holiday established in the first half of the fifth century A.D.[5] Centuries before translation into Russia began, an Armenian manuscript dating from the year 1240 described one translator as follows: "He had the gift of translating and always studied the writings of other nations. Whenever he encountered anything useful and not to be found in other literatures, he would diligently translate it himself, and also enlist in that task other translators."[6]

Yet it was from Western Europe (occasionally via Poland) that literary translation came to Russia; and the models emulated were Western. But it was not until the eighteenth century that *literary* translation made its appearance. Once introduced, it developed by leaps and bounds—so much so that by 1811 the first book appeared which discussed problems of Russian translation technique, "especially in respect to poetry." Characteristically, although the book was by a Russian and printed in St. Petersburg, it was written in French, the language of the educated aristocracy.[7] By the mid-nineteenth century, literary translation had become so firmly established in Russia that the earlier observations made by the Romantic poet and novelist Novalis (1772–1801) concerning Germany seem fully applicable to Russia as well:

> We Germans have been translating for a long time, and the desire to translate appears to be a national characteristic, since there is hardly a German writer of importance who has not translated, and who does not take as much pride in his translations as he does in his original works; and yet there seems to be nothing we know less about than—translation. Except for the Romans, we are the only nation which has felt the urge to translate so irrepressibly, and whose culture owes so immeasurably much to translation.[8]

Martin Luther's German New Testament dates back to 1522, and his Old Testament to 1534. William Tindale's work on an English Bible began

---

5. *Khudozhestvennyi perevod: Vzaimodeistvie i vzaimoobogashchenie literatur* (Erevan: Izdatel'stvo Erevanskogo universiteta, 1973), p. 95.

6. Ibid., p. 93.

7. Brower, *On Translation*, p. 275. Prince B. V. Golitsyn's treatise was titled *Reflexions sur les traducteurs russes*. The first Russian-language attempt at a systematic discussion of translation problems in Russia appeared only a full century later, an indication of the extreme scholarly neglect of the subject. It was by F. Batiushkov, K. Chukovskii, and N. Gumilev, *Printsipy khudozhestvennogo perevoda* (Petrograd, 1919). See Brower, *On Translation*, p. 280.

8. André Lefevere, *Translating Literature: The German Tradition from Luther to Rosenzweig* (Amsterdam: Van Gorcum, Assen, 1977), p. 65.

at approximately the same time; and the King James version appeared in 1611. According to one calculation, by the time printing was invented some five hundred years ago, parts of the Bible had already appeared in thirty-three languages; and by the beginning of the nineteenth century this number had increased to seventy-one.[9] However, Russia parted company with Western Europe in the very late appearance of a Russian (as distinct from Old Slavonic) rendition of the complete Bible. This delay, coupled with the very suspicious attitudes toward unauthorized Russian Bibles printed in non-Orthodox Western Europe, severely restricted the circulation of Biblical texts. As a consequence, the Bible had a relatively modest impact on the subsequent fortunes of Russian letters.

Although the Eastern Slavs were converted to Christianity at the end of the tenth century, not a single translation of the entire Bible into either Old Slavonic—the ancestor of all the modern Slavic languages—or into its medieval Russian descendant existed even as late as the fourteenth century. Only some renditions of individual books of the New Testament were extant (with a very few from the Old Testament). These contained many inaccuracies, some of them apparently *intentional*.[10] (As is well known, willful mistranslations of religious texts are usually a sign of heretical thought and sometimes even incipient schism.) Awareness of these dangers probably explains the suspicion with which Russian ecclesiastical authorities viewed translations of the Bible that were produced abroad.

The Psalms were translated in the fifteenth century into Church Slavonic from a Greek translation of the Hebrew. The translator was Kiprian (or Cyprian), metropolitan of All Russia, who (according to a later Russian source) apparently knew little Greek, and whose grasp of Church Slavonic was not only insufficient, but also betrayed his Bulgarian origin. At approximately the same time a convert from Judaism named Fedor, the protégé of Metropolitan Filip, translated the Psalms from the original Hebrew. His knowledge of Slavonic was also inadequate to the task; and like Kiprian, he allowed his Slavic vernacular to intrude into his Church Slavonic.* Finally in 1552 Maksim the Greek, famous for the "correction of the books" which later contributed to the schism of Old Belief in Russia, made another Slavic translation of the Psalms from Greek. (It is likely that

---

*By the fifteenth century the various Slavic vernaculars had deviated considerably from the comparatively unified spoken language which had formed the basis for the earliest translations into Old Slavonic in the ninth and tenth centuries.

9. Eugene Nida in Brower, *On Translation*, p. 11.
10. Rizhskii, *Istoriia perevodov Biblii v Rossii*, pp. 55, 45, 73, 111, 117, 123, 128–32, 139, 155, 183–86.

Tsar Peter the Great's later decree ordaining that translators render texts only into their *native* languages was inspired in part by these previous unsatisfactory efforts.)

The first Church Slavonic edition of the entire Bible appeared in Moscow in 1663. Though not yet in the spoken form of Russian—which diverged significantly from Old Slavonic—it represented an improvement over the previous state of affairs. The complete Bible was now at least partly understandable to speakers of the vernacular. The first *Russian* translation of the Bible was begun in 1683, though the project was soon abandoned due to the death of the translator, the Lutheran pastor Ernst Glück. A new version of the Slavonic Bible was commissioned by Peter the Great, with the text to be checked against the Septuagint. Peter himself (d. 1725) did not live to see it. Not published until 1751, this new Bible was not accepted by the Church as authoritative; and subsequent Russian biblical exegesis was never based on this version alone. No new Russian translation was undertaken until the British Bible Society (founded in 1804) helped organize a sister society in Russia in 1813. Tsar Alexander I favored producing a Russian Bible, as did Prince A. N. Golitsyn, procurator of the Holy Synod and minister of religious affairs and education. The Synod itself refused to cooperate. Nevertheless, by 1824 the Russian Bible Society had completed work on the entire New Testament and parts of the Old (the Pentateuch, the Psalms, and the Books of Ruth, Judges, and Joshua). The Russian text was printed parallel to the Church Slavonic—apparently a concession to ecclesiastic conservatives.

The penetration of English, French, and German Bibles into Russia, together with the dissemination of unauthorized Russian Bibles, pointed up a number of textual disparities among the various translations. These discrepancies produced a degree of religious ferment, including the controversy surrounding a new Russian translation of the Bible by Gerasim Petrovich Pavsky. Pavsky was attacked for rendering the Hebrew term *mashiah* as well as the Greek *hristos* as "anointed" (*pomazannik*), thus allegedly "destroying" a biblical prophecy. Christian believers traditionally had understood the prophecy of the coming of *hristos* as a reference to the actual name of Jesus Christ (in Russian, *Iisus Khristos*). Since Pavsky had obviously been influenced by Protestant Bible scholarship, he was ultimately forced to recant. The Holy Synod's own Russian translation of the Bible dates from 1876. In 1952 the American Bible Society issued a Bible in Russian that the Moscow Patriarchate found objectionable as allegedly influenced by Protestantism. A new Russian Bible authorized by the Patriarchate came out in 1956.

The Holy Synod's Russian-language Bible appeared too late to influence Russian literature during its formative years in the eighteenth century. Indeed, when the Russian Bible Society's New Testament came out in 1824, Pushkin was already a mature poet. Russia also was untouched by two other processes that in the West provided a powerful impetus to the development of translation: the Renaissance and the Reformation. By contrast, in neighboring Poland—a Slavic country but a Roman Catholic one—translations were a weapon of the rationalists in the sixteenth and seventeenth centuries in their struggles against the archconservative gentry. Łukasz Górnicki's *Dworzanin*, ostensibly a translation of Castiglione's *The Courtier*, was really an adaptation modified to appeal to Polish readers.[11] The lateness of the arrival of a Russian Bible left a permanent void in Russian letters, observable even in translations of modern Anglo-American writing. However, the theories and practices that antedate the arrival of literary translation in Russia had an impact that was ultimately felt, if only relatively briefly. Therefore it is worth summarizing some of their salient features.

In the Middle Ages the very concept of translation was not overly rigorous. For example, references to Aristotle by twelfth-century European authors may have been drawn from an Arabic rendition of a Syriac translation from the original Greek. Needless to say, a process of this kind could scarcely guarantee accuracy.[12] Furthermore, from the High Middle Ages until the end of the eighteenth century a translator treated the original as his own property. He felt free to eliminate or add literary personages and episodes, and he sometimes changed the ending of a book to suit his own times and his country. Only Greek and Latin texts were ordinarily safe from this cavalier treatment. When Abbé Gédoyn (1677–1744) remarked that "to translate, means to render into the vernacular a Greek or a Latin author," he probably was referring to the fact that in his day the so-called translations from one vernacular to another scarcely merited the designation. Other questionable practices included "translations" of fictitious travel accounts that were actually scissors-and-paste concoctions of excerpts from a variety of other travel literature.[13]

Translators of the time were as careless with language as they were with contents. To cite a specific example, Abraham Cowley, a translator of the

---

11. Michał Rusinek, ed., *O sztuce tłumaczenia* (Wrocław: Zakład Ossolinskich, 1955), pp. 210–11.
12. Savory, *Art of Translation*, p. 38.
13. Georges Mounin, *Les belles infidèles* (Paris: Cahiers du Sud, 1955), pp. 185–86.

Tudor era, wrote in 1647 in his preface to *Pindaric Odes:* "I have in those two odes of Pindar taken, left out, and added what I pleased; nor may it be so much my aim to let the reader know precisely what he spoke, as what was his way and manner of speaking."[14] Martin Luther's admonition in 1530 in his "Circular Letter on Translating" (*Sendbrief von Dolmetschen*) to respect the common vernacular was probably atypical, rooted in his own experience as a reverential translator of Holy Scripture that was intended to be read by simple folk: "It is not literature which should be consulted . . . but the mother at the hearth, the children in the street, the common man in the marketplace, looking them in the mouth to see how they are speaking—that is where translating begins."[15] However, Michel de Montaigne wrote in his "Apologie de Raimonde Sebonde" (ca. 1576) that it was difficult to reproduce language accurately: "It is easy to translate authors like this one, with hardly anything but subject matter to transfer; but it is risky to undertake those who have given their language much grace and elegance, particularly with a language of less power."[16]

The mid-sixteenth to mid-seventeenth century can be considered one of the two great periods of translation into English—the other being our own.[17] Yet the translators of that time typically ignored the style and background of their authors, wishing only to conform to the taste of their own day. They reflected a common belief in the superiority of one's own civilization, together with the conviction that one's own country and times are the best of all possible worlds. Thus in 1656 John Denham wrote in his preface to a London edition of *The Destruction of Troy,* an English rendition of the second book of the *Aeneid:* "If Virgil must needs speak English, it were fit that *he should speak it not only as a man of this Nation, but as a man of this age.*"[18] Katherine F. Philips echoed this view in 1663 in *Letters from Orinda to Poliarchus:* "The rule that I understand of translation . . . was to write to Corneille's Sense, *as it is to be supposed*

---

14. Helmut Liedloff, *Steinbeck in German Translation: A Study in Translational Practices* (Carbondale: Southern Illinois University, 1965), p. 4. Brower, *On Translation*, p. 274, gives the date as 1656. This example is inconsistent with Georges Mounin's claim that texts by classical authors were treated with greater respect than modern texts. Apparently they too were subject to translators' arbitrary revisions from time to time.

15. Quoted in Edmond Carey, "Prologemena for the Establishment of a General Theory of Translation," *Diogenes*, no. 40 (Winter 1962): 97.

16. Brower, *On Translation*, p. 274.

17. J. M. Cohen, *English Translators and Translations* (London: Longmans, Green, 1962), pp. 9–10.

18. Brower, *On Translation*, p. 274; emphasis added.

Corneille would have done, if he had been an Englishman not confined to his lines, nor his Numbers . . . but always to his meaning."[19]

Even venerable classics (to say nothing of more modern authors) were ruthlessly "civilized," in the sense that Huckleberry Finn was civilized for church services on Sunday. This procedure, we shall recall, left Huck cleaner and more decorous as well as tearful, pinched, itching, and otherwise uncomfortable, but above all, bearing little resemblance to Huck in his natural habitat. Madame Dacier (1647–1720), the French translator of *The Iliad* and *The Odyssey*, complained that Homer, while great, was also too vulgar and too crude. Homer, she wrote, is quite offensive to "people accustomed to our bourgeois protagonists who are ever so polite, so genteel, so proper." The reader would be revolted by the sight of ancient Greek warriors slaughtering animals and roasting them. She herself found this downright shocking (*choquant*). In her view, Homer's harshness and vulgarity would be intolerable in a French book published in her own century.[20] It hardly needs saying that Madame Dacier's Homer was thoroughly scrubbed and had his mouth washed out with soap to make him acceptable in polite society. A similar fate befell Shakespeare in the hands of Voltaire, which may account for the Englishman's sad fate on the French stage in years to come. Like Homer, Shakespeare was considered crude. Particularly objectionable were the many corpses that mar his plays.[21]

Eighteenth-century Neoclassicism as applied to translation theory and practice is sometimes defended as creating a kind of cosmopolitan "Esperanto of poetic diction in heroic couplets" that made Homer and Virgil, Chaucer and Tasso, Shakespeare, Milton, and Dryden all "converse in *one* language." On this assessment, it was "a noble conception and a noble achievement, worthy of the great age of cosmopolitan humanism."[22] However, this is very much a minority opinion. Scholars today generally believe that the experiment exacted too high a price, depriving individual literary works of the attributes specific to the time and place of their creation, to say nothing of their authors' artistic individuality.

19. Letter 19 (London, 1729); cited in Brower, *On Translation*, p. 274; emphasis added.
20. Mounin, *Les belles infidèles*, pp. 18–21.
21. Voltaire improved upon Hamlet's soliloquy ("to be or not to be") with the far more courtly "*Demeure, il faut choisir et passer à l'instant / De la vie à la mort et de l'être au néant*" (cited in Louis Trouffaut, "Les enjeux de l'ambivalence dans l'opération traduisante," *Meta*, 25 [December 1980]: 441).
22. Rudolf Sühnel, in G. A. Bonnard, ed., *English Studies Today*, 2d. ser., lectures and papers read at the Fourth Conference of the International Association of University Professors of English, Lausanne and Bern, August 1959 (Bern: Francke Verlag, 1961), p. 265.

As the eighteenth century drew to a close, attitudes toward literary translation began to change for the better in Western Europe. Romanticism brought with it a more respectful attitude toward other cultures, including those that earlier had been considered "uncivilized," while curiosity about distant nations and historical periods also implied recognition of the integrity of their literary texts. Neoclassicism's arbitrary "adjustments" of foreign writing in translation to suit its own notions of beauty and decorum were inconsistent with the new Romantic creed. Wilhelm von Humboldt (1767–1835) was among the first to express concern for preservation of the form of the translated literary work. However, he also believed that because each language reflects a specific *Weltanschauung*, the form of the original can be salvaged only in translations of purely factual accounts or rather primitive texts.[23] Humboldt insisted that a translation be faithful to the *entirety* of the source text, not just to its parts. Moreover, he favored multiple translations, since "many translations result, in the end, in a cumulative approximation of the original."[24] His contemporary A. W. Schlegel (1767–1845), famous for his collaboration with Ludwig Tieck (1773–1853) in translating the corpus of Shakespeare's works into German, set very high standards indeed when he demanded that renditions of a literary work into another language preserve the original's complexities of style and metrics and at the same time avoid the pitfall of "translationese."[25]

All of these early developments in the art of translation in Western Europe were ultimately to be repeated in Russia. Translation of translations was the rule in the eighteenth century whenever books from the lesser known foreign languages were involved. Even English novels were often turned into Russian from French translations. By the early nineteenth century, this practice had become less acceptable. Thus in 1811 in his introduction to an edition of La Rochefoucauld's *Maxims*, Prince Boris Golitsyn criticized Russian translators who worked not from original texts, but "from translations as inadequate and imperfect as their own." Golitsyn's attack was aimed at Sentimentalist writers like Karamzin who did, in fact, routinely produce Russian renditions from French translations of

---

23. Ralph-Rainer Wuthenow, *Das fremde Kunstwerk: Aspekte der literarischen Übersetzung* (Göttingen: Vandenhoeck & Ruprecht, 1969), p. 48.
24. Lefevere, *Translating Literature*, p. 40.
25. "Schlegel fordert, Versform und Stil, Eigentümlichkeiten und Schwierigkeiten des Originals auch in der Übersetzung noch zu wahren ohne deswegen eine deutsche Übersetzersprache zu schreiben" (Wuthenow, *Das fremde Kunstwerk,*) p. 51.

original works.[26] But although direct translation from the major Western European languages became the rule in Russia, the practice of translating from translations survives to the present day among those working with Turkic and other minority languages of the former Soviet Union.

It is fitting that the history of translation of secular books into Russian, including belles lettres, begins with Peter the Great (r. 1689–1725), the tsar who (against much opposition) sought to expose Russia to influences from Western Europe. It seems appropriate also that this autocratic sovereign's pronouncement on the subject of translation (referring primarily to scientific books) was formulated as an *ukaz* (decree) — foreshadowing the subsequent fortunes of the art of translation in Russia, at least during the two and a half centuries that followed. In 1724 Peter ordered that translations be clear and easy to understand, eschewing "lofty Slavonic words." He specified practical details as well. Translators conversant in the languages involved, but unfamiliar with the subject matter, were commanded to study the latter. The tsar also ordained that the language of translation be the translator's native tongue, and not the other way around — a stipulation obviously aimed against foreigners who translated into unidiomatic or substandard Russian.[27] Finally, in what was to become the inaugural statement on a subject stirring controversy to this day, Peter expressed his displeasure with the principle of literal translation, claiming that it destroys comprehensibility: "It obfuscates the meaning of the original, familiarity with which then becomes a virtual necessity for the Russian reader."[28]

Peter the Great's preference for nonliteral translation was soon echoed by Alexander Sumarokov (1718–77), a leading playwright and poet of the Neoclassical school. Like most Russian authors of that period, Sumarokov borrowed freely from Western sources and proudly acknowledged this fact: "His vanity was pleased when others referred to him as the Russian

---

26. Prince Golitsyn's foreword was, of course, written in French: *Reflexions sur les traducteurs russes et particulièrement sur ceux des maximes de la Rochefoucauld* (St. Petersburg, 1811). See Iu. D. Levin, "Ob istoricheskoi evoliutsii printsipov perevoda (K istorii perevodcheskoi mysli v Rossii)," in *Mezhdunarodnye sviazi russkoi literatury*, ed. M. P. Alekseev (Moscow and Leningrad: Izdatel'stvo Akademii Nauk SSSR, 1963), p. 23.

27. *Materialy dlia istorii Imperatorskoi Akademii Nauk* (St. Petersburg, 1885), 1: 79–80; cited in *Voprosy khudozhestvennogo perevoda: Sbornik statei*, comp. Vl. Rossel's (Moscow: Sovetskii pisatel', 1955), pp. 49–50.

28. *Zakonodatel'nye akty Petra I* (Moscow: Izdatel'stvo Akademii Nauk SSSR, 1945), p. 35; cited in Givi Gachechiladze, *Vvedenie v teoriiu khudozhestvennogo perevoda: Avtorizovannyi perevod s gruzinskogo* (Tbilisi: Izdatel'stvo Tbilisskogo universiteta, 1970), p. 26.

'Racine,' 'Molière,' or 'La Fontaine.' " Their Russian subject matter aside, Sumarokov's tragedies were transparent imitations of Racine or Shakespeare; his comedies were adaptations of Molière.[29] It may thus be argued that his antiliteralism was consistent with, and indeed an extension of, his own creative assimilation of Western literary material and technique. In the spirit of the times, Sumarokov expressed his views in verse. In "The Epistle on the Russian Language," he wrote:

> And as to which translation is praiseworthy, I shall
>   say thus:
>   Each nation has a style of its own.
> That which is most attractive in the French language
>   May be just the thing that is horrid in Russian.
> Do not assume, while translating, that the author offers
>   you a ready-made form. The author presents you with
>   ideas, but not with words to express them.
> Do not try to penetrate the structure of his speech.
>   Seek beauty in words that befit you. . . .
> If there be no order in your speeches and words,
>   Your translation will be like a riddle
> Which no one will ever solve. And it won't avail that
>   You have named every word with precision.
> Should you wish to translate, immaculately,
>   Reveal to me the author's spirit and power.[30]

Revealing the author's spirit and power—or even naming every word with precision—was no simple matter. In the eighteenth century a great many foreign words had as yet no equivalents in Russian. To cope with this

---

29. William E. Harkins, *Dictionary of Russian Literature* (New York: Philosophical Library, 1956), p. 373.

30. "Posem skazhu kakoi pokhvalen perevod: imeet v sloge vsiak razlichie narod. / Chto ochen' khorosho na iazyke frantsuzskom to mozhet v tochnosti byt' skaredno na russkom. / Ne mni perevodia, chto sklad v tvortse gotov: tvorets daruet mysl', no ne daruet slov. / V spriazhenie rechei ego ty ne vdavaisia i svoistvenno sebe slovami ukrashaisia. / Kol' rechi i slova postavish' bez poriadka, i budet perevod tvoi kak nekaia zagadka, / Kotoruiu nikto ne otgadaet vvek / to darom chto slova vse tochno ty narek. / Kogda perevodit' zakhochesh' besporochno. Ne to—tvortsov mne dukh iavi i silu tochno" (cited in P. I. Kopanev, *Voprosy istorii i teorii khudozhestvennogo perevoda* [Minsk: Izdatel'stvo Belorusskogo gosudarstvennogo universiteta, 1972], pp. 172–73).

problem the translator would sometimes merely adopt the foreign word and transcribe it in (phonetic) Russian. In other cases he would create a calque (that is, a copy), simply describe the item in question, or "adjust it to Russian customs."[31] Victor Zhirmunsky, a leading Soviet specialist in German literature, cited a specific example. Kozodavlev's eighteenth-century rendition of Goethe's drama *Clavigo,* while ostensibly very faithful to the original, strikes a modern reader as clumsy and overly intellectualized. In Zhirmunsky's view, these shortcomings were not simply a reflection of the translator's incompetence: "Apparently, prior to Karamzin, Russian prose lacked the linguistic resources required for the reproduction of the emotional style of sentimental drama, to say nothing of the impassioned tension and self-consciousness characteristic of the lexicon of personages from the plays of *Sturm und Drang.*"[32]

In eighteenth-century Russia translations were viewed as not very different from original works. Russians regarded them as equal components of the national literature, naturalized citizens recognizable as such by foreign-sounding names and faintly foreign accents, but in the final analysis just as indigenous as writings of native origin. Vasily Tred'iakovsky (1703–69), a founding father of Russian poetry as well as of Russian literary translation, was merely expressing accepted beliefs when he declared in 1730 that "the translator differs from the creator in name alone." That statement clearly expressed the Neoclassical belief that translation is not the reconstruction of a foreign literary work in a new language, but rather the creation of an *impersonal* new work seeking ever more closely to approach the ideal form, though of course without ever attaining it. This attitude, in turn, allowed the translator freely to revise the text of the original if, in his view, such revisions "improved" it. Only those works regarded as having already achieved perfection (Greek and Roman classics, for the most part) were to be treated deferentially. Clearly, no textual revisions were allowed in their case. However, these were the exceptions. For the majority of foreign works, substantial revisions were the rule. As Tred'iakovsky reasoned: "Why should readers care whether the words they read are mine or someone else's, as long as what they read is pleasurable, important, and useful?"[33]

Tred'iakovsky was appointed secretary of the Imperial Academy of Science, charged with translating from French into Russian anything he

---

31. Iu. D. Levin, in Alekseev, *Mezhdunarodnye sviazi russkoi literatury,* p. 10.
32. V. M. Zhirmunskii, *Gete v russkoi literature* (Leningrad: Nauka, 1981), p. 32.
33. Iu. D. Levin, *Russkie perevodchiki XIX veka i razvitie khudozhestvennogo perevoda* (Leningrad: Nauka, 1985), p. 9.

was assigned. For this he was to receive "360 rubles annually, inclusive of candles, firewood and lodgings commensurate with the rank of Secretary."[34] His duties included lecturing, completing his Russian grammar, continuing his predecessors' work on dictionaries, and "purifying" (*vychishchat'*) the Russian language through his writings. His son-in-law, the playwright Iakov Kniazhnin (1742–91), also did translations, with which he was as careless as in his financial dealings. Kniazhnin not only embezzled government funds (for which crime he was stripped of his army rank); he also produced sloppy translations for Russian bookstores, a practice that was to flourish in the nineteenth century and beyond. Nor was Kniazhnin the worst offender. Mikhail Chulkov (ca. 1743–92), the author of the picaresque novel *The Comely Cook, or the Adventures of a Debauched Woman*, a Russian *Moll Flanders* of sorts, complained bitterly that other men of letters were far more brazen. Chulkov wrote with heavy sarcasm of the apparently pervasive plagiarism of foreign literary works:

> A new fashion has come into being. Rarely are [writings] called translations. They are called instead [original] Works. However, since I have not altogether lost my conscience, the above appears to me quite unbecoming. Some contemporary authors . . . pilfer things from many works. They then claim them as their own. Not in the least are they afraid of being caught stealing the property of others. In this manner, many foreign authors have posthumously learned to speak Russian. Not only do they speak our language fluently, but they even write some very praiseworthy books in that language. Curiously, they never sign their names to them. One readily sees that they allow others to sign them instead.[35]

Perhaps the charge of outright plagiarism was overly harsh. Like their Western European predecessors, Russian translators of the Neoclassical persuasion viewed the originals as their property and thus felt free to do with them as they pleased—although replacing the authors' names with their own may have been carrying matters a bit far.

---

34. P. Pekarskii, *Istoriia Akademii Nauk v Peterburge*, 1870, p. 43; cited in T. Grits, V. Trenin, and M. Nikitin, *Slovesnost' i kommertsiia* (Moscow: Federatsiia, 1929), p. 151.

35. Ibid., pp. 148–49. Metropolitan Evgenii's report originally appeared in *Slovar' russkich svetskikh pisatelei* (Moscow, 1845), 1:289. Chulkov's was printed in his journal *I to i sio*, no. 41 (1769): 7.

As the term itself suggests, Neoclassical translators believed that perfection meant imitating the style of the ancient Greek and Latin authors. They quite consciously sought to bring the texts they translated into conformity with classical aesthetic norms. They omitted anything they considered superfluous, inartistic, or ineffective and added passages of their own to fill what they considered gaps. On the other hand, if the text at hand already conformed to the accepted norms, the translator would treat it with utmost care and humility, striving to render it word for word, or in the case of poetry, verse by verse.[36] Moreover, since classical aesthetic principles were supposed to be equally valid for all times and places, the Neoclassical translator assumed that the work he was translating had attempted to follow this model, whether successfully or otherwise. Accordingly, his task was to make the translation conform as well as possible to classical artistic principles (as the eighteenth century understood them). To a certain degree, even Greek and Latin works might receive this treatment. As one Soviet scholar explained:

> If the original was itself considered a model (say, Homer's poetry or the tragedies of Euripides), the translation edited or eliminated altogether everything that contradicted the Neoclassical interpretation of the norm. *Deviations from the norm in the original model were declared uncharacteristic and unessential.* In effect, translation was being replaced with adaptation. Original texts in foreign languages were adjusted to the norms of literary "good taste" of a given time and place.[37]

The insistence of eighteenth-century translators on fidelity to a norm (rather than to the text) is strongly reminiscent of the advice proferred in the twentieth century by Ivan Kashkin, a leading translator and theoretician of the Stalin era. Soviet translators, Kashkin wrote in 1968, must

> *first and foremost attempt to convey to our reader everything that is progressive* [in the work being translated], *all that is living and timely for our age.* They should retain that which can be preserved without impeding full, clear and correct understanding of the thought and imagery of the original. This should be accomplished without undue burdening of the text with unnecessary detail which

---

36. G. A. Gukovskii, in *Poetika: Sbornik statei* (Leningrad, 1928), 4:142–45; cited in K. I. Chukovskii, *Iskusstvo perevoda* (Moscow and Leningrad: Academia, 1936), pp. 116–17.

37. V. Mikushevich, in *Voprosy teorii khudozhestvennogo perevoda* (Moscow: Khudozhestvennaia literatura, 1971), pp. 42–43; italics added.

is characteristic only of the alien linguistic structure and *sometimes should not be translated at all.*[38]

The implications of Kashkin's pronouncements were fully in accord with the traditional precepts of Socialist Realism, the Soviet artistic doctrine obligatory for all creative writers from the mid-1930s to the early 1980s. Soviet translators were instructed to emphasize whatever was "typical" (and then only in its "revolutionary development," namely, that which Marxism-Leninism in its current interpretation *expected would become typical in the future*). This was done by using the translation as an opportunity to *magnify* whatever elements in the foreign literary work might suggest class struggle, possible admiration for Communism, or any incidents and realia lending support to Communist Party teachings or current Soviet practices. Conversely, whatever did not fit this description was to be minimized or, in extreme cases, blotted out completely. Thus Kashkin's advice to ignore "alien linguistic structure" could easily be interpreted as sanctioning "minor" censorship of foreign literary texts, such as deletion of sexually suggestive scenes or, more important, "casual" remarks disrespectful of the Soviet Union or the Communist Party. In my 1962 book, *Russian Classics in Soviet Jackets*, I called attention to some important similarities between Neoclassical and Soviet Socialist Realist original writing.[39] It should come as no surprise that analogous similarities can be found in Soviet translation doctrines as well.

For the just emerging secular Russian literature, the eighteenth century was a period of apprenticeship at the feet of the Western European masters. Notwithstanding the jingoistic scholarship of the Stalin era, there is nothing demeaning in this fact. On the contrary, it is remarkable that within only a hundred years Russian writing was able to overcome so large a time lag. As in any apprenticeship, unabashed imitation was the rule, as in the case of Sumarokov or Chulkov. Some of this emulation is still observable in one body of eighteenth-century literature that has survived the test of time on its own merits, and whose foreign origins only scholars remember: namely, the rhymed fables of Ivan Krylov (ca. 1769–1844).* Tens

---

*Although he lived well into the nineteenth century, Krylov is perceived as primarily an eighteenth-century writer.

38. Ivan Kashkin, *Dlia chitalelia-sovremennika: Stat'i i materialy* (Moscow: Sovetskii pisatel', 1968), p. 451; emphasis added.

39. Maurice Friedberg, *Russian Classics in Soviet Jackets* (New York: Columbia University Press, 1962), pp. 163–64.

of millions of Russian children annually memorize Krylov's tales, oblivious of the fact that these are rooted in La Fontaine or even Aesop. Indeed, not a few of these fables are "mere" translations of the most successful kind: namely, those that have acquired a life of their own, much as the King James Bible is a very major work of English prose. Apart from producing imitations (sometimes very close ones), practically all of Russia's more important eighteenth-century authors also translated Western writing. In addition to Krylov and Sumarokov, the list includes Kantemir, Lomonosov, Tred'iakovsky, Fonvizin, Bogdanovich, Kheraskov, Kapnist, Derzhavin, Karamzin, and Radishchev.[40]

The fact that literary translation was a rapidly expanding field in the middle of the eighteenth century is attested by the establishment in 1768 of the Association for the Advancement of Translation of Foreign Books into Russian, an organization that regulated translation activity in subsequent years. Nevertheless, much confusion persisted. Translations were published anonymously (most of the translators, presumably, were hacks); and the same work would sometimes become available in several competing Russian versions.[41] Nikolai Karamzin (1766–1826), an eminent historian and leading writer of the Sentimentalist school, whose renditions of Western writing have greatly enriched the Russian lexicon, brought out a translation of *Julius Caesar* in 1786. This was the second Shakespearean play to be put into Russian; Sumarokov's rendition of *Hamlet* had been the first. But unlike Sumarokov, who produced his version *from the French* (a common enough procedure with English books even in nineteenth-century Russia), Karamzin translated directly from the English, albeit in prose. He summarized his method as follows: "As far as my translation is concerned, I strove above all to translate faithfully, avoiding expressions incompatible [*protivnykh*] with our language. . . . I never changed the author's ideas, believing this to be inadmissible in a translation."[42]

The most political writer in eighteenth-century Russia (and the first to have his book confiscated and himself exiled) was Alexander Rad-

---

40. Rossel's, *Voprosy khudozhestvennogo perevoda*, p. 47.

41. Ibid., p. 55. The Russian name of the association was *Sobranie, staraiushcheesia o perevode inostrannykh knig na russkii iazyk*. Not that the problem is unknown in our times. Several years ago I wrote an introduction to a translation of a modern Soviet novel (Fyodor Abramov, *Two Winters and Three Summers*, trans. Jacqueline Edwards and Mitchell Schneider [San Diego, New York, London: Harcourt, Brace, Jovanovich, 1984]). Another translation of this Russian novel was brought out simultaneously by Ardis Publishers of Ann Arbor. Even in the USSR there were instances of similar duplication even though its publishing was highly centralized.

42. Rossel's, *Voprosy khudozhestvennogo perevoda* (1955), p. 51.

ishchev (1749–1802). Many of his radical ideas, incidentally, were inspired by the Founding Fathers of the newly independent United States of America. Radishchev's *Journey from St. Petersburg to Moscow* also has the distinction of containing what may be the first Russian comment on the subject of political censorship of literature (including translations, but apparently excluding Latin books)—though his remarks pertain to Western Europe, not Russia. In a long digression, Radishchev denounced political censorship as injurious to society. The reason he restricted his criticisms to Western practices was quite simple. The number of books published in Russia at that time was insufficient to warrant the establishment of censorship agencies. With the expansion of book publication, censorship (both political and ecclesiastical) gradually began to emerge in Russia as well.[43]

The translator most notorious in eighteenth-century Russia for his cavalier treatment of texts was Vladimir Lukin (1737–94). Known for his renditions of foreign plays "adapted to our [Russian] mores," Lukin justified his procedure on two grounds. In the first place, he argued, foreign authors do the same to one another.[44] More important, as a Soviet scholar wrote approvingly, Lukin "correctly justified his free translation of comedies, a genre which in his view was called upon to criticize Russian mores. It is for that reason that he deleted from French comedies everything that bore no resemblance to Russian life and customs."[45] The desire to make foreign literary works "relevant" to Russia extended even to substituting Russian proper names for the Western names of literary characters, and replacing exotic French or German realia with objects that Russian readers would find reassuringly familiar. Years later, Leo Tolstoy would denounce this practice (evidently criticizing one of Dostoevsky's translations): "Changing foreign stories such as *Eugénie Grandé* [sic] to suit Russian mores means depriving them of their value as documents of non-Russian life and of their realism above all."[46]

43. Ibid., p. 48.
44. V. I. Lukin, *Sochineniia i perevody* (St. Petersburg, 1868), pp. 112–15; cited in Rossel's, *Voprosy khudozhestvennogo perevoda*, pp. 51–52.
45. P. I. Kopanev, *Voprosy istorii i teorii khudozhestvennogo perevoda* (Minsk: Izdatel'stvo Belorusskogo gosudarstvennogo universiteta, 1972), p. 171.
46. "Peredelyvat' povesti inostrannye, kak Eugénie Grandé na russkie nravy znachit lishat' eti povesti interesa znaniia byta nerusskogo i glavnoe, real'nosti" (L. N. Tolstoi, *Polnoe sobranie sochinenii*, Jubilee edition [Moscow, 1935–36], 85:286–87; cited in *Russkie pisateli o perevode, XVIII–XX v.v.*, ed. Iu. D. Levin and A. V. Fedorov, with introduction by A. V. Fedorov (Leningrad: Sovetskii pisatel', 1960), p. 522.

Important authors, as I shall try to demonstrate, do not ordinarily make good translators. Conscious of their own status, they often "compete" with the original and indeed at times appear eager to "improve" it. Pasternak was one such translator, though in the twentieth century his type was comparatively rare. In the eighteenth and early nineteenth centuries the literary atmosphere was different. Leading Western European authors often produced translations, which was testimony both to the prestige of this activity and to the belief that an author might enhance his literary skills in the process. In England, for instance, until the middle of the nineteenth century "a [British] poet of major powers thought it a task perfectly worthy of him to devote his best energies either to getting a Greek or Roman classic into English or to modelling his own work on such a classic." After that time no important English poet devoted serious effort to this type of work.[47]

In France as well, important original poets and dramatists continued to translate during the first decades of the nineteenth century. "Chênedollé, Chateaubriand, Nerval, the Deschamps brothers, Henri de Latouche and many others integrated translation into their poetic activity." After about 1830, this practice became less common. Then "it was rather the second-rate or marginal innovating poets, i.e., the least mentioned but nevertheless original ones, who produced translations." Prose was "almost exclusively in the hands of 'specialists,' i.e., professional translators."[48] Nevertheless there were exceptions. Later in the nineteenth century and in the twentieth, major French poets would occasionally be seduced into translating foreign verse. Thus Charles Baudelaire (1821–67) translated Edgar Allan Poe (the same Poe who, in Dudley Fitts's estimation, "may not be much to begin with"!). This French rendition was clearly a great poet's labor of love. According to one expert, "Poe's stylistic idiosyncracies are more readily visible in Baudelaire's translation than in the original."[49]

Allowing for the usual time lag in the penetration of Western literary fashion, the pattern appears to have been followed in the Slavic lands as

---

47. G. S. Fraser, "On Translating Poetry," *Arion* 4 (Summer 1966): 129–30. In nineteenth-century America, the poet Longfellow (1807–82) translated mostly from the Spanish and Italian. Not that there was much need for it: Americans read British editions. Longfellow, incidentally, was a great-uncle of Ezra Pound, who did much translating.

48. Theo Hermans, ed., *The Manipulation of Literature: Studies in Literary Translation* (London: Croom Helm, 1985), pp. 160–61.

49. Jürgen von Stackleberg, in *Interlinguistica: Sprachvergleich und Übersetzung*, ed. Karl-Richard Bausch and Hans-Martin Gauger (Tübingen: Max Niemeyer Verlag, 1971), p. 585. Among major French poets of a later date, André Gide (1869–1951) translated Shakespeare and Conrad; Paul Valéry (1871–1945) translated Virgil.

well. To be sure, Poland's great nineteenth-century poets seem to have produced only two translations of major foreign works. Adam Mickiewicz supplied a Polish rendition of Byron's *Giaour,* while Juliusz Słowacki translated Calderón's *El Principe Constante* under the Polish title of *Książe Niezłomny.*[50] In Russia, on the other hand, a number of leading authors turned their hands to this work. As in England and France, this occurred most often in the first decades of the nineteenth century; subsequently the practice declined. V. M. Zhirmunsky provides a telling list of the quantity of verse by Goethe alone that was translated by Russian poets between 1820 and 1840. These calculations are most impressive, particularly if one remembers that German was not as well known as French in Russia at the time. The figures in parentheses indicate the number of Goethe's poems translated by individual authors: Bestuzhev-Marlinsky (8), Venevitinov (7), Apollon Grigor'ev (14), Zhukovsky (18), Lermontov (2), Maikov (7), Mei (3), Ogarev (4), Pleshcheev (2), Polonsky (1), Stankevich (2), A. K. Tolstoy (5), Ivan Turgenev (5), Tiutchev (16), Fet (18 poems, as well as *Faust* and *Hermann und Dorothea*), Derzhavin (1), Del'vig (1), and Griboedov (1). Even so, Zhirmunsky was disappointed that five of the major Russian poets (Pushkin, Batiushkov, Baratynsky, Iazykov, and Nekrasov) had *failed* to translate even one of Goethe's poems![51]

The greatest Russian poet of all, Alexander Pushkin, was not really interested in translation as such, though he found it useful for the study of poetic technique. In his unfinished study of Chateaubriand's French rendition of Milton's *Paradise Lost* (1837), which is cited in nearly every Russian work on literary translation, he was equally critical of literalism and of excessively free renditions. This posture was consonant with his own style of versification, which combines Neoclassical and Romantic elements. Pushkin's renditions of French verse (which are rather eclectic—some quite literal, others rather free) demonstrate that translation was to him a means to an end, an exercise aimed at enriching his own poetic equipment with forms and devices that already existed in French verse.[52] On one occasion Pushkin stated that translation is "the most difficult and the most thankless of all the literary genres I know." Accordingly, he shied away from it. At one time he had intended to translate Adam Mickiewicz's *Konrad Wallenrod*

---

50. Rusinek, *O sztuce tłumaczenia,* p. 16. That these were exceptions is indirectly attested by Paweł Hertz, who on page 219 of the same book asserts that no major Polish authors produced translations!

51. Zhirmunskii, *Gete v russkoi literature,* pp. 25–26.

52. Alekseev, *Mezhdunarodnye sviazi russkoi literatury,* pp. 31–32.

(1828), a long poem of patriotic revenge through treason, but ultimately abandoned the project. "I don't know how to translate," he wrote; "I don't know how to submit to the translator's hard work."[53]

Pushkin's sentiments regarding the difficulty of translation were later echoed by another major poet, Nikolai Nekrasov (1821–78), who insisted that translating poetry is more arduous than composing original verse.[54] Fedor Tiutchev and Mikhail Lermontov, like Pushkin, considered translation mainly as an activity that facilitated their writing of original verse. Similarly, Fet, Grigor'ev, and Pleshcheev all produced their renditions of foreign verse while still young.[55] This was perhaps just as well. Pushkin's confession that he did not know "how to submit to the translator's hard work" is applicable to the majority of great poets. Not content with the humble role of translator, they often usurp the function that properly belongs to the author of the original. This tendency inspired Vissarion Belinsky, the first great Russian literary critic, to write:

> In a translation of Goethe we want to see Goethe and not his translator. Even if Pushkin himself were to translate Goethe, we would insist that he too present Goethe to us and not himself.[56]

After 1840 translation ceased to be viewed as primarily a literary activity, but rather as part of commercial publishing. Translation became a profession. Such post–1850 professionals as Berg, Mei, Miller, Min, and Kostomarov produced renditions of very different foreign authors that sounded remarkably alike. Their opponents, the so-called revolutionary democrats (such as Kurochkin, Pleshcheev, Minaev, and Mikhailov), strove instead to exploit translation for political ends. They produced popular renditions of rebellious poets like Béranger. The overall artistic level of Russian translations declined.[57] Nonetheless, some authors best known for their original writings brought out occasional translations. Dostoevsky launched his literary career with a rendition of Balzac's *Eugénie Grandet;* Turgenev translated two of Flaubert's novellas; and Tolstoy's "Françoise" is

53. Cited in P. Toper, "Traditsii realizma," *Druzhba narodov*, no. 5 (1953): 229–30.
54. Rossel's *Voprosy khudozhestvennogo perevoda*, p. 54.
55. German Ritz, *150 Jahre russischer Heine-Übersetzung* (Bern, Frankfurt am Main, Las Vegas: Peter Lang, 1981), pp. 10–11.
56. V. G. Belinskii, *Polnoe sobranie sochinenii* (Moscow, 1955), 9:277; cited in Alekseev, *Mezhdunarodnye sviazi russkoi literatury*, p. 35, and in Ginzburg, *Nad strokoi perevoda*, p. 52.
57. Ritz, *150 Jahre*, pp. 10–11.

but a Russian version of Maupassant's "Le Port."[58] Included in the group of translators were three of Russia's leading literary critics, Belinsky, Dobroliubov, and Chernyshevsky, and the playwright Alexander Ostrovsky.[59]

During the first half of the nineteenth century the destinies of literary translation in Russia were dominated by Vasily Zhukovsky (1783–1852), a leading early Romantic poet. In fact, the publication in 1802 of his free rendition of Thomas Gray's "Elegy Written in a Country Churchyard" is sometimes considered the advent of Russian Romanticism. "Without Zhukovsky," Belinsky insisted, "we would not have Pushkin."[60] In view of this high praise from the country's leading critic, it comes as something of a surprise to discover that Zhukovsky was primarily a translator, although arguably the single most important Russian translator of all time.

"Zhukovsky's poetry is an unusual poetic universe," Belinsky mused. "His most original works somehow look like translations, and his translations look like original works."[61] Gogol made a similar observation:

> When you read the titles of his [Zhukovsky's] poems, you see that one is Schiller's, another Uhland's, a third Walter Scott's, a fourth Byron's. . . . But after reading a few, you ask yourself, whose poems have you read? And it is not Schiller you'll see before your eyes, nor Uhland nor Walter Scott. You will see a poet distinct from each of them, yet worthy to sit not at their feet, but side by side with them, as an equal among equals.[62]

Zhukovsky himself concurred with this verdict. "Such is the general character of my literary work. Almost everything I have written is someone else's or inspired by someone else. Yet all of it is my very own." A German correspondent once asked Zhukovsky for some translations into German of *his own* Russian verse. In response, Zhukovsky sent him a list of foreign poems he had translated. Appended was a note: "While reading them, make believe that they are all translations from Zhukovsky's Russian originals, or vice versa."[63] Zhukovsky, in other words, was the kind of

---

58. Gachechiladze, *Vvedenie v teoriiu*, p. 38.
59. Rossel's, *Voprosy khudozhestvennogo perevoda*, p. 47.
60. Levin, *Russkie perevodchiki*, p. 8.
61. V. G. Belinskii, *Polnoe sobranie sochinenii* (Moscow: Akademiia Nauk SSSR, 1954), 5:550.
62. Cited in Levin, *Russkie perevodchiki*, p. 20.
63. Ibid., pp. 12–13.

author of whom Tred'iakovsky had written: "A translator differs from the creator in name alone."[64]

Zhukovsky obviously saw no conflict between a smooth translation and a faithful one. In a much-quoted statement, he declared that "when one translates a novel the most pleasant [*priiatnyi*] translation is, of course [*sic*], the most faithful as well."[65] In another famous pronouncement, he declared that a translator of prose is a slave, while a translator of verse is a rival. Belinsky commented on this: "The latter assertion is only half true. He [the translator] is a rival in language, style and metrics, in other words—in [poetic] form, but not in thought, not in content. Here he is a slave. A translator's gift is a gift in form, assuming, of course, an ability to penetrate the spirit of another poet's works, to feel their aesthetic charms."[66] According to Yuri Levin, what Zhukovsky meant was not merely that verse translation requires as much effort as the writing of the original, or even that it demands poetic gifts of the same magnitude. Rather, he wanted to call attention to the fact that a translated text becomes part and parcel of the literature in the target language, and as a literary work in its own right, it becomes a "rival" of the text that was its inspiration.[67]

Zhukovsky's own contemporaries treated his translations as essentially original works, and their reviews usually emphasized his independence from his sources. Commenting on Zhukovsky's translation of Byron's *Prisoner of Chillon,* one Russian critic wrote: "We even dare to state emphatically that to translate as Zhukovsky translates, is the same thing as creating." Another noted: "Many of Zhukovsky's translations are better than their originals, since euphony and versatility of language adorn the accuracy of his expression." Belinsky agreed: "They say that Zhukovsky has little of his own, that it is almost all translation: a mistaken opinion! *Zhukovsky is a poet, and not a translator.*"[68]

---

64. "Perevodchik ot tvortsa tol'ko chto imenem roznitsia," in V. K. Tred'iakovskii, *Sochineniia Tred'iakovskogo* (St. Petersburg, 1849), 3:649; cited in Alekseev, *Mezhdunarodnye sviazi russkoi literatury*, p. 6.
65. V. I. Rezanov, *Iz razyskanii o sochineniiakh V. A. Zhukovskogo* (St. Petersburg, 1906), pp. 351–53; cited in Chukovskii, *Iskusstvo perevoda*, p. 118; also cited in Levin, *Russkie perevodchiki*, p. 13.
66. Cited in Levin, *Russkie perevodchiki*, p. 101. The statement appears in Belinskii, *Polnoe sobranie sochinenii*, 277.
67. Levin, *Russkie perevodchiki*, pp. 11–12.
68. The quotations from Pletnev, Bestuzhev, and Belinskii are taken from Michael R. Katz, *The Literary Ballad in Early Nineteenth-Century Russian Literature* (Oxford: Oxford University Press, 1976), p. 46; emphasis added.

Zhukovsky in 1808 and Pavel Katenin in 1816 each published a Russian "translation" of Gottfried August Bürger's poem *Lenore*. Zhukovsky's version was provided with a Russian name, *Liudmila,* which accurately reflected its Russified contents; it was dubbed an "imitation." Katenin's *Lenore* was—for variety's sake?—rechristened *Ol'ga,* and Ol'ga-Lenore's beloved was made to join the Russian army of Peter the Great.[69] It was characteristic of the then prevalent views about the nature of translation that when the playwright A. S. Griboedov and the poet and translator N. I. Gnedich argued about the relative merits of Zhukovsky's *Liudmila* and Katenin's *Ol'ga,* they discussed these works as *Russian ballads:* Bürger's German original was hardly mentioned. It was as a Russian ballad that Gnedich liked Zhukovsky's *Liudmila* and Griboedov did not. Similarly, Orest Somov's devastating criticism of Zhukovsky's *Fisherman* viewed it as a bad Russian poem, not as an unsuccessful translation of Goethe's German original.[70]

As for the charge that Zhukovsky's renditions of Schiller, Byron, and Goethe all look alike, Belinsky considered this a *virtue:* "He remained faithful to himself."[71] In other words, Belinsky judged Zhukovsky's translations as one would judge original writing. But as N. A. Polevoi noted, Zhukovsky selected at random the works that he chose to translate. It mattered little to him whether the author of the original was Schiller or Bürger or Oliver Goldsmith, as long as the theme was "the anguish of love, with quiet joy, the sacrifice of love or a meeting in the hereafter."[72] Zhukovsky was interested in the subject matter of the original—which would be retained in his very free renditions, and therefore had to be in harmony with his own poetic predilections. But he displayed indifference toward the artistic peculiarities of the original, which in any case would be obliterated in his Russian re-creations. To cite Belinsky again: "His so-called translations are very imperfect as translations, but they are superb as his own creations."[73]

Zhukovsky was influenced by Sentimentalism, which like Neoclassicism viewed the original text as an excuse for the creation of a "new" Russian literary work. The euphony and pleasing quality (*priiatnost'*) of the latter,

---

69. See Rossel's, *Voprosy khudozhestvennogo perevoda,* pp. 57–58.
70. Iu. D. Levin, "O russkom poeticheskom perevode v epokhu romantizma," in *Rannie romanticheskie veianiia* (Leningrad: Nauka, 1972), pp. 237–38.
71. Ibid.
72. Levin, *Russikie perevodchiki,* p. 19.
73. Ibid., p. 20.

its smoothness, readability, and *ability to sustain the illusion that it is an entirely original work,* were to be its foremost virtues, not fidelity to the foreign author. As the Soviet scholar V. V. Tsoffka observed: "In Zhukovsky's time, translation of verse was viewed as equal in importance to the writing of original poetry. Zhukovsky's contemporaries believed that verse translation belonged in greater degree to the translator than to the creator of the original. To Zhukovsky, translation of verse was first and foremost a means for self-expression, while his contemporaries viewed it above all as a device whereby Russian literature was enriched."[74]

Needless to say, such beliefs sanctioned the introduction of arbitrary textual changes by the translator. Obviously aware that to a Soviet reader "textual changes" implied political censorship, in 1960 the translator Vladimir Rossel's hastened to assure his readers that such changes were prompted by "the then prevalent aesthetic norms" rather than "reactionary impulses." But other commentators detected a pattern of right-wing political malice in Zhukovsky's renditions. For instance, they pointed to his softening the blasphemy in Bürger's *Lenore* (in its 1808 incarnation as *Liudmila*), "his blunting the edge of Heine's irony, and his insertion of Slavonicisms into the translation of Schiller's *Ode to Joy,* which transformed a work inspired by the French Revolution into something resembling a religious hymn."[75] Kornei Chukovsky (1882–1969), a leading Soviet theoretician and translator, concurred with this view, adding to the list of Zhukovsky's transgressions his renditions of Byron's *The Prisoner of Chillon* and some German verse of Ludwig Uhland. Chukovsky insisted that all of this was done with malicious intent: "I repeat. These systematic departures from the text on Zhukovsky's part, which were not in the least accidental, are the more noticeable because with very few exceptions his translations miraculously reproduce the most minute intonations of the original."[76]

According to Rossel's, eighteenth-century French notions of propriety suggested that "ennobling" of texts was appropriate.[77] But apparently even an "ennobled" Cervantes was not noble enough for young Zhukovsky. At the age of twenty he undertook the task of translating *Don Quixote.* It

---

74. V. V. Tsoffka, "Ob evoliutsii V. A. Zhukovskogo-perevodchika," *Vestnik Moskovskogo Universiteta,* 9th ser., *Filologiia,* no. 1 (1983): 58–61.

75. P. A. Nikolaev, ed., *Russkie pisateli o perevode Biobibliograficheskii slovar'* (Moscow: Prosveshchenie, 1990), 1:14–15.

76. Kornei Chukovskii, *Vvsokoe iskusstvo: O printsipakh khudozhestvennogo perevoda* (Moscow: Iskusstvo, 1964), p. 29.

77. VI. Rossel's, "Teoriia khudozhestvennogo perevoda—oblast' literaturo-vedeniia," *Voprosy literatury,* no. 5 (1960): 157.

seems he knew little Spanish and translated the novel from Florian's rather free French adaptation. He noted approvingly that Florian had "toned down [Cervantes'] expressions that were overly crude, eliminated repetitions, and through his verbal agility, found substitutes for those charms [of the Spanish language] which his [own] language lacked."[78] Still he considered the novel's "smooth" French prose unsatisfactory: "*Don Quixote* contains excesses and lapses of good taste—why not get rid of them?"[79] As he explained in his introduction to the 1803 edition of his translation:

> There are imperfections in Cervantes. Certain jokes are repeated too often, while others are overly long. Also there are some distasteful scenes. Cervantes' taste was not always pure. . . . I took the liberty to change a few things, to tone down some overly blunt expressions. I changed many lines and eliminated repetition. . . . People who are not overly strict and believe that translators have some sense and taste will trust that I love Cervantes and have eliminated from my translation only that which is unworthy of him.[80]

Occasionally Zhukovsky would return to an old translation and rework it, sometimes more than once. Thus he produced three versions of Gray's *Elegy* and two of Johann Gottfried Herder's *El Cid*.[81]

The advent of Romanticism marked a turn toward literalism in translation, reflecting the Romantic movement's interest in and respect for alien cultural traditions. In the latter part of his life Zhukovsky claimed to be a convert to this aesthetic, which postulated *respect for the content*, if not the form of the original. His two renditions of Gottfried August Bürger's *Lenore* illuminated his road to Damascus. The 1808 version, which he christened *Liudmila*, was very free. More than twenty years later, Zhukovsky came out with *Lenora*. The date of its publication, 1831, ostensibly marked his repudiation of Sentimentalism's very free treatment of the text undergoing translation. It also symbolized his new allegiance to the Romantic creed, which mandated respect for the textual integrity of the original. Yet even so, the more faithful text of *Lenora* bears "a stronger

---

78. Levin, *Russkie perevodchiki*, p. 13.
79. Rezanov, *Iz razyskannii o sochineniiakh V. A. Zhukovskogo*, pp. 351–53; cited in Chukovskii, *Iskusstvo perevoda*, p. 118.
80. Ibid., pp. 118–19.
81. Tsoffka, "Ob evoliutsii V. A. Zhukovskogo-perevodchika," pp. 58–62.

resemblance to Zhukovsky's own [earlier] *Lyudmila* than to Bürger's *Lenore*. Any 'translation' by Zhukovsky must indeed be considered as the creation of an original poet."[82]

Half a century later a leading Russian translator reached a similar conclusion. Petr Veinberg wrote in 1889:

> *Zhukovsky's translations can in no case be regarded as such in the full sense of the term.* Nearly every one of them attests to the translator's gifts. They also reflect the poet's spiritual kinship with the original. However, these are imitations, transformations, what we sometimes call "variations on the theme of"—in short, anything you please except translations. When compared with the original, a great many verses of the renditions reveal the most serious disparities. Consciously or unwittingly, the translator has eliminated a great many idiosyncracies and individual traits of the original.... We can hardly be entirely happy with [Zhukovsky's rendition of] *The Prisoner of Chillon* when we know that in many ways what we are reading is not Byron, but his translator.[83]

Veinberg's refusal to recognize Zhukovsky as a translator in the proper sense of the term, like Belinsky's similar comment of an earlier date, referred to translations done *after* Zhukovsky's alleged conversion to the Romantic doctrine![84]

Zhukovsky and other Russian Romantics were less rigorous in their creed as translators than were the Romantics of Western Europe, who gravitated toward strict literalism. One example was the English poet Robert Browning, who wrote in his preface to Aeschylus's *Agamemnon*: "I have spared no effort to be literal at every cost save that of absolute violence to our language.... I would be tolerant for once—in the case of so intensely famous an original—of even a clumsy attempt to furnish me with the very turn of each phrase in as Greek a fashion as English will bear."[85]

At the opposite extreme was the Russian prose translator Irinarkh Vvedensky (1813–55), whose renditions were filled with the additions and

---

82. Katz, *Literary Ballad*, p. 50.
83. *Perevod—sredstvo vzaimnogo sblizheniia narodov: Khudozhestvennaia publitsistika* (Moscow: Progress, 1987), p. 276; emphasis added.
84. Tsoffka, "Ob evoliutsii V. A. Zhukovskogo-perevodchika," p. 62.
85. L. G. Kelly, *The True Interpreter: History of Translation Theory and Practice in the West* (New York: St. Martin's Press, 1979), pp. 78–79.

emendations that the Russians call *otsebiatina*. While Vvedensky's foremost achievements were his renditions of Dickens and Thackeray, whom he regarded as the greatest novelists of his age, he also translated Cicero (from Latin) and several church fathers (from Greek), as well as some nonfiction from French and German. His first translation from English was Oliver Goldsmith's *The Vicar of Wakefield*.[86] Vvedensky was an exceptionally hard-working and productive translator, particularly considering his heavy teaching obligations. He claimed in 1851 that in the previous four years he had translated 5,248 pages. In 1841 he translated James Fenimore Cooper's *Deerslayer;* this was one of the earliest Russian versions of American writing. Charlotte Brontë's *Jane Eyre* followed in 1847, and Caroline Norton's *Stuart of Dunleath* in 1851. Within the five-year period from 1847 to 1852 Vvedensky rendered into Russian Thackeray's *Vanity Fair* and four of Dickens's novels: *Dombey and Son, The Pickwick Papers, David Copperfield,* and *The Haunted Man.*

In 1853 Vvedensky undertook a journey to Western Europe. He was unimpressed by France and by the French, finding the latter irresponsible and somewhat decadent. By contrast, as befitted a translator of English novels, he fell in love with Great Britain and praised it extravagantly. Naturally he had hoped to meet Dickens and Thackeray, but both novelists were out of town. Vvedensky regarded English literature as the best in the world. In his words, "Human intellect revealed itself in all of its splendor and glory in this literature alone"; and he described the English novel as "one of the most brilliant rays in English literature's shining wreath of glory." Curiously, Vvedensky seems to have been less impressed by the aesthetic merits of English novels than by their value as social documents. He valued in particular their descriptions of British factories, law offices, debtors' prisons, and various other social realia.

According to the poet Afanasy Fet (1820–92), who was himself an important translator, Vvedensky's pronunciation of foreign languages was awful, but he had a perfect command of written German, French, English, and Italian and was also fluent in Latin. However, the literary historian Yuri Levin subsequently showed that Vvedensky's English left much to be desired, since he mistranslated such terms and idioms as "handcuffs," "speaker" (of Parliament), and "many happy returns."[87] Kornei

86. Ibid., pp. 118–20. Curiously, the Russian title of Thackeray's *Vanity Fair* that is in use today is not Vvedenskii's *Bazar zhiteiskoi suety,* but that used by an earlier and less illustrious translator, *Iarmarka tshcheslaviia.*
87. Levin, *Russkie perevodchiki,* pp. 109, 113–18, 107–8, 135.

Chukovsky recalled editing Vvedensky's rendition of *David Copperfield*, which required the correction of some *three thousand* mistakes. Moreover, he had to remove about *nine hundred* instances of Vvedensky's own *otsebiatina*—concoctions that purported to explain and improve on the original.[88] However, the latter blended so nicely with Dickens's own prose that Chukovsky was willing to forgive Vvedensky his transgressions.[89] Equally willing, apparently, were other critics, publishers, and the reading public. Though widely known to be inaccurate, Vvedensky's renditions continued to be republished until the early twentieth century, while at least one, that of *Dombey and Son*, was reprinted in the Soviet period.[90]

It was not only in Russia that numerous errors and sheer misunderstandings of a translated text were at times considered acceptable. One of Vvedensky's literary ancestors was Jacques Amyot, bishop of Auxerre, who in 1559 translated Plutarch's *Lives of Famous Greeks and Romans*. Though teeming with inaccuracies, his achievement was widely hailed; and Amyot became known as the "prince of translators."[91] The French bishop's defects as a translator were no secret. As the Polish literary critic Wacław Borowy pointed out, as early as 1635 a scholar named Meziriac had demonstrated at a meeting of the Académie Française that Amyot's version of Plutarch contained no fewer than *two thousand* mistakes. The translator had made additions and cuts to the text and changed various expressions and imagery. In spite of this, Amyot's translation continued to be regarded as a great work of French literature, since in the seventeenth (and eighteenth) centuries, such departures from the original were viewed as "the translator's sacred right."[92]

Coming as they did *after* Romanticism's relatively faithful translations, Irinarkh Vvedensky's free-wheeling and wildly "creative" renditions represented a throwback to Neoclassicism. Thus in translating *David Copperfield* he composed his own ending to chapter 2, provided a new beginning for chapter 4, and so on. What could have encouraged this particular regression? One conjecture is that Vvedensky was influenced by Belinsky's

---

88. Literally, "from oneself." The "-tina" suffix and ending, analogous to such terms as *teliatina* (veal), *kuriatina* (chicken meat), or *gusiatina* (goose flesh), impart to the term a comic flavor.
89. Chukovskii, *Iskusstvo perevoda*, pp. 104–5.
90. Levin, *Russkie perevodchiki*, p. 123
91. Savory, *Art of Translation*, p. 39.
92. Rusinek, *O sztuce tłumaczenia*, p. 24.

defense of Nikolai Polevoi's very "creative" renditions of *Hamlet*. Eager to popularize Shakespeare among newly literate Russian readers, Belinsky sanctioned such translations as temporarily justified, believing that with the growth of literary sophistication among the Russian public they would be supplanted in time by more literal renditions. According to this theory, Vvedensky assumed that Belinsky's reasoning was equally applicable to Victorian novels and proceeded to create a very sloppy and inauthentic Russian rendition of *Vanity Fair* teeming with his own explanatory insertions. He explained his reasoning in an essay comparing his own and a competitor's Russian versions of the novel: "Transpose the writer under those skies and into the society in which you live, and ask yourself the following question. How would the writer express his ideas if he were to live and write in your circumstances? . . . Granted, my renditions are not literal, and *I readily concede that in my Vanity Fair there are passages created by my own pen. Please note, however, that my pen was attuned to Thackeray's manner of expressing his thoughts.*"[93]

And so it was. Vvedensky's patches of his own cloth, so impertinently grafted onto his renditions of the novels of Thackeray and Dickens, were themselves woven from deceptively Dickensian and Thackerayan thread, blending completely with the fabric of the English novelists' prose. Vvedensky took great pride in his singular gift, and on one occasion gleefully pointed out that certain passages in his Russian version of *Vanity Fair*, which even his detractors conceded were excellent, did not originate with Thackeray at all, but were translator's *otsebiatina!*[94] Even Kornei Chukovsky, who was shocked to discover thousands of mistakes in Vvedensky's *David Copperfield*, fell under the spell of this translator's magic:

> Nevertheless, his renditions are wonderful. What does it matter if he is a liar and an ignoramus who distorts nearly every sentence! The fact is that without him we would have no Dickens at all. He alone brought us closer to [Dickens's] work, immersed us in his flavor, infected us with his temper. He did not understand Dickens's words, but he understood Dickens himself. . . . We heard Dickens's real voice, and we came to love it. In his translations Vvedensky seems to

---

93. Irinarkh Vvedenskii, "O perevodakh romana Tekkereia *Vanity Fair* v Otechestvennykh zapiskakh i Sovremennike," *Otechestvennye zapiski*, 1851, no. 9, pp. 69–70; cited in Alekseev, *Mezhdunarodnye sviazi russkoi literatury*, p. 41; emphasis added.
94. Levin, *Russkie perevodchiki*, p. 129.

have dressed himself up in Dickens's costume and mask; he appropriated his gestures and manner of walking. . . . Of course, one cannot tolerate a translator's adding his own words to the text [*otsebiatina*], but some of Vvedensky's [additions] are so much in the spirit of Dickens, are so much in harmony with his general tone, that one hates to cross them out. Indeed, one wonders whether Dickens would have crossed them out himself, had he chanced upon them![95]

Chukovsky's enthusiasm for Vvedensky's versions of Dickens did not go unchallenged. Evgeny Lann (1896–1958), who in collaboration with his wife Alexandra Krivtsova (1896–1958) produced new Russian renditions of both *David Copperfield* and *The Pickwick Papers*, maintained that what Vvedensky did was not translation at all, but only a paraphrase that paid almost no attention to the stylistic peculiarities of Dickens's prose. The Soviet scholar Yuri Levin saw Vvedensky's methods as *an aspiration to co-authorship* which overstepped the permissible limits of the translator's art.[96]

Specifically, as pointed out by the novelist and journalist A. V. Amfiteatrov in 1911, Vvedensky tried to establish a link between Dickens and Gogol in the mind of the Russian reader. Thus in A. I. Levitov's story "It Happened in St. Petersburg" one of the characters speaks of Vvedensky's Russian versions of Dickens and Thackeray as continuers of the Gogolian tradition.[97] More to the point, regardless of whether one shares Chukovsky's rapture or Lann's disapproval of Vvedensky's art, it is difficult to challenge Levin's judgment that up to the present time no other translated author has been as influential in Russian literature as Dickens and, to a lesser extent, Thackeray.

By the 1830s Russian literary translation was becoming more professional, and renditions from French translations increasingly rare. To be sure, most practitioners of the art had to earn their livelihoods in other pursuits. One of these was Mikhail Vronchenko (1801 or 1802–55), a military geographer with the rank of major general, who resided during his career in several cities that afforded him opportunities to associate with local men of letters. While living in the Estonian city of Tartu he struck up a friendship

---

95. Kornei Chukovskii and Andrei Fedorov, *Iskusstvo perevoda* (Leningrad: Academia, 1930), pp. 61–62.

96. Levin, *Russkie perevodchiki*, pp. 142–43; emphasis added.

97. Alexander Levitov (1846–77) was a minor novelist. *Peterburgskii sluchai* describes the author's childhood. See Nikolaev, *Russkie pisateli*, 1:402.

with the Russian poet N. M. Iazykov, and in Vilnius (then Vilno) he was befriended by the Polish poet Adam Mickiewicz. Vronchenko's translations reflect the changes wrought by the new fashions of the late 1820s. Translators were now called upon to reproduce, insofar as possible, not merely the content, but also the form, style, artistic peculiarities, and above all the *national* traits of the original. The poets and translators N. I. Gnedich and P. A. Viazemsky, formerly partisans of Zhukovsky's "pleasing" free renditions, now demanded that the translator *submit* to the author of the original, rather than aspire to equal fame, and be content with having accomplished "a good deed." Vronchenko's renditions include *Hamlet* (from the original, not from a French adaptation), *Macbeth*, Byron's *Manfred*, six of Thomas More's *Irish Melodies*, parts of *Faust* and of *Paradise Lost*, Mickiewicz's *Forefather's Eve*, and a part of his *Konrad Wallenrod*. As a translator, Vronchenko espoused literalism: "I translated nearly always verse by verse and often word by word, resorting even to rarely used locutions. I endeavored to create for my contemporaries the closest possible facsimile of Shakespeare's *Hamlet*. However, this required the retention of a nearly inimitable aesthetic splendor. And it was precisely this that I could not guarantee." Vronchenko's literalist *Macbeth*, however, was a commercial failure. Belinsky reported in 1840 that it had sold only *five* copies. Possibly for that reason Vronchenko subsequently moderated his literalism. Still, whenever he departed from a word-by-word rendering, he alerted readers to that fact by means of a footnote; and he always strove to reproduce the original as faithfully as he could. Even in his *Faust* one finds no interjections of his own, no *otsebiatina*.

If Major General Vronchenko was regarded by the Imperial Russian authorities as a patriotic gentleman, as seems safe to assume, Nikolai Gerbel' (1827–83) was certainly considered politically questionable. His renown as a poet was easily eclipsed by his notoriety as the publisher in the West of Russian literary works that were banned by the Imperial censorship. (The term *tamizdat* [published abroad] had not yet been coined, but the activity itself was already familiar.) Gerbel' printed abroad such rebellious Decembrist poets as Wilhelm Küchelbecker, A. I. Odoevsky, S. I. Murav'ëv-Apostol, and K. F. Ryleev, as well as about a hundred of Pushkin's poems. His publications were then smuggled into Russia, inaugurating an illustrious tradition that continued until the collapse of the Soviet Union in 1991. Gerbel' himself was only modestly gifted as a poet; he often employed clichés, platitudes, or awkward turns of phrase. As a translator, he is remembered chiefly for his renditions of Byron, the complete sonnets of Shakespeare, the prose and poetry of Schiller and Goethe (he always translated verse in verse), and scenes from Marlowe's *Edward II*.

As a publisher, however, Gerbel' was enterprising and influential. His foremost nonpolitical achievement was a two-volume edition of Schiller in Russian translation.[98] The project involved forty-nine translators, which may have set an unfortunate precedent. Such collective efforts inevitably result in a bewildering variety of translating styles, making it virtually impossible for the reader to guess what the original might really be like. On the other hand, the defects of this collective method were partly mitigated by the fact that a few of Schiller's poems were printed in as many as five renditions apiece.

Among nineteenth-century Russian literary translators, Mikhail Mikhailov (1829–65) represented the radical extreme on the political spectrum. He was the descendant of serfs, although his father, a provincial government official, had been ennobled. Like Vvedensky, Mikhailov was a friend of the radical critic Chernyshevsky; and during his stay in England and France in 1858–59 he met with the revolutionary exiles Alexander Herzen and Nikolai Ogarev. Subsequently he became associated with other radicals, such as P. L. Lavrov and N. V. Shelgunov. For disseminating their leaflets Mikhailov was arrested and exiled to Siberia, where he died.[99]

As a young man (roughly from 1845 to 1854), Mikhailov did not distinguish between original and translated verse and often omitted to name the foreign authors whose works he put into Russian. Subsequently, however, he was to insist that all translations faithfully reproduce the original texts. Failure to do so, he wrote, makes even a smooth and polished rendition quite worthless. He spared no effort to preserve the formal features of the originals, since he believed these characteristics to be closely tied to the contents of his sources. The fact that he was not always successful is another matter, presumably a reflection of his poetic limitations. Only later in life did Mikhailov realize that the same meter and stanzaic construction can create different effects in different languages, a discovery leading him to seek emotional rather than formal equivalents.

Mikhailov was a prolific translator. He produced renditions of Schilller, Goethe, Uhland, Lenau, Rückert, Chamisso, Byron, Sappho, and An-

---

98. Levin, *Russkie perevodchiki*, pp. 142–43, 36–37, 26–35, 38–39, 46–47, 163–70, 174.

99. Mikhailov was in love with Shelgunov's wife, with the husband's full knowledge. It may well be that this love triangle served as a model for the one found in Chernyshevskii's *What Is To Be Done?*

acreon. He owed his fame, however, to his translations of Heinrich Heine's satirical, iconoclastic verse. Indeed, Mikhailov's popularity among liberal and radical Russian readers in the nineteenth century can hardly be exaggerated. He declared in 1848 that he had translated nearly everything Heine ever wrote. In 1857, a year and a half after the German poet's death, he undertook to publish a four-volume edition of his Heine translations, but ultimately abandoned the project.

At the opposite end of the political spectrum, Alexander Druzhinin (1824–64) was a conservative. At one time he was also a major presence in Russian letters. His novel *Polin'ka Saks* (1847), which dealt with the shocking new subjects of extramarital love and divorce, was one of the most widely read books of its time. Druzhinin was also an influential literary critic, a conservative counterpart of Belinsky and Mikhailov. Erudite and well read, particularly in English prose, he wrote essays about Samuel Johnson, Sheridan, Crabbe, Walter Scott, Thackeray, Richardson, Goldsmith, Anne Radcliffe, and Charlotte Brontë. As a translator of Shakespeare, he had to contend with considerable competition: the harvest of renditions from the 1840s included N. M. Katkov's *Romeo and Juliet*, N. M. Satin's *The Tempest* and *A Midsummer Night's Dream*, and the four translated plays by A. I. Kroneberg (*Hamlet, Macbeth, Twelfth Night*, and *Much Ado About Nothing*). All of these Russian translators tended toward compromise between a literal and a free method. To create a smooth and graceful effect, they simplified Shakespeare's language, replacing unusual or complex images with more familiar ones. But they all avoided the arbitrary translator's insertions [*otsebiatina*] for which translators like Vvedensky had been famous.[100]

Nowadays Druzhinin is chiefly remembered for his translations of four Shakespearean plays, particularly *King Lear*, which he completed in 1856. Prior to his time there had been three other Russian versions of this play: N. I. Gnedich's (1808), which was an adaptation of a French translation; V. A. Iakimov's very literal version, which was quite devoid of poetry; and V. A. Karatygin's highly abridged and rather ponderous rendition. However, such was Druzhinin's "reactionary" reputation that even in the twentieth century he was taken to task by Soviet critics for his *choices* of Shakespearean dramas to translate. In Chukovsky's opinion, Druzhinin selected *Coriolanus*, a play based on Plutarch's *Lives*, in order "to settle political scores with [the radical] Chernyshevsky and his followers." (The play

---

100. Levin, *Russkie perevodchiki*, pp. 202–4, 183–93, 150.

contains angry diatribes by the Roman patrician Coriolanus against popular rule.) As for *King Lear*, Chukovsky grumbled, Druzhinin must have viewed it as a paean to conservative virtues, devoted old servants, and the like. Such arguments are not very convincing. Surely the choice of texts to be translated falls within the translator's prerogatives and calls for no apology. It was not Druzhinin's *King Lear* that warranted criticism for political bias, but Gnedich's, or more precisely, the French rendition on which it was based. In Gnedich's text Lear's insanity was suppressed, the better to highlight the moral injustice of robbing an anointed monarch of his lawful throne.

Druzhinin's own 1856 translation of *King Lear* was, in his own words, "poetic" in the sense that Belinsky had used the term in his evaluation of Polevoi's (very free rendition of) *Hamlet*. It was neither literal nor complete, but it did attempt to reproduce at least some of the poetry of the original. Druzhinin admitted that he had "abandoned any exaggerated worship of the letter of the original" and "toned down or eliminated metaphors or locutions incompatible with the spirit of Russian" in order to "explain and simplify" Shakespeare's poetry for Russians. While he believed that Shakespeare's metaphorical quality was a superficial trait not *worth* salvaging, he did strive to preserve the Bard's unusual locutions, thus earning recognition as an early representative of Russian Realistic translation.[101] Interestingly, Druzhinin regarded "poetic" translations as only temporarily tolerable until such time as the Russian public had reached a level of sophistication adequate for understanding and appreciating literal renditions. Actual developments took a different path. Russian translators in the latter part of the nineteenth century grew more "creative," and their renderings bespoke progressively less resemblance to the works that had inspired them.

Dmitry Mikhailovsky (1828–1905), an official in the Ministry of Finance, wrote original verse reminiscent of Nikolai Nekrasov's civic poetry of social protest and also did much translating. His own poetry was quite undistinguished, filled with conventional imagery and banal epithets presented in a monotonous stanzaic structure. In his translations he at first favored congenial subjects, such as Thomas Hood's "The Bridge of Sighs" and other works that, as he wrote to Nekrasov, "contained ideas" of protest against inequality. Mikhailovsky was also the editor of a three-volume set of Byron in Russian and a similar edition of Shakespeare. He himself translated Byron's *Mazeppa* and half of Longfellow's *Hiawatha*. (The latter

---

101. Chukovskii, *Vysokoe iskusstvo*, pp. 30–31, 34–36, 150–51.

would be overshadowed in the twentieth century by Ivan Bunin's haunting translation of the full text.) Mikhailovsky also produced renditions of five of Shakespeare's plays: *Julius Caesar, Richard II, Henry V, Romeo and Juliet,* and *Antony and Cleopatra*. In addition, he wrote mediocre original verse inspired by foreign poets. From the 1870s to 1890s Mikhailovsky forsook themes of social protest in favor of translations of poetry that probed the subjects of melancholy, foreboding, and death. During this latter period he produced renditions of Baudelaire, Musset, Sully Prudhomme, and the Swiss poet Dranmore, whose pessimistic verse bears the imprint of the philosopher Schopenhauer. A conventional translator, Mikhailovsky criticized Afanasy Fet's version of *Julius Caesar,* charging it with excessive concern with form at the expense of content as well as excessively rigid literalism, which even did violence to good Russian usage.[102]

Fet (1820–92), a leading Russian poet, was indeed an unbending literalist. His translation practices were viewed as extreme even in his lifetime, and he had neither unconditional allies nor faithful pupils.[103] This is not to say that no other partisans of literalism existed in his day. When Petr Viazemsky (1792–1878), a poet, critic, and close friend of Pushkin, became a convert to Romantic principles of translation, he embraced literalism with such fervor that in order to avoid compromises with its dogmas he began to render poetry in prose. This practice was common enough in France but exceedingly rare in Russia.[104] The poet Nikolai Gnedich (1784–1833) toyed with the idea of translating literally even if this entailed disregarding Russian usage, though he never actually went so far. Instead, he rendered the *Iliad* very impressively in Russian hexameters and majestically archaic language. "Free translation," he wrote, "benefits the translator rather than the original. I chose to benefit Homer rather than myself."[105] Vronchenko, as mentioned earlier, was also a literalist. Yet it is Fet who continues to be regarded as the standard-bearer of nineteenth-century literalism in Russian translation history, both on account of his steadfast adherence to literalist principles and because of his stature as a poet.

Fet's rendition of *Faust* was not merely literal in its reproduction of Goethe's text. It also copied the metric structure and syntax of the original (a formidable feat, given the difficulty of converting German sentence structure into Russian) and reproduced even those features of German that

---

102. Levin, *Russkie perevodchiki*, pp. 235–53.
103. Alekseev, *Mezhdunarodnye sviazi russkoi literatury*, p. 53.
104. Levin, *Russkie perevodchiki*, pp. 37–38.
105. Ibid., p. 38.

are rare in Russian or altogether alien to it. The resulting clumsy rendition was a forerunner of Symbolist translation practices.[106] Fet believed that ultimately there can be *no* substitute for reading a literary work in the original. Homer, he insisted, must be read in ancient Greek. A translation is no equivalent, and certainly is not a work of art in its own right. What Fet really advocated was the learning of foreign languages.[107] Implied by the rigidity of his literalist views was the notion that a translation is merely a "crib," a "pony." However, he stood ready to defend his creations as the best possible approximations to the original works:

> Even the poorest photograph or [the hearing of] an organ grinder offers a better opportunity to see Venus de Milo or the Virgin, or to hear [the opera] Norma, than any verbal descriptions can. The same may be said of the translations of works of genius. Lucky the translator who succeeds in capturing even a part of that graceful form without which a work of genius is unthinkable. This should bring supreme happiness both to the translator and to his reader.[108]

Fet's somewhat stilted renditions offered an easy target to opponents of literalism. One Soviet critic, himself not a native speaker of Russian, went so far as to accuse the great Russian poet of using not only clumsy metric constructions, but even poor grammar.[109] Fet's literalism, however, was not unprovoked. It was an "elitist" reaction to the sloppiness, incompetence, and disrespect for the integrity of the literary text that characterized the efforts of commercial translators whose work was aimed at newly literate readers. It is probably true that the majority of readers failed to appreciate Fet's painstaking Russian reconstructions. But it is just as likely that these readers did not appreciate Fet's exquisite original lyric poetry either, preferring instead the crude civic outpourings of the "progressive" versifiers of the day.

Fet was atypical of the translators of his age, both as an exponent of literalism and as a major author in his own right. Most competent Russian literary translators bore greater resemblance to Dmitry Min (1818–85), a practicing physician, professor of medicine, and editor of a medical journal who translated in his free time. Besides Schiller and Byron, who were

---

106. Zhirmunskii, *Gete v russkoi literature*, pp. 430–32.
107. Rossel's, *Voprosy khudozhestvennogo perevoda*, pp. 81–87.
108. Nikolaev, *Russkie pisateli*, pp. 326–27.
109. Gachechiladze, *Vvedenie v teoriiu*, pp. 57–58.

translated by scores of other Russians, Min provided renditions of George Crabbe, an English Realist poet whose poems "The Borough" and "The Parish Register" depicted provincial towns and parishes. Min's most important achievements were his renditions of Torquato Tasso's *Jerusalem Delivered* (which his radical colleague Mikhail Mikhailov liked, while the conservative Alexander Druzhinin did not) and of Dante's *Divine Comedy*. Of the five Russian versions of Dante's classic produced in the nineteenth century, Min's was reputedly the best. Even so, the Symbolist poet Valery Briusov (1873–1924) complained some years later that Min's translation "impoverishes" Dante. This was undoubtedly true: Min was at best a skillful versifier. A superior rendition of *The Divine Comedy* was completed in the 1930s by Mikhail Lozinsky, one of the best translators of the Soviet period.

Those of Min's contemporaries who deserve mention include Nikolai Ketcher (1809–86), who translated some works of Schiller and E. T. A. Hoffmann as well as *all* of Shakespeare's plays; Andrei Kroneberg (1814–55), whose renditions of *Hamlet, Macbeth,* and *The Twelfth Night* "were once recognized as canonical, and were reprinted for nearly a century"; and Pavel Kozlov (1841–91), who produced the first complete Russian rendition of Byron's *Don Juan,* one of the longest narrative poems in world literature. (The protagonist of Nabokov's *Pnin* uses Kroneberg's translation to recite the scene of Ophelia's drowning in the incongruous setting of a postwar American college campus.)

Petr Veinberg (1831–1908), a professor of Russian literature in Russian-ruled Warsaw and in St. Petersburg, was an exceptionally active man of letters. He wrote lackluster, cliché-ridden original poetry as well as much literary and social commentary; published the weekly magazine *Vek* (age, or century); and served the literary community through his work with a charitable association offering assistance to aging and needy authors, a forerunner of the Soviet *Litfond*. Veinberg brought out a twelve-volume set of Russian renditions of Heine (he was himself a leading translator of the German poet), a six-volume set of Goethe (originally he had envisaged ten volumes), and editions of other foreign authors. He was also a prolific translator who aimed to introduce the Russian reading public to the best of Western writing.

Veinberg's success in disseminating Western literature is borne out by an incomplete list of his activities. He translated Lessing, Schubart, Uhland, Chamisso, Lenau, Gutzkow, Herwegh, Freiligrath, Sheridan, Burns, Shelley, Barrett-Browning, Musset, Dumas, Sardou, Barbier, Longfellow, Bret

Harte, Anderson, and Ibsen. He was particularly attracted to the translation of plays. This proved a boon to Russia's theaters, which suffered (as they still do!) from the seemingly perpetual shortage and inadequacy of native repertory. All in all, Veinberg translated twenty-three plays, including nine of Shakespeare's—*Othello, Timon of Athens, Henry VIII, The Merchant of Venice, As You Like It, The Comedy of Errors, Love's Labor Lost, The Merry Wives of Windsor,* and *All's Well That Ends Well.*[110] While his versions of these plays have been rendered obsolete by more modern translations such as Boris Pasternak's, they continue to live in the Russian language as commonly used quotations from Shakespeare.[111]

Veinberg wrote in 1889 that a translation should strive to reproduce the *impressions* that the content of the original makes on its readers, not just the artistically pleasant sensations but the unpleasant ones as well.[112] Unfortunately, his modest literary talent often precluded the realization of his theories in practice, and exacted a price for his insistence on reproducing the original "in full." His renditions are verbose and puffy or, as Yuri Levin called them, "diluted" (*razbavlennye*). In Veinberg's English translations the number of lines, stanzas, and words is far greater than the usual fifteen percent increase common in Russian verse translations of English poetry. (The latter is an unavoidable consequence of the much greater length of inflected Russian words.) His translations of Schiller required twice as many verses as the original. This was not only because Russian words are longer than German ones (to say nothing of the English), but because Veinberg's poetic lexicon was less taut and concise than that of the foreign original.

A number of Western European poets—Byron, Schiller, and Heine, for instance—exerted a strong fascination on nineteenth-century Russia. But Goethe alone was viewed with awe as both a poet and a seer, much as Tolstoy would be regarded some decades hence. This subject is explored in Viktor Zhirmunsky's 1981 study, *Goethe in Russian Literature.* Not surprisingly, many Russian translators, including important poets—especially in the nineteenth century but also in the twentieth—have tried to capture the essence of Goethe's art and thought. *Faust* appeared in no fewer than

---

110. Levin, *Russkie perevodchiki*, pp. 214–32, 289–90, 273, 274–85.
111. For example, "Ona menia za muki poliubila / A ia ee za sostradan'e k nim" [She loved me for the dangers I had pass'd / And I love her that she did not pity them] (Othello, 1.1.158); "Chudovishche s zelenymi glazami" [It (jealousy) is the green-eyed monster] (Othello, 3.3.165).
112. See Levin, "Ob istoricheskoi evoliutsii," pp. 51–52.

five nineteenth-century Russian translations, not counting Mikhail Vronchenko's partial version: by Nikolai Kholodkovsky (1858–1921), Edward Guber (1814–47), Alexander Strugovshchikov (1808–78), Afanasy Fet, and Valery Briusov. This number attests to an exceptional interest in Goethe's poetic masterpiece and in Western writing generally. Nevertheless, efforts to produce more satisfying modern versions continued into the twentieth century, culminating in the one by Boris Pasternak.

Goethe's nineteenth-century translators revealed a number of different and sometimes conflicting approaches to literary translation as such. Guber, whose version of *Faust* appeared in 1838, created a very literal translation. Indeed, he even tried to retain Goethe's meter and stanzaic structure, saying:

> Insofar as possible, I endeavored to salvage in my rendition all the meters of an original work in which form is so closely linked to thought, in which it corresponds so vividly to the feelings and position of the characters. Even in those instances where Goethe resorted to so-called *Knittelverse,* a rigid uneven meter of German folksongs and sixteenth-century *Minnesänger,* I strove to preserve the color of the original, disregarding the fact that this entailed sounds to which the Russian ear is unaccustomed.

Guber's poetic limitations, like Veinberg's, resulted in such tell-tale traits as verbosity (with nine lines of the original *Faust* corresponding to fourteen in the translation), very long paraphrases of concise passages, and the loss of Goethe's idiosyncratic language, which became submerged in the translator's "generic Romantic" clichés.

Among Goethe's nineteenth-century Russian translators, Alexander Strugovshchikov (1808–78) was one of the most picturesque. Working during the 1830s and 1840s, when interest in Goethe was at its peak—a period when translators of Goethe included such leading Russian poets as Lermontov, Fet, and Apollon Grigor'ev—he nevertheless succeeded in gaining recognition as the foremost Russian interpreter of the great German poet. Financially independent (his family was quite wealthy, and he had a well-paying position at the Ministry of War), Strugovshchikov was impervious to pressures from publishers and reviewers. He also had reason to trust his own judgment. His lengthy residence in Germany and fluency in spoken German (attributes which his rivals lacked) allowed him to escape the feeling of awe that Goethe generally inspired. This led him to take great liberties with Goethe's works, rearranging the text, translating some parts, rearranging others, and even inserting passages of his own. He never claimed authorship of these works, however, but saw himself in the "modest role of a good translator."[113]

Strugovshchikov seemed quite literally possessed by Goethe. Not only did he know *Faust* by heart. Intent on producing a perfect rendition of the original without ever repeating himself, he translated it six times, sealing each version in an envelope, locking it in a separate drawer, and throwing the key into the Neva river. Only after completing the sixth version did he create a composite of all the variants.[114] The resulting Russian-language *Faust* read reasonably smoothly and was on the whole faithful to the original. Nevertheless it was not well received, since it suffered from the common nineteenth-century afflictions of verbosity and Romantic cliché. Strugovshchikov was also addicted to Sentimentalist euphemisms, which destroyed much of Goethe's impassioned German narrative as well as the natural simplicity of Gretchen's speech.[115] These shortcomings were unavoidable, since Strugovshchikov's craft proved inadequate to Goethe's art.

Earlier, however, Strugoshchikov had considered himself to be something of a rival of the authors he translated. Thus he titled a collection of his works *Poems by Alexander Strugovshchikov Borrowed from Goethe and Schiller,* implying that the poems were *primarily his own.*[116] Indeed, he openly proclaimed that a reasonably free translation becomes the sole property of the translator: "When your translation ceases to look like one/ Sign your own name to it, and assume responsibility for it." That Strugovshchikov's views rather closely resembled Zhukovsky's may also be seen from his 1841 pronouncement: "As for the so-called mistakes in my translations (and a good many of these may, indeed, be found), they are the result of a little rule I always observe. *Do not translate what the poet wrote, but what he tried to express by what he wrote.*"[117]

It hardly needs emphasizing that, by implication, this position sanctioned even extreme conjecture. Strugovshchikov practiced what he preached. He confessed that while translating he would often forget or

---

113. Levin, *Russkie perevodchiki*, pp. 285, 60, 62–65, 72–75, 83.
114. Lev Ginzburg, *Nad strokoi perevoda: Stat'i raznykh let* (Moscow: Sovetskaia Rossiia, 1981), pp. 52–53.
115. Levin, *Russkie perevodchiki*, pp. 92–93.
116. Ibid., pp. 83–84. The Russian title of the book was *Stikhotvoreniia Aleksandra Strugovshchikova zaimstvovannye iz Gete i Shillera.*
117. Levin, *Russkie perevodchiki*, p. 85; emphasis added.

simply disregard details of the original text while trying instead to reproduce his *impressions* of it: "It happens sometimes that memories impress one's psyche more strongly than the phenomena themselves."[118] Nor was he alone in this careless treatment of original texts. Nikolai Berg (1823–84), a translator of Petrarch, Byron, and Slavic folklore, believed that "verse is not important, spirit is, impressions are. Why follow the painter's brush trying to ascertain whether he had smeared this spot red and that spot white? What we used is acceptance of the completed portrait as a likeness of the original."[119] V. D. Radchuk, a Soviet Ukrainian critic, commented that Berg was "fearful of everything unusual or strange, and he mutilated, discolored, rendered neuter or Russified songs of other nations to the point where they lost all resemblance to the original."[120]

Aleksei K. Tolstoy (1817–75), poet, playwright, novelist, and distant cousin of Leo Tolstoy, is chiefly remembered nowadays as the co-creator of a literary mystification, the nonsense poetry attributed to "Koz'ma Prutkov." He also did some translating. In 1867 he described his method in rendering Goethe's *The Bride of Corinth:*

> Insofar as possible, I try to remain faithful to the original, but only on condition that precision and faithfulness *not obstruct the artistic effect.* I will not for a moment hesitate to abandon literal precision if the latter might result in Russian in an impression different from [that of] the German original. I believe that one should not translate *words* — and sometimes not even the *meaning* — but above all convey the *impression.* The reader of translations should be transposed into the same *milieu* as the reader of the original. The translation should touch the same nerves.

It is worth noting that subsequently a Symbolist like Sergey Solov'ëv thought highly of A. K. Tolstoy's *Bride of Corinth.*[121]

The 1840s mark the end of Russian Romanticism not only in original literature, but also in the translation doctrine that insisted on relative fidelity to the original text. Not everyone was pleased with this development. Belinsky was greatly irritated by the contemptuous attitude toward

---

118. Nikolaev, *Russkie pisateli*, p. 210; cited in *Teoriia i praktyka perekladu* (Kiev), no. 1 (1979): 44.
119. Nikolaev, *Russkie pisateli*, p. 317.
120. *Teoriia i praktyka perekladu*, no. 1 (1979): 44.
121. Zhirmunskii, *Gete v russkoi literature*, pp. 349–50; italics in the original.

original works that had recently become fashionable among translators. His comments on Alexander Strugovshchikov's very free renditions of Goethe were sharply worded:

> We have begun to notice that Mr. Strugovshchikov does not always merely translate. Sometimes he [also] introduces textual revisions. Indeed, Mr. Strugovshchikov makes no secret of it. He has expressed somewhere in print the opinion that in a translation one should have the foreign author write as he would do if he were to write in Russian. . . . But who gives one the right to modify, change, abbreviate or expand the thought of a writer of genius, to change his creation? Only another genius! What is the purpose of a translation? To convey the most faithful impression possible of a foreign literary work as it really is.[122]

Needless to say, Belinsky's wish has since been followed as often in the breach as in the observance. Confusion has been compounded by the fact that while only a few of the translators (say, Pasternak or Akhmatova) could aspire to poetic greatness, the overwhelming majority of original texts were not written by geniuses, either. Not infrequently the translator could, in all honesty, "improve" on the original. Sometimes he felt that it was his duty to do so, precisely because the artistic idiosyncrasies of the original were not viewed as precious in themselves.

According to Efim Etkind, a leading Soviet (and later émigré) specialist on poetic translation, professional Russian translators of verse at the close of the nineteenth century fell into four categories. The group that included Nikolai Berg, Dmitry Min, and Mikhail Mikhailov envisaged its mission as contributing to the cultural enrichment of readers and also as introducing new forms to Russian poetry itself. Closely allied to this group were translators who wished to acquaint their readers with aesthetic notions different from those in the Russian tradition. In a third category were the established poets such as A. K. Tolstoy and Aleksei Apukhtin (1841–93), who used renditions of congenial foreign authors as an opportunity to "express their own poetic creed." Indeed, their style of translation is understandable only in the context of their original work. The final category includes translators active in the radical revolutionary movement like Vasily Kurochkin (1831–75), Dmitry Minaev, and Viktor

---

122. Cited in ibid., p. 357.

Burenin (1841–1926), who utilized translations of Western authors to propagate their own revolutionary democratic ideals. In Etkind's words, "Statements of Russian political positions were concealed behind a famous foreigner's name."[123]

Professional translators of verse and (to a lesser degree) drama were, so to speak, the aristocracy of the craft. Translation of prose was a different matter. Here the dilettantes and proletarians of the profession were to be found, those to whom translation was either a hobby or a means to eke out a meager livelihood. Representatives of both groups are familiar even to casual readers of nineteenth-century Russian literature. The wealthy bureaucrat Famusov in Griboedov's comedy *Woe from Wit*, at a loss to describe the occupation of the aristocratic Byronic drifter Chatsky, calls him a "translator." In *Crime and Punishment*, when a kindly soul seeks to help the starving and feverish Raskolnikov by finding him some employment, the work specifically mentioned is translation. A veritable chasm separated translation of lowly prose from that of the nobler genres.

Nineteenth-century prose translations did not invariably identify the author of a text on the title page. The translator might claim the work as his own; conversely, he might attribute to a foreign author something he had actually written himself. This was a familiar occurrence in France;[124] and analogous phenomena were to be found in Russia as well. I have already referred to some of them. It should also be added that pseudo-translations were written in Russia not only by hacks, but in one case by Pushkin himself. He was the real author of poems falsely attributed to the French poet Evariste Parny (1753–1814).

Drastically abbreviated Russian versions of foreign novels were also common in the nineteenth-century, when two or even three renditions of the same novel occasionally were serialized in competing journals. *Notes of the Fatherland* (*Otechestvennye zapiski*), a reputable magazine that had published Vvedensky's translations of Dickens and Thackeray, pointed an accusing finger at the very popular *Library for Reading* (*Biblioteka dlia chteniia*) for publishing a rendition of *The Pickwick Papers* that compressed the text into one-third of its original length. It was not that the *Library* was trying to save paper or avoid burdening its readers with an overly long text. On the contrary, while cutting Dickens's prose it added some witticisms

---

123. E. G. Etkind, ed., *Mastera russkogo stikhotvornogo perevoda: Vstupitel'naia stat'ia* (Leningrad: Sovetskii pisatel', 1968), pp. 59–60.

124. Hermans, *Manipulation of Literature*, pp. 158–59.

and opinions of its own—opinions to which Dickens could not possibly have subscribed.[125]

The Library for Reading, organized by the reactionary journalist, scholar, and literary entrepreneuer Osip Senkovsky (1800–1858), who called himself Baron Brambeus, was a major employer of the translator underclass. This class comprised mostly women, who were mercilessly exploited. To earn a pittance, they had to translate very fast and certainly could not afford the luxury of painstaking work. According to Kornei Chukovsky, these women worried only about meeting their deadlines and preserving the plots of their stories. Thus "Flaubert came out resembling Spielhagen, and Maupassant resembled Bret Harte." Trollope and George Sand, Balzac, and Eugène Sue were all rendered in the same colorless Russian prose. Not one of the *Library*'s translations was worth preserving for posterity.[126] However, Senkovsky's enterprise was hardly an exception in this respect. In Chukovsky's opinion, Russian translation between the 1870s and 1890s was on the whole God-awful. All writers came out sounding alike, since translators paid no heed to rhythm or style.[127]

Chukovsky was not alone in his unflattering appraisal. N. A. Rubakin, a leading Russian publisher and bibliographer, wrote in 1897: "The vast majority of great West European authors appear on the Russian book market in such miserable [*skvernye*] renditions (some abridged, others 'rewritten' by translators, still others mutilated by censorship, or simply obsolete) that on the basis of them Russian readers cannot form any notion of what the originals are like." Two major Soviet translation specialists concurred with this estimate. Vladimir Rossel's agreed with Rubakin that isolated successes by major translators "drown in this torrent of mediocre fiction."[128] Genrikh Mitin used similar language, urging "courage to voice unquestionably honest conclusions from the failures of [Russian] translation in the nineteenth century."[129]

---

125. I. N. Bushkanets, "Angliiskii roman i stanovlenie printsipov realisticheskogo perevoda v rossii," in *Russkaia literatura i osvoboditel'noe dvizhenie: Sbornik sed'moi* (Kazan': Ministerstvo Prosveshcheniia RSFSR, 1976), p. 92. To add insult to injury, *The Library for Reading* identified *Pickwick Papers* as a novel written in the early seventeenth century.

126. Chukovskii, *Vysokoe iskusstvo*, p. 294.

127. Chukovskii and Fedorov, *Iskusstvo perevoda*, p. 27. Karolina Pavlova's early nineteenth-century rendition of Schiller's *The Death of Wallenstein* is a rare exception: it is still reprinted. See Ginzburg, *Nad strokoi perevoda*, pp. 55–56.

128. Vladimir Rossel's, *Skol'ko vesit slovo: Stat'i raznykh let* (Moscow: Sovetskii pisatel', 1984), pp. 12–13.

129. L. A. Annenskii, comp., *Khudozhestvennyi perevod: Problemy i suzhdeniia: Sbornik statei* (Moscow: Izvestiia, 1986), p. 360.

Moreover, it appears that command of foreign languages among the educated classes of nineteenth-century Russia was less exemplary than is usually assumed. Belinsky, for one, adorned his articles with French quotations long before he had learned French, while Pushkin's German and English were decidedly poor. As for Russian renditions of foreign writing: "For a long time translated books were viewed as inferior literature for 'simple folk.' " The commissioning of translations in nineteenth-century Russia reflected this low esteem. Publishers often treated the translation of all types of writing—say, a mathematical treatise, a cookbook, or a volume of verse—in the same manner. All three might be entrusted to a single student, who engaged in this work for the money. Typically the student was instructed to produce a specific number of pages and observe certain deadlines. Fidelity to the original text was hardly an issue.[130] The resulting translations usually contained many factual errors and gross inaccuracies. Some were scarcely more than paraphrases. Others suffered from substandard language, inordinate use of calques, unwieldy sentences, and limited vocabulary. Many were also marred by references to specifically Russian realia, or by having foreign personages use Russian proverbs and sayings in their speech.[131]

Symbolism, a neo-Romantic literary movement arising in Russia at the turn of the century, resurrected much of the translation aesthetics of the earlier Romantic movement. Symbolist writers reverted to their predecessors' respectful stance toward original texts, including the self-effacing implication that *no* translation could rival the original. Valery Briusov, for example, often treated an original text downright deferentially. Logically this position often led to literalism, which now survived in Russia until its suppression during the 1930s. Indeed, Briusov asserted in 1911 that translations of verse are really an impossible task. His fondest hope, he said, was that his Russian renditions of Paul Verlaine might encourage *two or three Russians to read him in French*. This extreme position was strongly reminiscent of similar dicta of Afanasy Fet. Although in 1923 Briusov criticized Georgi Shengeli's clumsy literalist translations of Emile Verhaeren, his own unsuccessful rendition of the *Aeneid* also attested to literalist tendencies.[132]

Indeed, Briusov had earlier defended his own translations of Verhaeren from the criticism of Maksimilian Voloshin by insisting that a translation should reproduce even the shortcomings of the original. The Soviet linguist

---

130. Ibid., p. 193.
131. A. V. Fedorov, *Osnovy obshchei teorii perevoda* (Moscow, 1968), pp. 87–88.
132. Alekseev, *Mezhdunarodnye sviazi russkoi literatury*, pp. 54–59.

A. V. Fedorov sided with Briusov, arguing that those features of the original which the translator might consider clumsy, the author might regard as an important feature of his style. Essentially the same point was made on one occasion by the lexicographer Vladimir Dal' (1801–72) in an exchange with the publisher Aleksei Suvorin (1834–1912). One may be sorely tempted to "correct" Gogol's quaint Russian, Dal' argued, until one realizes that therein lies Gogol's idiosyncratic art.[133]

Fedorov, who was quite devastating in his evaluation of nineteenth-century Russian literary translation, spoke rather positively of Symbolist translators like Briusov (1873–1924), Innokenty Annensky (1856–1909), and Fedor Sologub (1863–1927). "Most of them," Fedorov wrote, "captured those peculiarities of the original poems which the Russian Symbolists considered important and attractive (as well as characteristic of the originals), setting them off against the background of French literature."[134] Fedorov was right. The Russian Symbolists produced excellent, sensitive translations, but only when the foreign poets whom they translated were Symbolists themselves and at least equal in poetic stature to their Russian counterparts. Otherwise, their tendency was to fashion the foreign poets into their own image—resembling their French Symbolist predecessors in this respect. For example, in translating Heinrich Heine into French, the poet Gérard de Nerval turned him into more of a Symbolist than Heine's own text would warrant. Nerval regarded translation as a creative act, and believed that the translator of poetry must necessarily be a poet himself.[135] The great French poet Charles-Pierre Baudelaire—an only occasional translator—was driven to render the tales of Edgar Allan Poe into French "because he resembled me." In opening one of Poe's books, he wrote, "I saw, with horror and delight, not only the subjects I had dreamed of, but *phrases* of mine, written by him twenty years previously."[136]

Russian Symbolists produced a number of translations of Goethe. As if following Verlaine's admonition in *Art poétique* ("De la musique avant toute chose / Et tout le reste est littérature"), they tried at all costs to salvage the rhythm and musical aspects of the original, even at the expense of the poem's contents. As Viktor Zhirmunsky noted, such practices distorted Goethe, a poet whose work emphasizes simplicity, directness, and

---

133. Chukovskii and Fedorov, *Iskusstvo perevoda*, pp. 212–13.
134. Ibid., pp. 219–20.
135. Marilyn Gaddis Rose, ed., *Translation Spectrum: Essays in Theory and Practice* (Albany: State University of New York Press, 1981), pp. 118–19.
136. Ibid., p. 120.

wholeness in the perception of life. Valery Briusov's rendition of *Faust* (the first part of which was printed in the fall of 1928, the second in 1932) reflected the translator's own philological erudition. Even so, he experienced difficulties in conveying the poem's philosophical content, though he succeeded admirably in reproducing Goethe's music and rhythm. Other Symbolist translators likewise endowed Goethe with traits characteristic of their own original work. Thus Viacheslav Ivanov (1866–1949) imparted a dense metaphysical suggestiveness to the German poet, while Innokenty Annensky overemphasized the preoccupation with death that was a hallmark of "decadent" Russian writing.[137]

Konstantin Bal'mont (1867–1943), an immensely popular Symbolist poet, was a prolific translator who "actually sought out foreign poets as a means of self-expression." However, his uniform style tended to obliterate the distinctions between dissimilar poets, making all sound somewhat alike.[138] Bal'mont's translation of Walt Whitman substituted classical Russian rhymes for Whitman's free verse—a point singled out for disapproval by Vladimir Rossel's.[139] Kornei Chukovsky was far more scathing. He maintained that Bal'mont could not abide Whitman's simplicity, even occasional crudeness, and made him reek of the same cheap perfume that was the scent of Bal'mont's own verse. He even changed Whitman's straightforward title *Leaves of Grass* (*List'ia travy*) to the more refined and genteel *Shoots of Grass* (*Pobegi travy*).[140] Bal'mont loved showmanship and adored high-flown language and complex imagery—none of which can be found in Whitman. As a result, according to Chukovsky:

> The translation turned into a *tug-of-war* between the translator and the poet being translated. That was unavoidable because basically Bal'mont hated the American bard. Accordingly, he would not let him remain as he was. Bal'mont tried to improve on Whitman in every way by imposing on him his own mannerisms, the elaborate and pretentious modernistic style that Whitman so detested. . . . Thus Bal'mont would not allow Whitman to speak in the language of the street and the newspapers. Bal'mont replaced Whitman's simple words with precious Church Slavonicisms. . . . Above all,

---

137. Zhirmunskii, *Gete v russkoi literature*, pp. 467–72.
138. Ritz, *150 Jahre*, pp. 12–13.
139. Rossel's *Skol'ko vesit slovo*, p. 36.
140. Chukovskii and Fedorov, *Ikusstvo perevoda*, pp. 13–16.

Bal'mont hated the prosaic, matter-of-fact tone that Whitman strove to achieve.[141]

Bal'mont was to achieve notoriety in the history of literary translation with his outwardly mellifluous, seductively sentimental renditions of Shelley. These were naturally popular with a public ignorant of English because "they read smoothly." Little did these Russians know that it was Bal'mont they read, not Shelley. The myth of Bal'mont's successful Russian versions of the English poet was finally exploded by Chukovsky, then still a brash young critic, who recalled: "I believe it was not until I read Shelley's verse in Bal'mont's renditions that I fully comprehended the extent to which a translator can distort the appearance of an author he has translated in order to make it resemble his own. . . . [Bal'mont's] additions solidified into a cohesive whole. They were glued to each other by a perfumed, stilted style of tawdry love songs. And this was a thousand times more harmful to Shelley than individual mistakes in translation."[142] Chukovsky christened Bal'mont's translations of Shelley *Shel'mont,* a nickname that also suggested the Russian word for "scoundrel" or "rogue," *shel'ma.* That label was to haunt Bal'mont for years to come.

Unbeknownst to him, Bal'mont's treatment of Shelley was a case of poetic justice (no pun intended!). It so happened that Shelley himself had done translations from classical Greek, German, Italian, and Spanish. As a translator, he very much resembled Bal'mont. His careless renditions abound in inaccuracies. Moreover, Shelley also felt free to "improve" the original text by "substituting himself" for whatever he did not like in the foreign author.[143] Translators of Russian novels into French sometimes treated their texts in the same way. Turgenev complained bitterly that he could not find *four properly translated lines* in the French version of his *Sportsman's Sketches.* Charrière, his French translator, arbitrarily omitted some passages in the book and changed others at will. Indeed, the Frenchman actually *introduced a personage not found in the Russian original* and proceeded to describe him in considerable detail. Similarly, Leo Tolstoy had

---

141. Chukovskii, *Iskusstvo perevoda*, pp. 18–19; original emphasis.
142. Ibid., p. 23.
143. Timothy Webb, *The Violet in the Crucible* (Oxford: Oxford University Press, 1976), as cited in Dewey R. Faulkner, "Late and Later Romantics," *Yale Review* (Spring 1978): 442–45.

been appalled by his French translators, who made Caucasian mountaineers play Spanish castanets instead of native tambourines.[144]

Russian literary translation in the nineteenth century has generally been held in low esteem by prerevolutionary and Soviet observers alike. Their arguments are convincing enough, but cast much doubt on later Soviet claims of excellence in translation, since Soviet translation practice was itself deeply indebted to nineteenth-century traditions. However, the present writer wishes to register dissent from what he regards as an overly harsh estimate of translation in tsarist Russia. In a number of ways it carried out its mission admirably. Translation introduced a newly literate nation (or more precisely, the nation's educated class) to secular writing and to the pleasures of reading. It provided Russia's men and women of letters with models for emulation. Translation served to educate literary taste and helped sustain the repertory of the young Russian theater. It established firm links between the artistic and intellectual life of Russia and that of Western Europe. Finally, without the benefit of translations from Western European languages, the rich body of Russia's own literature (as distinct from the works of individual authors) might not have come into being, let alone have succeeded in becoming the equal of the old and established literary traditions within the course of a single century.

---

144. Mounin, *Les belles infidèles*, pp. 9–10.

2

Theoretical Controversies

Except in the case of short poems, few literary translations can fully sustain the illusion that one is reading an original text. Unfamiliar circumstances intrude, as do foreign names, strange customs, and alien landscapes. This effect is even more pronounced in the theater and the cinema, where exotic natural surroundings, costume, and music clash with the language of the actor and the spectator. Three incidents stand out in my memory. One is an American Western in a Munich cinema in which the cowboy hero, armed with two pistols, instructed the regulars of a frontier saloon to get out by shouting in German, "*Alle raus!*" Another was a Russian film version of Jack London's *The Fighter,* in which sombreros, cacti, and the guitar strains of a Mexican song clashed with the Russian speech of the desperados. Finally, there was the performance in Israel of Gogol's *Inspector General* in which an actor, dressed in authentic nineteenth-century Russian costume, crossed himself in front of an icon and then said "*shalom.*"

True, a monolingual spectator's reactions would most likely have been more subdued. In the final analysis, we are all aware that most translations contain an element of make-believe. We must stand ready to suspend incredulity to the degree necessary for the acceptance of a dubbed film in which Japanese fishermen converse in English, or courtiers of Louis XIV chat in German, or a Chicago gangster says "*bonjour*." To a significant extent this suspension of disbelief is also required for the printed word that portrays settings, personages, and events that normally preclude the use of the language of the text. More basic misgivings about translation have been expressed in the past. Early in the twentieth century the philosopher Benedetto Croce, as if paraphrasing the old Italian saying *traduttore-traditore* ("Translators are traitors") declared that falsification is inevitable in translation.[1] And the poet Paul Valéry, who translated all of Virgil's *Eclogues*, some of Poe's *Marginalia*, a Petrarch sonnet, and Thomas Hardy's *Felling a Tree* into French, insisted that a poet "is never profoundly, intimately, and completely understood and felt except by his own people: he is inseparable from the speech of his nation. . . . The prose writer, the novelist, and the philosopher can be translated, and often are, without too much damage. But to the poet belongs the privilege and inevitable disadvantage that his work cannot be translated either into prose or into a foreign language. A true poet is strictly untranslatable."[2]

While similar views were not uncommon in the past, they are comparatively rare today. Theories of the impossibility of translation are "elitist." They naturally belong to historical periods like the eighteenth century, when literary culture was limited to a narrow, privileged class that was educated in foreign languages and able read foreign texts in the original.[3] In the Soviet Union, which defined itself as a workers' state, the theory of translation unanimously held that *anything* could be translated. Nevertheless, it is obvious that a perfect, definitive translation simply cannot exist. If we view the text in the target language as a translation, it never achieves perfection because we observe that it is not an entirely faithful reproduction of the original; and we can always conjure up yet another translation. On the other hand, if we see it as an *original* creation, it cannot simultaneously be viewed as a perfect translation because we now regard it as an autonomous literary work that has severed its ties to the original that inspired it.[4]

1. L. G. Kelly, *The True Interpreter: A History of Translation Theory and Practice in the West* (New York: St. Martin's Press, 1979), p. 216.
2. Cited in Reuben A. Brower, ed., *On Translation* (New York: Oxford University Press, 1966), pp. 73–75.
3. Georges Mounin, *Les belles infidèles* (Paris: Cahiers du Sud, 1955), p. 30.
4. Levon Mkrtchian, *Cherty rodstva* (Erevan: Izdatel'stvo Aiastan, 1973), p. 78.

Most translators—whether artists or hacks—are strictly practitioners of their craft and see no need for theoretical guidance, any more than do most poets or painters. It is therefore telling that Ivan Kashkin (1899–1963), arguably the most influential Russian translator of the era of Socialist Realism, insisted, as a good Marxist should, on the need for firm theoretical underpinnings:

> A translator who is not guided by a theory, a translator who is not interested in general principles, is but an artisan. On occasion he may even be a self-taught master, but he is an artisan nevertheless. Most frequently, however, he is just an ordinary artisan working in isolation. Within the limits of his gifts, he is capable of accidental successes. At the same time, however, he is vulnerable to slips and even disastrous failures, and this should come as no surprise. He rediscovers the wheel and seeks solutions to problems that were solved ages ago.[5]

The problem is that very few theoretical studies of translation exist in any language, and even fewer satisfying ones. In Russia Ivan Kashkin's own collection of essays does not really fit the bill, nor do the more adequate monographs of Kornei Chukovsky.[6] The 1791 *Essay on the Principles of Translation* by Alexander Fraser Tytler (Lord Woodhouselee) was "the first and only book written directly and only on the problems of translation until the end of the nineteenth century," according to Helmut Liedloff. Tytler laid down three rules which ought to be observed in all renditions: (1) the translation should give a complete transcript of the ideas of the original work; (2) the style and manner of writing should be of the same character as that of the original; and (3) the translation should have all the ease of the original composition. Tytler did authorize the translator to "clarify" ambiguities of the original and, as befitted Neoclassical aesthetics, allowed him

---

5. I. A. Kashkin, in *Masterstvo perevoda, 1963* (Moscow: Sovetskii pisatel', 1964), p. 452.

6. See Ivan Kashkin, *Dlia chitatelia-sovremennika: Stat'i i materialy* (Moscow: Sovetskii pisatel', 1968). A contrary opinion is offered by Lauren G. Leighton, who calls Kornei Chukovskii's *Iskusstvo perevoda* (*The Art of Translation*) the "first major study in world literature of the art of translation." Chukovskii's later popularization, *Vysokoe iskusstvo*, led Leighton to write that "its author was the most expert theorist and critic of the art of translation who ever lived." See Lauren G. Leighton, trans. and ed., *Kornei Chukovsky's A High Art* (Knoxville: University of Tennessee Press, 1984), pp. ix, xi. My own view of Chukovskii as a literary critic is decidedly less positive.

to "improve" even on Homer whenever the original might be offensive to modern tastes.[7] In that respect he was in full agreement with Madame Dacier (1647–1720), the French translator of the *Iliad* and the *Odyssey*, who found Homer excessively vulgar and crude.

According to a 1930 essay by Roman Jakobson, transferring a text from one language to another is but one of three types of translation, the others being paraphrase in the same language and "inter-semiotic translation," that is, formulating the signs of one semiotic system with the signs of another, as in the verbal description of a painting.[8] Jakobson's range of scholarly interests was exceptionally broad, so it was natural for him to write that a linguist should be sensitive to the poetic function of language and *vice versa*. Andrei Fedorov, the coauthor of Kornei Chukovsky's 1930 volume *The Art of Translation*, was a linguist of that kind. However, Fedorov and Jakobson were exceptions among scholars. In his 1975 book *Translating Poetry*, André Lefevere rightly bemoaned the fact that modern linguistics provides little guidance for literary scholars. He then quoted approvingly the statement of G. Leech that "no one has produced a complete account of language in general, or even of a single language, or even of one major area of the semantics of a single language." Yet precisely this, in Lefevere's view, constitutes "the very heart of the matter in literary translation."[9]

Efim Etkind cautioned that any linguistic theory of translation necessarily holds that the essence of translation is merely the change from one linguistic medium to another. What really impedes the development of translation theory, in his view, is insufficient recognition of the fact that literary translation is both an art and a science. This makes it subject to conflicting demands. Etkind advocated the study of comparative stylistics, which combines the linguistic and the literary aspects of translation: "A comparison of the stylistic resources of two languages is an absolute precondition for the formulation of a theory of translation."[10]

---

7. Helmut Liedloff, *Steinbeck in German Translation: A Study in Translational Practices* (Carbondale: Southern Illinois University, 1965), p. 5. Liedloff misspells the name as "Alexander Frazer Tyler." Information on Tytler may also be found in Theodore Savory, *The Art of Translation* (London: Jonathan Cape, 1957), pp. 42–43.

8. Irzhi Levyi [Jiří Levý], *Iskusstvo perevoda*, trans. Vl. Rossel's (Moscow: Progress, 1974), pp. 35–36.

9. André Lefevere, *Translating Poetry: Seven Strategies and a Blueprint* (Amsterdam: Van Gorcum, Assen, 1975), p. 6. The quotation is from G. Leech. It appears in his *Semantics* (Harmondsworth: Penguin, 1974), p. 70.

10. E. G. Etkind, "Khudozhestvennyi perevod: Iskusstvo i nauka," *Voprosy iazykoznaniia*, no. 4 (1970): 17 and 27.

At the present time we lack a systematic exposition of such theory. In the absence of one, I have relied on a wide variety of sources. Jiří Levý's Czech monograph was the most helpful Slavic book. Thoroughly grounded in Western European as well as Slavic translation theory and practice, it is far more erudite and sophisticated than any of the Soviet sources. André Lefevere's two studies were exceptionally useful for their insights as well as for the rigor with which they identify the weaknesses and strengths of the different approaches to translation practice.[11]

In 1684 in his *Essay on Translated Verse,* Wenworth Dillon, fourth earl of Roscommon, wrote:

> Then seek poet who your way do's bend,
> And chuse an author as you chuse a Friend,
> United by this sympathetic bond,
> You grow familiar, intimate and Fond;
> Your thoughts, your Words, your Stiles, your Souls agree,
> No longer his interpreter, but he.[12]

The recommendation to translate only what one loves has often been repeated since Roscommon's time. Moreover, his counsel continues to be dispensed three centuries after his death. The same (or similar) advice has been proffered by critics as different from each other as the American professor Justin O'Brien and the Soviet theoretician Kornei Chukovsky. O'Brien warned, "*Never translate anything one does not admire.* If possible, a natural affinity should exist between translator and translated."[13] In 1930 Chukovsky advised: "A translator should avoid authors whose temperament or literary bent he finds alien or hostile. A translator partial to Hugo should not be translating Zola: he would be doomed to failure."[14] And in 1936 he added the sage Marxist recommendation: closeness of the rendition to the original is achieved when the translator and the author

---

11. Levyi, *Iskusstvo perevoda;* André Lefevere, *Translating Literature: The German Tradition from Luther to Rosenzweig* (Amsterdam: Van Gorcum, Assen, 1977), and Lefevere, *Translating Poetry.*

12. Quoted in Kelly, *True Interpreter,* p. 61.

13. Reuben A. Brower, ed., *On Translation* (Cambridge: Harvard University Press, 1959), p. 85; original emphasis.

14. Kornei Chukovskii and Andrei Fedorov, *Iskusstvo perevoda* (Leningrad: Academia, 1930), p. 29.

belong to the same social class. This, he intoned, could already be observed in the USSR.[15]

Personally, I find Chukovsky's, O'Brien's, or—for that matter—Roscommon's advice unconvincing. Musicians and actors, who in their professions most closely resemble literary translators in that they provide individual interpretations of immutable musical scores or plays, do not always give their best performances when they play "congenial" works. Nor do lawyers when they defend clients whom they admire, or even just believe to be innocent. In fact, *a translator's skills may be challenged most severely by a literary work he does not particularly like but, for example, finds stylistically interesting or simply difficult to convey in the target language.*

The German Romantic Novalis (1772–1801) saw the virtues of a poetic translation not in "fidelity to the original, but in the striving toward the ideal."[16] What is an ideal translation? No single, unequivocal answer to this question is possible, any more than to such seemingly analogous queries as to what an "ideal" novel or play should be like. Indeed, it was a serious weakness of Soviet scholarship at the end of the Stalin era that it *implied* the existence of a single translation theory that might in turn provide beneficial guidance to translators of various kinds of fiction, poetry, and drama intended for audiences ranging from children and uneducated readers to sophisticated intellectuals. Fortunately, the theoreticians' advice was generally ignored by the better translators.

As early as the seventeenth century, John Dryden (1631–1700) in his preface to Ovid's *Epistles* identified three main types of translation: metaphrase (that is, literalism), "turning an author word by word, line by line, from one language into another"; paraphrase, "where the author is kept in view by the translator, so as never to be lost, but his words are not so strictly followed as his sense"; and "imitation, where the translator (if now he has not lost that name) assumes the liberty, not only to vary from the words and sense, but to forsake them both as he sees occasion."[17] Somewhat differently, the eighteenth-century German theorist Johann Jakob Bodmer (1698–1783) recognized just two basic types of translations, those that strive to retain the formal traits of the original and those that essentially are interpretations of its thought.[18]

---

15. Kornei Chukovskii, *Iskusstvo perevoda* (Moscow and Leningrad: Academia, 1936), pp. 52–53.

16. Iu. D. Levin, *Russkie perevodchiki XIX veka razvitie khudozhestvennogo perevoda* (Leningrad: Nauka, 1985), p. 13.

17. Cited in *Delos*, no. 2 (1968): 167.

18. Lefevere, *Translating Literature*, p. 18.

Many observers have recognized that a need exists for different translation styles, depending upon the readers for whom the work is intended. In contrasting the French (Neoclassical) with the German (Romantic) way of translating Homer, Johann Gottfried Herder (1744–1803) strongly implied that *for French readers* their method may be the correct one (although he described it with heavy sarcasm):

> The French, who are overproud of their national taste, adapt all things to it, rather than try to adapt themselves to the taste of another time. Homer must enter France a captive, and dress according to fashion, so as not to offend their eye. He has to allow them to take his venerable beard and his simple clothes away from him. He has to conform to French customs, and where his present coarseness still shows, he is ridiculed as a barbarian.

The German style he depicted with mock humility:

> But we poor Germans, who still are almost an audience without a fatherland, who are still without tyrants in the field of national taste, we want to see him the way he is. . . . I should not like to think that poetry and hexameters should be lacking in his translation; but they should be poetry and hexameters in the Greek taste, even if they only serve to draw our attention to the extent to which our language and poetry lag behind.[19]

Johann Wolfgang Goethe (1749–1832) also apparently disapproved of the French style of translation, though without quite branding it illegitimate. He described it as a mere approximation to the foreign text, reproducing its content in the translator's own sense: "In most cases men of wit feel called to this kind of trade. The French use this method in their translations of all poetic works. . . . Just as the French adapt foreign words to their pronunciation, just so do they treat feelings, thoughts, even objects: for every foreign fruit they demand a counterfeit grown in their own soil."[20] For some purposes, such as Luther's rendering of the Bible, Goethe thought that a simple prose translation was appropriate. But the highest and best

---

19. Ibid., pp. 32–33.
20. Ibid., pp. 35–36. An English translation of excerpts from Goethe's *Noten und Abhandlungen zu besserem Verständnis des Westöstlichen Diwan* may also be found in *Delos*, no. 1 (1968).

translation method is one which strives to make the original identical with the translation.[21] Still better is to read the original. "Translators should be looked upon as busy matchmakers who advertise a half-veiled beauty as being very lovely: they arouse an irresistible desire for the original."[22]

Echoes of Goethe's distinction between an ideal and a merely acceptable rendition may be detected in Belinsky's classification of translations as either "poetic" (*poeticheskii*) or "artistic" (*khudozhestvennyi*). According to Levin, he viewed the former as "an idealized expression of the subjective," and therefore inferior to the latter, which was to him an "objective reflection of reality." In Belinsky's own words: "In *artistic* translation there should be no excisions, no additions, no changes. If the original has shortcomings—these too should be faithfully reproduced. The purpose of such translations is to replace the original, insofar as possible, for those [persons] to whom the original is inaccessible because of the language barrier. [The translation] thus provides them with the means to judge and enjoy it."[23] Belinsky believed that textually intact "artistic" renditions are obviously intended for an elite. This makes them unsuitable for the rank and file. Translations should not be just for the chosen few but for the entire reading public, namely, those who cannot read the originals. Similarly in the theater, a play should impress not just the wealthy viewers in the expensive seats but also the ordinary folk in the cheap ones. For the general public, Belinsky recommended "poetic" renditions *that are really adaptations of the original text*. In other words, "The translator should strictly conform to the taste, the education, and the nature and demands of the public . . . *the more heterogeneous the public for whom he is working, the more incumbent it is on him to make cuts, additions and changes* [in the text]."[24]

Similar sentiments have been expressed over the years by other critics, particularly those sympathetic to literalism. Rudolph Pannwitz wrote (in German) in his *The Crisis of European Culture* (1917) that *all* renditions are overly free, that *none* are literal enough. (Pannwitz used no capital letters, and tolerated no punctuation except periods. The translator of the following passage repeated this feature of the original.)

> our translations even the best proceed from the false principle they want to germanize hindi greek english instead of hindiizing greciz-

21. Lefevere, *Translating Literature*, pp. 35–36.
22. Ibid., p. 39.
23. Levin, *Russkie perevodchiki*, p. 100; emphasis added.
24. Ibid.

ing anglicizing german. they have a much more significant respect for the usages of their own language than for the spirit of the foreign work. . . . the fundamental error of the translator is that he maintains the accidental state of his own language instead of letting it be violently moved by the foreign language.[25]

This suggestion, later repeated *verbatim* by Walter Benjamin (1892–1940) in "The Tasks of the Translator," was neither abstract nor altogether unexpected.[26] The fact that translations expand the target literature's assortment of genres and poetic meters has long been recognized as self-evident. Why not enhance the language itself? Pannwitz explained (this second translation ignored the idiosyncratic capitalization and punctuation of the original): "He [the translator] should expand his native language with the help of the foreign tongue. This offers virtually limitless opportunities for its enrichment and evolution for which a potential exists in every language. There is no more difference between languages than between the dialects of a single language. All this, of course, assumes that the problem is approached not lightly but with the seriousness it deserves."[27] In Russia, literary translation has in fact been "expanding," and indeed "violently moving," the nation's language ever since the onset of translation into Russian in the eighteenth century. It has greatly enlarged the lexicon of standard Russian, and in so doing has helped pave the way for the emergence of Russian literature itself.

Its extremism aside, Pannwitz's defiant affirmation of literalist principles was but another salvo in the eternal war between the proponents of literal and free translation. Eternal, because it is precisely that disagreement which serves, overtly or by implication, as the common denominator of most theoretical battles in literary translation. Eternal also because the problem at issue does not lend itself to any definitive resolution that would settle it for all time. Periodic flareups in Soviet Russia of variants of the literalist heresy, long ago declared dead, attested to this fact. The choice between literalist tendencies and freer rendition is a matter of the individual translator's taste, made even more unpredictable by the exigencies of a particular author's style, the peculiarities of specific literary genres, and on

25. Rudolph Pannwitz, "krisis europäischen kultur," *Delos*, no. 4 (1970): 198.
26. See Walter Benjamin, "The Tasks of the Translator," in *Illuminations*, trans. Harry Zohn (New York: Harcourt, 1968), p. 81.
27. Rudolf Pannwitz, *Die Krisis der europäischen Kultur* (Nuremberg: Verlag Hans Karl, 1917), p. 243.

occasion even by the nature of the audience for whom a given rendition is primarily intended. As a translator, Pushkin (whose original work bears the imprint both of Neoclassicism and Romanticism) provides a telling example. Some of his renditions are quite free, while others are virtually literal.

To decide between literal and free renditions is really to choose between the *authentic* and the *familiar,* between the *genuine* and the *comfortable,* between exploring the exotic and surrending to the force of habit. We face similar choices in buying a recording of folk songs: some are crude and sung *a capella* by nonprofessionals, while others are arranged, provided with accompaniment, and performed by singers with trained voices, as in the Soviet Moiseyev ensemble. In the Russian theater we find both the tradition of Konstantin Stanislavsky's meticulous imitation of reality and Vsevolod Meyerhold's defiantly ostentatious theatricality, in which the actors make no pretense of being "real" people from the play. Nor are the dilemmas limited to artistic choices. We make similar decisions when planning to go to a foreign restaurant. Which will it be: a truly "native" eatery, or one in which spicing is moderated to appease foreign palates unaccustomed to hot foods? Similar choices must often be made when traveling abroad. Shall we forgo private bathrooms and stay in hostels catering to the natives, or make reservations at the local Sheraton-Hilton? The choices are rarely clear-cut and should certainly not be made "on principle." There are times when we crave adventure, and other times when we are tired and comfort is of the essence. Regrettably, it is only in retrospect that we are in a position to evaluate the wisdom of our choices—which unfortunately is of little value in informing our future decisions in similar, though not identical circumstances.

Stiva Oblonsky, we read in *Anna Karenina,* was a ladies' man and a gourmet who disliked any religious restrictions on his pleasure-seeking life. Accordingly, Tolstoy noted sarcastically, he *had* to be a secularist liberal. A similar logic helps explain why proponents of free translation have naturally always been more numerous than literalists. Literalism is "elitist." It requires a degree of literary sophistication from both translator and reader (as free renderings do not), to say nothing of solid command of both the source language and the target language on the part of the translator. By contrast, free translation prizes "readability," thus exempting the reader from the need to exert much intellectual effort. Free renderings also absolve the translator from the need to master the foreign language, or even to know its grammatical rudiments: an interlinear crib ("trot" or "pony") will normally suffice. Nor does the author of a free rendition require much familiarity with the historical data and literary allusions found in the original. Accordingly, a learned translator can produce *either* a free or a literal rendition. An ignorant one can aspire to free rendition alone. Last but not least, a literal rendering requires considerable modesty and self-abnegation from the translator, a constraint that must have been taxing to Vladimir Nabokov—a celebrated writer himself—while working on his (exceedingly literal) English version of *Eugene Onegin*.

In the twentieth century, literalism has rarely been given a fair shake. Its relatively few Russian proponents (such as Evgeny Lann, Georgi Shengeli, or Adrian Frankovsky) have all too often been dismissed as eccentrics and fanatics. (The fact that Nabokov was at least taken seriously was due to his stature as an American and Russian novelist.) Much the same situation prevails in Western Europe and the United States. Indeed, our period is one of rampant excesses of "free" and "creative" translations (both adjectives, it should be noted, are universally viewed as positive modifiers, in contrast to ossified literalism). In the West, "free" renderings and their various mutants, such as imitations and variants, often serve as fig leaves for the translator's ignorance of foreign languages and exaggerated notions of his or her own literary gifts. In addition, "free" renderings were favored in the USSR because they often served as sublimation for the talents of authors unable to publish original work, while at the same time providing them with a literary livelihood. Translators by necessity (rather than by choice) included such celebrated poets and prose writers as Pasternak, Akhmatova, Mandelshtam, and Zoshchenko; and from all indications, the Soviet authorities approved of the existence of translation as a purgatory for authors in disfavor. Moreover, the philosophy of non-literal translation both justified and facilitated minor censorship of foreign literature. Passages objectionable for political or moral reasons could thus be deleted inconspicuously.

Authenticity versus comfort is one way of viewing the choice between literal and free renditions. Another useful dichotomy was proposed by the Czech scholar Josef Čermak, who viewed the choice as one between "undertranslated" (*sous-interprétée*) versus "overtranslated" (*sur-interprétée*) works. The former strategy emphasizes the components of the text at the expense of the whole, making the rendition literal. The latter focuses on the whole at the expense of its parts, which ultimately results in a free rendering. Undertranslation brings the rendering closer to the author, while overtranslation moves it closer to the reader. According to Čermak, literalist views are rooted both in the idea that the original work should remain intact and (more fundamentally) in a belief in the essential *impossibility* of translation generally. An overly free rendition (or an overly literal one, for that matter) ultimately *ceases to be a translation altogether.*[28]

Čermak's dichotomy recalls the dictum of Friedrich Schleiermacher (1768–1834): "Either the translator leaves the author undisturbed—insofar as this is possible—and moves the reader in his direction, or he leaves the reader undisturbed and moves the writer in his direction."[29] This statement, in turn, was essentially a reformulation of Goethe's distinction between renderings that "make the foreigner look like a compatriot" and those that require the reader to adjust to foreign manners and mores.[30] Even earlier, Wilhelm von Humboldt (1767–1835) had written: "To me, all translating seems simply to be an attempt to solve an impossible problem. Thus every translator must always run aground on one of two reefs: he either adheres too closely to the original, at the expense of the taste of his nation; or he adheres too closely to the characteristics of his nation at the expense of the original." Humboldt concluded: "A compromise between them is not only difficult, but simply impossible."[31] (In reality, of course, most modern translations are compromises between doctrinaire literalism and totally free renderings. Most of them probably conform to the German rule of thumb [*Faustregel*]: "As faithful as possible, as free as necessary" [So treu wie möglich, so frei wie nötig].[32] The common sense of this piece of German folk wisdom is, on the surface, too obvious to provoke any objections.) Nonetheless, the dilemma described by Goethe and Humboldt

---

28. In an extremely free rendition, "Le texte original n'est que le point de départ et il peut résulter une manifestation littéraire très indépendante, tendant à devenir une oeuvre propre du traducteur." In a literal rendering, by contrast, "Le traducteur littéral n'a qu'un seul but: pénétrer, à partir de sa propre langue, dans une langue étrangère. Pour lui la traduction n'est qu'un chemin menant à l'oeuvre. Elle n'est pas une forme littéraire autonome comme le texte original, elle en est séparée par sa propre substance." See *The Nature of Translation: Essays on the Theory and Practice of Literary Translation,* ed. James S. Holmes, Frans de Haan, and Anton Popovič (Bratislava: Publishing House of the Slovak Academy of Sciences, 1970), pp. 34–36.

29. "Entweder der Übersetzer lässt den Schriftsteller möglichst in Ruhe, und bewegt den Leser ihm entgegen; oder er lässt den Leser möglichst in Ruhe und bewegt den Schriftsteller ihm entgegen" (H. J. Störig, ed., *Das Problem des Übersetzens* [Darmstadt: 1963], p. 47; cited in Lefevere, *Translating Literature,* p. 103).

30. Goethe's remarks are found in his speech honoring the memory of the poet and novelist Christoph Martin Wieland. See J. W. Goethe, "Zu brüderlichem Andenken Wielands," *Gesamtausgabe* (Munich, 1961–63), 29:210; cited in Rano Faizullaeva, *National'nyi kolorit i khudozhestvennyi perevod* (Tashkent: Izdatel'stvo "FAN," Uzbekskoi SSR, 1979), p. 19.

31. Cited in Liedloff, *Steinbeck in German Translation,* p. 3.

32. Hilde Spiel, "Freuden und Leiden des Übersetzens," *Maske und Kothurn: Internationale Beiträge zur Theaterwissenschaft* 3 (1977): 225.

has never been resolved. Jiří Levý restated it in essence almost two centuries later when he categorized all translations as either *illusionist* or *anti-illusionist*. The illusionist ones resemble theater productions with "authentic" decorations and costumes, which aim to create the impression that the reader has the *original* work facing him, while anti-illusionist ones defiantly flaunt their "artificiality."[33]

Presumably few people would disagree with the proposition that a completely faithful, literal translation—if at all feasible—would be ideal. However, the opponents of literalism usually argue that no such feat can be achieved. The issue is not merely how to reproduce the semantic meaning of the original, but also how to capture such far more elusive qualities as subtext, allusions, flavor, and style.

Some early—and continuing!—controversies about the merits of literal versus free translation have been inspired not by aesthetic, but by theological differences. The Fathers of the Christian Church asserted that the Jewish rabbis adhered stubbornly [and erroneously] to the letter rather than the meaning of Holy Scripture. Contrasting the [Christian] *sensus mysticus* with the *sensus judaicus,* they accused the rabbis of a rigid literalism. This prejudice persisted even in Renaissance France. In a curious gloss on the Latin cliché *ad litteram,* one sixteenth-century French writer stated that "to 'Judaize' is to cling more to words than to sense." In other words, "To appropriate the Jewish letter is to don the shroud of mortality, *to remain blind to Old Testament figurative truths rich in latent christological meaning.*"[34] In the seventeenth century Pierre d'Ablancourt, the leading exponent and theoretician of the "belles infidèles," denounced the "Judaic superstition of tying oneself to the words" of a source text rather than communicating their meaning.[35] Similar accusations have continued down to our own day, though naturally expressed in more polite terms.

---

33. Levýi, *Iskusstvo perevoda,* pp. 47–48.

34. Glyn P. Norton, *The Ideology and Language of Translation in Renaissance France and Their Humanistic Antecedents* (Geneva: Librairie Droz, 1984), pp. 61–62; emphasis added. The best known example of superimposition of a christological meaning on the Hebrew Bible is found in Isaiah 7:14. In Jewish Bibles the verse is translated as "Therefore the Lord himself shall give you a sign; Behold, the young woman [*ha-alma*] shall conceive, and bear a son, and shall call his name Immanuel." In Christian Bibles, instead of "the young woman" we find "a virgin," thus permitting the text to prophesy the birth of Jesus Christ.

35. Theo Hermans, ed., *The Manipulation of Literature: Studies in Literary Translation* (London: Croom Helm, 1985), p. 112. This observation appears in d'Ablancourt's preface to the 1637 edition of Minucius Felix's *Octavius.*

The Jews, understandably, resisted the imposition of christological meanings on the Hebrew Bible. Besides, in the Middle Ages and beyond, Judaic scholars held that any sacred text "is susceptible to two levels of analysis, *peshat* and *derash*, the literal and the homiletical. Without first breaching the plain linguistic truths derived in *peshat*, the exegete's venture into *derash* becomes little more than a flight of imaginative fancy. There just emerges . . . a basic hermeneutic principle: 'No verse in Scripture can lose its literal (plain, simple) meaning.' "[36] The medieval Jewish theologian Maimonides (1135–1204), the single most authoritative voice in postbiblical Judaism, was clearly no adherent of literalism. He stated unequivocally that a translation should seek to extract the meaning of a text and convey it with clarity, even if this entailed major stylistic and lexical emendations. Maimonides (who lived in Muslim Egypt) wrote his *Guide for the Perplexed* in Arabic, but a short time afterward it was translated into Hebrew. Concerned about the quality of this rendition, he wrote to his translator, Samuel ibn Tibbon:

> The translator who is set to render a certain word in the original with its precise equivalent and to adhere to the precise sentence structure of the original is bound to encounter great difficulties, and the result will be an inadequate and hard to read text. It is wrong, therefore, to translate in this manner. It is advisable that the translator first clarify for himself the meaning of what he is translating and then render it in a manner that is clearly expressed. This is impossible if he does not make necessary changes in the order of the sentence, by substituting several words for one word, or one word for several words, omitting some expressions and adding others, so that the thought of the original text and its rendition in the translation are clear and idiomatic.[37]

The Jews were not alone in their attachment to the sacred biblical text. Martin Luther, himself a famous translator of the Bible, believed that renditions of Scripture should be "translucent," with the hallowed original shining through. One recent German scholar, Anneliese Senger, even discerned a special affinity for Luther's quasi-literalist position on the part of

---

36. Norton, *Ideology and Language*, pp. 61–62.
37. Cited in *The Jewish Spectator* (Spring 1987): 6.

twentieth-century Jewish translators with a theological background, "*especially Jewish translation theorists (Buber, Rosenzweig, Benjamin)*."[38]

The French scholar Louis Trouffaut expanded on this argument, though in his opinion Walter Benjamin's literalist longings did not reflect theological proclivities, but rather the anti-authoritarianism of the Frankfurt school. Trouffaut thought that Benjamin's translation theories resembled the anti-authoritarianism of psychoanalysis, in which the doctor does not lecture the patient, nor attempt to impose his own views, but merely *listens*. Curiously, Trouffaut also accepted Senger's suggestion that mysterious links exist between literalism in translation and Judaism: "*The majority of theoreticians and practitioners who have emphasized the importance of the signifier in translation have links to Judaism. The same is true of the great investigators of language. For them, language is a manifestation of unifying and creative authority.*"[39]

Justified or not, the views of Senger and Trouffaut were apparently intended as innocent scholarly speculation; they brought no harm to anyone. In the USSR, on the other hand, the charge of literalism was used as a weapon against Jewish translators. Ivan Kashkin, the foremost Soviet translator of the era of Socialist Realism, made this point in an article that appeared at the height of Stalin's anti-Semitic purges in December of 1951. (It should be recalled that in the campaign against Jews in the arts, the Soviet press regularly referred to Jews by such euphemisms as "Formalists" and "cosmopolitans": after all, the witch-hunts were not *officially* supposed to be anti-Semitic. "Formalism" vaguely denoted neglect of Communist content; "cosmopolitan" suggested contempt for Russian culture and "kowtowing" to the West.) In an article in the Moscow *Literaturnaia gazeta* blandly titled "On the Language of Translation," Kashkin wrote: "In their striving for artificial complexity, Formalist translators mutilated the Russian language. Even when this was not predicated by the stylistic peculiarities [of the original], such as the need to reproduce local color or features of direct speech, they intentionally tried to use alien languages as guides."[40] Nor was Kashkin above naming specific names. According to

---

38. Anneliese Senger, *Deutsche Übersetzungstheorie im 18. Jahrhundert* (Bonn: Bouvier, 1971), p. 87. Of the three, Martin Buber and Franz Rosenzweig (but not Walter Benjamin) had strong theological backgrounds. Cited in Lefevere, *Translating Literature*, p. 66; emphasis added.

39. Louis Trouffaut, "Les enjeux de l'ambivalence dans l'opération traduisante," *Meta* 25 (December 1980): 436–37; emphasis added.

40. Cited in Levyi, *Iskusstvo perevoda*, p. 43.

Simon Markish, a prominent Moscow translator who later emigrated to the West, Kashkin called Evgeny Lann a "cosmopolitan," a very dangerous accusation in Stalin's declining years. Lann (real name Lozman), a leading literalist translator and a Jew, committed suicide in 1958 together with his wife, A. V. Krivtsova.

Literalism in the Soviet Union was held in nearly universal disrepute. The term itself suggested a machine-like rigidity, clearly inappropriate for renditions of belles lettres. (Although machine translation has its uses, this is clearly not one of them.) Moreover, literalism requires of translators a degree of self-effacement that makes the activity quite unattractive. Not unreasonably, Soviet translators preferred to view themselves as writers in their own right, particularly since their function was indispensable. Without them many original works would have been totally inaccessible to millions of readers, gathering dust in libraries like musical scores without performing musicians. Though *inspired* by the foreign originals, the Soviet translators' prose, poetry, and drama was what Russian audiences actually read.

Our present age prizes originality, creativity, and unconventionality, all of which are held to be incompatible with literalism, but conducive to free translation. Some proponents of this latter method may be attracted to it by its comparatively relaxed practices. In producing free renditions, difficult problems are often simply brushed aside.[41] The American translator Burton Raffel even argued for free translation on the ground that although "it is not hard to learn a language" [really?], it is hardly worth the effort because *"linguistic knowledge is not the best or even a good road toward a good translation."*[42] Finally, free renditions are thought to benefit the reader: they require less effort on his part and thus offer far more enjoyment.

Against this reasoning, the relatively few proponents of literalism can produce just one argument: their renditions, at least in theory, are closer approximations to the original. And even though literalism (except in scientific translation) is generally viewed as defeated, passions continue to run high. In the former Soviet Union, literalism was treated as being beyond the pale of respectability; while even in the United States, complaints can be heard that at scholarly translators' symposia, persons sympathetic to literalism are "deliberately excluded from the panel[s]."[43]

---

41. Holmes, de Haan, and Popovič, *The Nature of Translation*, p. 37.

42. Burton Raffel, *The Forked Tongue: A Study of the Translation Process* (The Hague: Mouton, 1971), pp. 104–5; emphasis added.

43. William Arrowsmith and Roger Shattuck, eds., *The Craft and Context of Translation* (Austin: University of Texas Press, 1961), p. 1.

Jiří Levý postulated that the value of a literary translation is measured by two criteria, the degree of its success in recreating the original work with fidelity, and the aesthetic criterion of beauty. Those who emphasize the first, Levý suggested, are the literalists, while those stressing the second are partisans of free (or more precisely, adaptational) translation. While conceding that a translation should be "as faithful as possible in its reproduction of the original," he also emphasized that the translation should be in itself "a worthwhile literary work."[44] Levý's "adaptational" bias is obvious. By not insisting on a *minimal* degree of literal fidelity to the original, he recognized any "worthwhile literary work," however distant from the original, as a valid translation. This, of course, is unacceptable to the literalists.

Opponents of literalism often charge it with insensitivity to aesthetic values. Therefore it is curious that some of its foremost exponents in Russia have been distinguished writers and poets whose original work was *very* sensitive to aesthetics, often at the expense of social involvement. Afanasy Fet (1820–92) was such a poet, and he was also a staunchly literalist translator: "However clumsy and unpolished it [the literalist rendition] may appear in the unaccustomed surroundings of an alien tongue, a reader with intuition will always discern the power of the original in such a rendition. By contrast, in a rendition that desperately strives to provide the reader with a pleasantly familiar form, the public as a rule reads the translator rather than the author."[45]

In this century the single most publicized event in the sphere of translation was arguably the appearance in 1964 of Vladimir Nabokov's literalist English rendition of Pushkin's *Eugene Onegin*. The choice of this particular work as the vehicle for an unyieldingly aggressive literalism actually made good historical sense. Rigid literalism has traditionally been defended as appropriate in renditions of "ideal" Greek and Latin classics; and to a Russian, Pushkin's masterpiece is similarly an object of unquestioned veneration. *Eugene Onegin* is generally acknowledged as *the* supreme work of Russian literature of all time.

In his introductory remarks, Nabokov identified three types of poetic translation:

1. Paraphrastic: offering a free version of the original, with omissions and additions prompted by the exigencies of form, the conventions

---

44. Levyi, *Iskusstvo perevoda*, pp. 92–93.

45. *Perevod—sredstvo vzaimnogo sblizheniia narodov: Khudozhestvennaia publitsistika* (Moscow: Progress, 1987), pp. 413–14.

attributed to the consumer, and the translator's ignorance. Some paraphrases may possess the charm of stylish diction and idiomatic conciseness, but no scholar should succumb to stylishness and no reader be fooled by it.

2. Lexical (or constructional): rendering the basic meaning of words (and their order). This a machine can do under the direction of an intelligent bilinguist.
3. Literal: rendering, as closely as the associative or syntactical capacities of another language allow, the exact contextual meaning of the original. Only this is a true translation.[46]

What is curious here is that Nabokov was a rather late convert to the literalist faith. In 1923 at the age of only twenty-four, he published his Russian translation of Lewis Carroll's *Alice in Wonderland*.[47] This rendition was a prime example of what Nabokov was to denounce and ridicule forty years later. It was, to put it mildly, quite cavalier in its treatment of the original. The little heroine's name and consequently also the book's title (which in Russian should have been simply *Alisa*) was gratuitously Russified as *Ania*, much as young Zhukovsky had unnecessarily substituted *Liudmila* for *Lenore*.[48] The English poems and songs in the original were cleverly replaced with delightful parodies on poems that Russian children traditionally had to memorize in school.[49] And as if following in the footsteps of Pavel Katenin's Russified *Ol'ga* of a century earlier, young Nabokov had his Ania-Alice listen to the Mouse reciting an old textbook account of the fortunes of Vladimir Monomakh and of his son Mstislav in medieval Kiev.[50] Nabokov's subsequent conversion to a quasi-Romantic literalism from the kind of "Neoclassical" translation doctrine that sanctions such arbitrary adaptation of a text to suit national taste would not in itself be unusual. However, it is difficult to understand why this celebrated novelist in 1976 authorized the republication of an "embarrassing" rendi-

---

46. Aleksandr Pushkin, *Eugene Onegin*, trans. Vladimir Nabokov (New York: Pantheon Books, 1964), 1:vii–viii.

47. Its reprint was titled *The Nabokov Russian Translation of Lewis Carroll's Alice in Wonderland—Ania v strane chudes* (New York: Dover Publications, 1976).

48. Incidentally, "Ania" is a diminutive of "Anna," not of "Alisa."

49. These included parodies on Lermontov's "Cossack Lullaby" and "Borodino" (e.g., "*Voi* [instead of *spi*—i.e., "howl" instead of "sleep"], *mladenets moi prekrasnyi*, "my lovely baby"); on Krylov's fables; and on Pushkin's "Tale of Oleg the Wise." See Nabokov, trans. *Ania v strane chudes*, pp. 53, 42–43, 90–91, 94.

50. Ibid., pp. 22–23.

tion that contradicted all that he then preached so passionately and that could at best be excused as a youthful indiscretion.

Literalism flourished in Soviet Russia in the 1920s (its proponents liked to call themselves partisans of "technologically exact renditions"). The leading practitioners of this method were Evgeny Lann, Adrian Frankovsky, and Georgi Shengeli. In retrospect, it appears that this early Soviet literalism was a reaction against the excesses of free translation in the prerevolutionary period. (Similar circumstances had encouraged the emergence of literalism in nineteenth-century Russia.) Then the victory of free translation in the 1930s produced another problem, *that of cavalier disregard of the original by the translator who imposes his own predilections on the text, becoming, in effect, its self-appointed coauthor.* In the 1970s such tendencies were particularly noticeable among translators who used interlinear "ponies."[51]

It is clear that Russian literalist translators expanded the lexicon of literary renditions, and in general benefited translation in much the same way that dry textual scholarship helps inform literary criticism. Even after literalism had lost favor in the Soviet Union, its earlier contribution to the art of translation was recognized. Because of its emphasis on closeness to the originals, literalism aided in the scholarly understanding of foreign texts.[52]

Mikhail Lozinsky (1886–1955), perhaps the best Soviet translator of verse, provided a rare defense of literalism in 1936 in an address delivered at the First All-Union Conference of Translators. He identified two ways to translate a literary text. The first he called "reorganizational" (*perestraivaiushchii*), allowing the translator to reshape the work to suit his literary tastes and/or ideological predilections. The second, which he called "reproductive" (*vossozdaiushchii*), is a maximally faithful replica of the form and content of the original. Lozinsky concluded: "It goes without saying that only a rendering of the second type may be called a translation. Its aesthetic and cognitive significance cannot even be compared with that of the 'reorganizational' translation. As a matter of fact, the latter is not even a translation, but rather an act of retelling, or imitation. It is an independent genre in its own right, but it can never replace the true translation, the 'reproductive' one."[53]

---

51. V. V. Koptilov, *Teoriia i praktyka perekladu* (Kiev: Vyshcha shkola, 1982), p. 27.

52. Iu. D. Levin, in *Aktual'nye problemy teorii khudozhestvennogo perevoda* (Moscow, 1967), 1:89; cited in *Voprosy teorii khudozhestvennogo perevoda*, Comp. Vl. Rossel's (Moscow: Khudozhestvennaia literatura, 1971), p. 179.

53. M. Lozinskii, "Iskusstvo stikhotvornogo perevoda" (1936), reprinted in *Druzhba narodov*, no. 7 (1955): 160.

What Lozinsky called "reproductive" translation was, to all intents and purposes, literalism. Obviously, literalist renderings are far more difficult to execute than run-of-the-mill free translations. Are they worth the extra effort? Who stands to benefit from them? It is generally agreed that they are useful to students. M. P. Alekseev, while still a young teacher in Siberia, attested to their pedagogical value, though with the caveat that they are no substitute for the originals.[54] Stanley Burnshaw, who distrusted all translation, recommended that persons intent on understanding a poem in a foreign language turn to "a literal rendering plus commentary." Taken together, they should make it possible to *understand* the poem and begin to "experience it as a poem."[55] The classicist D. E. Hill argued that only "unmodernized" masterpieces are acceptable in the classroom: "A student should read Virgil to find out what is there and to understand how and why it was all achieved. He cannot do that if he is unwilling to tolerate anything that is alien, anything that is unclear at first sight. . . . The object of our courses is not to make Virgil seem like a modern but so to attune our sensibilities to him and to his time that we feel some sense of comprehension of that alien world and thereby, one hopes, a deeper understanding of our own."[56]

Opponents of literalist translations, however, question even their pedagogical value. André Lefevere described them as possibly useful to students of anthropology, history, or semantics, but "meaningless" and "positively harmful" to the student of literature. They are "pseudo-literary," "sacred monsters with no appeal at all to the student." He went on to say:

> The many "improvements," archaisms, and ready-made utterances encountered in literal translations suggest that the literal translation is definitely intended to be some form of literature—an antiquated one, no doubt, but the result does not change the translator's intention. This is precisely what makes the literal translation unacceptable from the literary point of view. . . . The only way in which a really literal translation could be of any help to the semi-bilingual

---

54. M. P. Alekseev, "Problema khudozhestvennogo perevoda," in *Sbornik trudov Irkutskogo gosudarstvennogo universiteta*, vol. 18, no. 1 (Irkutsk: Izdanie Irkutskogo universiteta, 1931), p. 166.

55. Stanley Burnshaw et al., eds., *The Poem Itself* (New York: Holt, Rinehart & Winston, 1960), p. xi; original emphasis.

56. D. E. Hill, "What Sort of Translation of Virgil Do We Need?" *Greece and Rome* (Oxford) 25 (April 1978): 60–62.

reader is in the form of an interlinear version forever vegetating on the boundary between the literary and the non-literary.[57]

As the editor and co-translator of two volumes of Russian short stories with facing Russian and English texts, which have been used by several generations of undergraduates, I must register my dissent from Lefevere's unconditional dismissal of such publications. Though not by any means strictly literalist, our renditions understandably leaned in that direction. Nevertheless they proved rather successful pedagogically, and were of much assistance in helping semi-bilingual students enjoy the Russian originals as literature.[58]

Soviet theoreticians and practitioners of translation were generally unwilling to concede even a limited usefulness to literalist renditions. M. P. Alekseev was slightly more generous in acknowledging their pedagogic value, but nevertheless insisted in 1931 — long before such translations were anathematized in the USSR — that

> the average reader, whose needs and objectives are different [from those of the student], does not require literal, word-for-word precision. He does not understand the fine points of the lexical and stylistic departures of the rendition from the original. Since he does not actually see the original, he forgets about its existence. . . . That is why intentional changes in renditions are, in a way, necessary and useful. No rendering can do without them if it is to acquire an independent existence and literary significance.[59]

---

57. Lefevere, *Translating Literature*, pp. 96–97.
58. The books in question were Maurice Friedberg, ed., *A Bilingual Collection of Russian Short Stories*, vol. 1 (New York: Random House, 1964), and Maurice Friedberg and Robert A. Maguire, eds. and trans., *A Bilingual Collection of Russian Short Stories*, vol. 2 (New York: Random House, 1965). The first volume included Tolstoy's "Father Sergius," Dostoyevsky's "The Christmas Tree and the Wedding," Vsevolod Garshin's "The Red Flower," Dmitri Mamin-Sibiryak's "Wintering Station on Chill River," and Nikolai Leskov's "The Tale of the Squint-Eyed, Left-Handed Smith of Tula and the Steel Flea." The second volume contained Valerii Bryusov's "In the Mirror," Vasilii Rozanov's "Dream Through a Crack," Venyamin Kaverin's "The Great Game," Fyodor Sologub's "A Little Man," Isaac Babel's "How Things Were Done in Odessa," Aleksei Remizov's "The Conflagration," Vsevolod Ivanov's "How Burial Mounds Are Made," Yurii Olesha's "The Cherry Stone," Boris Pilnyak's "Mahogany," and Yurii Tynyanov's "Second Lieutenant Asfor."
59. Alekseev, "Problema khudozhestvennogo perevoda," p. 166. Similar sentiments were expressed to me in the 1980s (i.e., half a century later) by émigré Russian translators in Europe, Israel, and the United States.

Similarly, Lev Ginzburg, a leading translator of German poetry into Russian, dismissed literal renditions as "useless and senseless": "Specialists who know the language of the original have no need of such renderings, while the reading public does not require literalist meticulousness. Those who wish to see the work in its 'pure' form, without any 'additives,' should turn to the original."[60] An even more dogmatic pronouncement came from Nikolai Liubimov, the translator of *Madame Bovary* and *Don Quixote*, whose very ingenious rendition of proper names in *Gargantua and Pantagruel* is a model of free translation. He asserted categorically: "Literary translation, whether of prose or verse, is an art. Art is the fruit of creation. And creation is incompatible with literalism." What other writers might call "free" or "creative" translation, Liubimov termed "artistic precision": "Artistic precision alone enables the reader to penetrate the author's thoughts and moods, and to perceive concretely his unique stylistic system. . . . Only artistic precision neither mutilates nor embellishes the author."[61]

To be sure, misgivings about the feasibility of literal translation had been expressed in Russia even in the early nineteenth century. Pushkin complained that Chateaubriand's literal French rendition of Milton's *Paradise Lost* distorted the sense of the English original. This he believed was less the fault of the translator than of the method:

> Literal renditions can never be faithful. Every language has its idioms, its figures of speech, its established expressions which analogous words cannot render into another language. For instance, take such random sentences as "comment vous portez-vous" or "how do you do." Try translating them literally into Russian.[62]

Similar objections were voiced by Belinsky in his comments on a Russian translation of *Hamlet*:

> Closeness to the original implies reproduction not of the letter of the work but of its spirit. Every language possesses means, peculiarities, and properties that are characteristic of it alone. Moreover, these are

---

60. Lev Ginzburg, *Nad strokoi perevoda: Stat'i raznykh let* (Moscow: Sovetskaia Rossiia, 1981), p. 15. Analogous claims may be found in pronouncements by other Soviet translators.

61. Nikolai Liubimov, *Perevod-iskusstvo* (Moscow: Sovetskaia Rossiia, 1977), p. 3.

62. A. S. Pushkin, *Polnoe sobranie sochinenii* (Moscow: Akademiia Nauk SSSR, 1940), 10:311–12.

so pervasive that at times, if a sentence or an image is to be reproduced correctly, it must be fundamentally reshaped in translation. An analogous sentence or image will not always contain analogous words. It is the inner life of the translated expression that should correspond to the inner life of the original.[63]

Belinsky's sentiments were echoed by Gogol:

> Sometimes one must intentionally move away from the words of the original, in order to remain closer to it. . . . In a translation, one ought to be most attached to the idea and least of all to the words, however enticing the latter may be.[64]

André Lefevere's attack on literalism was many-pronged. He argued that superimposing the syntax of the source language onto the target language encourages circumlocutions, the use of clichés, and the translator's tendency simply to omit inconvenient words.[65] Semantics presents another insuperable obstacle, because in literalist translations "one has to uphold the fiction that a satisfactory sense equivalent for each and every word in the source language exists in the target language." This is untenable because (here he quotes Uriel Weinreich) "the semantic mapping of the universe by a language is, in general, arbitrary, and the semantic map of each language is different from [that of] all other languages." As a consequence: "The work of the literal translator is therefore the record of a long series of more or less strategic retreats from the principle that he (and his readers, who enjoy the sense of pseudo-scientific 'security' that reading his work gives them) pay lip service to."[66]

Advocates of literalism occasionally attempt to create the illusion of precise translation by reproducing the verse form of the original. Lefevere regarded this stratagem as doomed to failure because (quoting J. S. Holmes) "no verse form in any language can be entirely identical with a verse form in any other, however similar their nomenclatures and however

---

63. Cited in Liubimov, *Perevod-iskusstvo*, p. 4.
64. N. V. Gogol, *Polnoe sobranie sochinenii* (Moscow: Akademiia Nauk SSSR, 1940), 10:311–12.
65. Lefevere, *Translating Poetry*, pp. 33–36.
66. Ibid., p. 28. Quotation from Uriel Weinreich, in J. Greenberg, ed., *Universals in Language* (Cambridge, Mass.: Harvard University Press, 1963), p. 142.

cognate the languages."⁶⁷ In short, literalism in the translation of verse is a nasty form of elitism. Its proponents really believe that one should master the languages involved, and readers must therefore rest content even with unsatisfactory renditions. This is clearly unrealistic, according to Lefevere. It would require several lifetimes to learn "Hebrew, Sanskrit, Greek, Latin, English, various European languages, a major Indian language and Japanese."⁶⁸ Although teachers of the classics or "exotic" languages frequently are partisans of literalism, they too are elitists who prefer not to share their wisdom with the masses.⁶⁹ To that condemnation the present writer, a teacher of "exotic" Slavic languages and onetime member of a Classics department, can only add, *nostra maxima culpa*.

This litany of literalism's sins and vulnerabilities could be extended. Few rigidly literal translations can be understood without copious annotation, as demonstrated by Nabokov's *Eugene Onegin*. Furthermore, literal renditions are as subjective as free ones. This may easily be demonstrated in a classroom. No two strictly literal student versions of the same text will be exactly alike.

In view of these facts, what is the usefulness of literalist translations? As suggested above, they are helpful as teaching aids, but they also benefit the enterprise of literary translation as a whole. The existence of literalist versions offers protection from an unchecked invasion by so-called translations that are overly free, imaginative to excess, dazzlingly creative, and only vaguely reminiscent of the works they purport to reproduce. In other words, literalist renderings serve as border markings that warn the reader of unmapped expanses where vegetation may be lush, but is no longer to be considered genuine. After all arguments have been heard, literalism's foremost virtue remains its insistence on respect for the integrity of the original work. For over half a century, literalism was banished from Soviet translation practice; and its absence definitely was felt. Soviet renderings of poetry, in particular, contain "smooth," "imaginative," and even "brilliant" verse produced from interlinear cribs by established and even major poets who did not know the languages of the originals. In the absence of modest literalist renderings, these "beautiful but unfaithful" Russian versions often bear little similarity to the spirit—or occasionally even to the letter—of the originals. They fly in the face of Belinsky's insistence that even if Pushkin

67. Lefevere, *Translating Literature*, pp. 37–38. Quotation from J. S. Holmes, ed., *The Nature of Translation* (The Hague: 1972), p. 95.
68. Lefevere, *Translating Poetry*, pp. 97–98.
69. Lefevere, *Translating Literature*, p. 97.

himself were a translator, we would still demand that the rendering give us the original author, not Pushkin.

In practice, rigidly literalist renditions, in Russian or in other languages, are as rare as their totally uninhibited free opposites that still aspire to the status of translations. In the dedication of his English *Aeneid,* John Dryden wrote in 1697 that he "thought fit to steer betwixt the two extremes of paraphrase and literal translation," attempting in the process "to make Virgil speak such English as he would himself have spoken, if he had been born in England, and in this present age."[70] The latter desideratum found resonance in nineteenth-century Russia (or was reinvented there independently). Belinsky's sentiments resembled Dryden's: "There is but one rule for translating literary works, which is to convey the spirit of the original. And this, in turn, can be accomplished only by rendering it into Russian as the author himself would have written it in Russia if he had been Russian himself."[71]

Outwardly reasonable, Belinsky's suggestion was in reality quite untenable. Where in the nineteenth century could one conceive of a Russian counterpart of Heine, a baptized Jew writing German verse in Paris? When in the history of Russia had there ever been a period of cultural tensions comparable to those that produced Dante, Boccaccio, or Rabelais—authors rebelling against the constraints of Christianity who were attracted to the classical world? The profound historical differences between Roman Catholicism and Russian Orthodoxy would in themselves have precluded such parallels. The impossibility—in a vast number of cases—of creating the impression that the translated author had actually written in the target language finds confirmation in the experience of several bilingual authors. Rainer-Maria Rilke related that he had tried on several occasions to write the same story in German and in French, but to his great astonishment the tale came out differently in each language.[72] Likewise the bilingual Russian authors Nabokov (in Russian and English) and Elsa Triolet (in Russian and French) wrote in quite dissimilar fashion in the two languages. Both strongly disliked translating their own work from one language into the other. Nabokov, for example, wrote to Zinaida Schakovskoy that putting *Otchaianie* [*Despair*] into English was "a terrible thing, translating oneself,

70. Hermans, *Manipulation of Literature,* p. 126.
71. V. G. Belinskii, *Polnoe sobranie sochinenii* (Moscow, 1953–59), 2:427; cited in Levin, *Russkie perevodchiki,* p. 102.
72. *Khudozhestvennyi perevod: Voprosy teorii i praktiki* (Erevan: Izdatel'stvo Erevanskogo universiteta, 1982), p. 128.

sorting through one's own innards, then trying them out for size like a pair of gloves."[73]

Only in the twentieth century was the insistence of Dryden and Belinsky that the translator improvise an equivalent of the source language in the target language finally laid to rest. Instead we find the continuation of a line of reasoning employed in the nineteenth century by Matthew Arnold: it is the effect, not the means, that really matters. Arnold argued in 1861 in *On Translating Homer* that a translation should affect foreign readers in the same way as the original may be supposed to have affected its first listeners. Conceding that no one knows with certainty how Homer affected the Greeks, he therefore offered a "practical test": "The translation should give to those who both know Greek and have an appreciation of poetry the same sensation as does the original."[74] Similarly, Vilém Mathesius, one of the founders of the Prague Linguistic Circle, wrote in 1913: "Poetic translation should exert on the reader an impact identical with that of the original, even if this must be achieved by artistic devices different from those of the original . . . because identical or similar artistic devices frequently produce different impacts. The postulate that identity of artistic impacts is more important than the application of similar artistic devices should be observed most strictly in translations of poetry."[75]

The Russian translator Petr Veinberg (1831–1908) also argued for preserving in translation the impressions created by the original work. He believed that the works of really great poets "contain nothing superfluous, nothing unintentional, nothing organically unrelated to their personality or the poet's vision of reality." Therefore:

> Such works should be translated not only with all their virtues intact, but with all of their weaknesses as well. . . . [The translator]

---

73. According to a study of the subject by Elizabeth Klosty Beaujour, bilingual authors who attempt to self-translate *typically* hate it. See Beaujour, *Alien Tongues: Bilingual Russian Writers of the "First" Emigration* (Ithaca: Cornell University Press, 1989), p. 51. Beaujour also cites the experience of the Bulgarian-born Tzvetan Todorov, now an influential critic writing in French, who on one occasion began to translate his own speech into Bulgarian. "Working in Bulgarian, he reacted to his argument as would the Sofia intellectuals, one of whom he would have been had he not left Bulgaria. *In Bulgarian, he felt obliged to replace his initial argument with its contrary*" (ibid., pp. 48–49; emphasis added).

74. Cited by Savory, *Art of Translation*, pp. 44–45. However, a contemporary of Matthew Arnold, Professor F. W. Newman, held an exactly opposite theory of translation. We thus see that the "illusionist" / "anti-illusionist" controversy is by no means a recent development.

75. A. Mathesius, "O problémech českeho překladatelstvi," *Přehled* (Prague) 11 (1913): 808; cited in Levyi, *Iskusstvo perevoda*, p. 36.

should attempt to evoke in his readers not only impressions that are artistically pleasing, but to convey to them also those which, for whatever reason, may impress them unfavorably.[76]

As Yuri Levin explained, Veinberg believed that a translation

should have no additions and no deletions, and should retain its historical and national flavor. The translator should not overshadow the author. Finally, the rendition ought to be poetic and written in idiomatic Russian, without forced calques, but also without Russification. All this represented an achievement of Russian translation theory in the nineteenth century.

However, these principles pertained to the *contents* of the original, not its poetic form. Veinberg's view that the effect of the original must be preserved in translation reflected actual Russian practice in the nineteenth century, as well as the prevalent belief that only geniuses can salvage the formal features of the original.[77]

Essentially similar ideas may be found in Roman Jakobson's important essay "On the Translation of Verse" ("O perevode stikhov") and in the writings of the Polish theoretician Zenon Klemensiewicz.[78] As the Soviet translator and scholar Vladimir Rossel's pointed out, these ideas are also consonant with what he called the Gorky-Chukovsky-Kashkin doctrine of literary translation, the main premises of which he summarized as follows:

1. *Any* literary text is translatable.
2. A translator, like an original author, should study not only the text, but life itself.
3. In literary [*khudozhestvennyi*] translation, literary aspects are more important than linguistic ones.
4. A literary translation should be neither "precise" (that is, literal) nor "free," but "should strive to achieve an artistic impact on readers of the translation that equals the impact of the original on the author's countrymen."

76. Levin, *Russkie perevodchiki*, p. 278.
77. Ibid., pp. 278–79.
78. Levyi, *Iskusstvo perevoda*, pp. 36–37.

This could be accomplished, according to Rossel's, provided that the translator makes no attempt to copy the artistic devices of the original.[79]

In reality, equaling "the impact of the original on the author's countrymen" is much easier said than done. In the case of older literature, the impact is almost impossible to ascertain. For example, what exactly is the effect on a modern Spaniard or Argentinian of *Don Quixote*, published in 1605? Another case in point is the literary treatment of religion or human sexuality. Bawdy scenes and crude language that would once have been thought shocking arouse little reaction now. At least in the Western world, contemporary readers are no longer scandalized by blasphemy or obscenity. Graffiti are more likely to feature a racial slur or a swastika. In short, equal impact is attainable (if at all) only if the original was written by a modern author. Otherwise it is a matter of pure conjecture.

The Soviet scholar Leonid Barkhudarov made exactly this point in an essay published in 1982. Recalling the advice of Irinarkh Vvedensky, the nineteenth-century translator of Dickens and Thackeray, that the translator should *imagine* how the foreign author would have written the text in Russian if he had lived under Russian conditions, Barkhudarov commented:

> [According to Vvedensky] a translation should look as if the author of the original had lived in identical circumstances with speakers of the target language. That means, if he had been a member of another culture and a speaker of another language. Naturally, this requirement cannot be realized in practice. *If the author had lived elsewhere, at some other time, and if he had also spoken another language, he would have chosen another plot and other protagonists. He would not have been who he was in actual fact.*[80]

The Belgian scholar Jacques Perret made a similar observation concerning French renditions of the Greek and Latin classics. As he pointed out, if Virgil had lived in the seventeenth century (or later), he would not have written *any* epic, let alone an *Aeneid*. Perret argued that a translation should read like a translation and not pretend to be what it is not.[81]

---

79. Ibid., p. 12.
80. *Khudozhestvennyi perevod* (Erevan, 1982), p. 208.
81. Jacques Perret, in *Problèmes littéraires de la traduction* (Leiden: E. J. Brill, 1975), pp. 18–22. (See Introduction, note 12.)

Nor is the criterion of "reacting to the translation as to the original" very useful, according to Barkhudarov: "The works, let us say of Pushkin, Tolstoy, and Blok bring forth different reactions from the old and the young, from people trained in the humanities and engineers, or from someone without any college training, from literary scholars and nonspecialists, and so forth."[82] Thus irrespective of the qualities of the translation, its readers cannot possibly react to it as readers of the original would react. No qualities of the translation can overcome the emotional obstacles created by historical distance, social differences, and above all by ethnic barriers. To readers of the original, the author is a compatriot. To readers of the translation he is a foreigner, an alien. Therefore an ideal rendition is one "to which readers would react as if they were native speakers of the author's language reading the work in the original."[83]

As we see, Barkhudarov came perilously close to denying the principal article of faith of Soviet translation doctrine, which held that any literary text is translatable. Actually some years earlier another Soviet writer, V. Stanevich, had advanced an even more extreme idea. He asserted that not even an impeccable command of the language of the original enables a foreigner fully to appreciate another nation's literary work. According to Stanevich, even a Russian who is completely fluent in English or French cannot possibly understand Shakespeare or Balzac as fully as a native Englishman or Frenchman. This is because "a language contains within itself the biography of a nation as well as the biography of each one of us." The thoughts and rhythms of our native language have an additional dimension for us, suggesting "supplementary meanings and associations that are beyond the grasp of a foreigner."[84] Such a statement implies that we might be well advised to limit our reading to *native* literature, if foreign writing, even in the original, is really beyond our grasp. Stanevich did not merely question the efficacy of translation, but suggested a rationale for cultural isolationism.

One formal feature of foreign poetry that Russian translators thought important to retain in translation was verse. From the eighteenth century up to the present time, Russians have generally subscribed to the idea that verse should be rendered in verse. This was in striking contrast to the French, whose theories of translation were otherwise quite influential in

82. *Khudozhestvennyi perevod* (Erevan, 1982), pp. 208–9.
83. Ibid., p. 212.
84. V. Stanevich, "Tvorcheskii perevod khudozhestvennoi prozy," *Druzhba narodov*, no. 8 (1958): 239.

Russia. To be sure, in centuries past some Frenchmen likewise believed that poetry should be translated in verse, as Chukovsky and Fedorov reminded their readers. For example, Jacques Abbé de Lille, whom the two Soviet scholars described as one of the finest theoreticians of translation in the eighteenth century, had not been impressed by the allegedly superior faithfulness of prose. "The accuracy of prose renditions of verse is always inaccurate," de Lille declared in a paradoxical formulation:

> The nature of prose is vastly different from the nature of verse. The latter's attributes are courage, which frightens away the timidity of the former; liveliness of motion, which clashes with the former's heaviness; spontaneity that is beyond the reach of the slowness of prose. That which is merely blunt in verse becomes coarse in prose; the daring becomes meaningless. The prose translator [of verse], retreating unconsciously before this manner of writing, replaces strength with weakness, allegoric with literal expression, measured speech with unmeasured, the magic spell of conquered obstacles with the vulgarity of common prose. This said, the prose translator [of verse] may be just a trifle more faithful to the literal meaning of a few words or to the construction of a few sentences. The verse translator [of verse] will readily concede to him this apparent accuracy which cannot, however, compensate for the real inaccuracy—since we assume that the virtue of poetry consists of courage, liveliness, and harmony.[85]

Poetry is generally translated in verse in Polish as well, in spite of the fact that Polish, like French and unlike Russian, has a fixed stress. The penultimate stress in Polish makes masculine rhymes as difficult to attain as feminine rhymes are in French. Therefore it is telling that one of the very few Poles to defend the French practice of translating poetry in prose was Tadeusz Boy-Żeleński (1874–1941), a leading Polish translator of French literature. He was sympathetic to the French method because (and this is the standard French justification) all too often translators waste so much effort on finding appropriate rhymes that they neglect the contents of the poetry. To illustrate his point of view, he compared two renditions of a Sophocles tragedy: one in French prose by the poet Leconte de Lisle, the other in German verse by the scholar Wilamowitz-Moellendorff. Since

---

85. Chukovskii and Fedorov, *Iskusstvo perevoda*, pp. 96–97.

he generally preferred prose translations, Boy-Żeleński naturally found de Lisle's version more satisfying. "Such prose translations have an additional virtue: anything can be translated in this manner. Thus one may plan in advance to translate the entire corpus of world literature without awaiting the appearance of a congenial poet like [Julian] Tuwim, who was moved to translate [Pushkin's] *Bronze Horseman*. Besides, one need not exclude the other. An excellent prose translation *should exist*, while an ideal verse translation may occur."[86]

Other writers were highly critical of prose translations of verse. (Indeed, the French remain a minority in employing this method.) The English poet Coleridge (1772–1834) wrote: "I do not admit the argument for prose translations [of verse]. I would, in general, rather see verse in so capable a language as ours. The French cannot help themselves, of course, with such a language as theirs."[87] Evidently Belinsky also disliked prose translations. Though generally an admirer of French letters, his view of the French language was uncomplimentary. In an aside to his review of Nikolai Polevoi's translation of *Hamlet* (1893), he remarked: "The French language, this poor, pitiful language, has an exceptional capacity to cheapen [*oposhlivat'*] everything that is not vaudeville or bombastic rhetoric."[88] Earlier the dramatist Lessing (1729–81) had been scandalized by a German prose rendition of Pope, whom he described as "a poet whose great, not to say greatest merit lay in what we call the mechanics of poetry, whose whole endeavor was to put the richest, most poignant sense into the fewest, most melodious words; to whom rhyme was not a matter to be trifled with. To translate such a poet into prose is to disfigure him in a worse way than Euclid would be disfigured if he were translated into verse."[89]

A convincing enumeration of the limitations and tradeoffs of prose renditions was provided by André Lefevere:

> Translations of poetry into prose have, for some time, been favourably received by both readers and critics. They are usually fairly elegant in language, avoiding most of the distortions and verbal antics one finds in verse translations. They are accurate, closer to the

---

86. Edward Balcerzan, ed., *Pisarze polscy o sztuce przekładu, 1440–1974: Antologia* (Poznań: Wydawnictwo Poznańskie, 1977), pp. 240–42; original emphasis.
87. Cited in Paul Selver, *The Art of Translating Poetry* (Boston: The Writer, 1966), p. 13.
88. Cited in *Perevod—sredstvo vzaimnogo sblizhenniia narodov*, pp. 42, 82. Balcerzan, *Pisarze polscy o sztuce przekładu*, pp. 240–42; original emphasis.
89. Cited in Lefevere, *Translating Literature*, p. 27.

source text than a verse translation could ever be. They are happily liberated from the deadening restraints of the doggedly word-for-word technique.

On closer investigation, however, prose translation turns out to be less respectable than tradition would have us believe. It results in an uneasy, hybrid structure, forever groping toward a precarious equilibrium between verse and prose and never really achieving it. . . . Because of its very form, prose is unable to direct the reader's attention towards certain words the way poetry can; it can neither make a word stand out through its position in the line, nor can it, without losing its quality of elegance, repeat a word too often.[90]

Since the translation of poetry in verse is a Russian tradition, Soviet scholars rarely examined the issue of prose renditions of poetry. By contrast, they frequently defended linguistic theories of translation (the idea that translation is merely the change from one linguistic medium to another). Their defense was weakened, however, by a failure to distinguish literary ("artistic" or *khudozhestvennyi*) translation from the communicative types, for example technical or synchronic.[91] In the late 1960s and early 1970s another heresy, seemingly rooted in the ideas of A. V. Fedorov,[92] advanced the notion that a translation should be *adekvatnyi* and *polnotsennyi*, that is, "commensurate" and "offering full value." As one exponent of the theory put it, this implies "a level of translation which exerts on the reader an emotional impact commensurate with the original."[93] In practice, "commensurability" (*adekvatnost'*) resulted in "interpretations" that had very little in common with the original. In the final analysis, judgment as to what was "commensurate" was left to the translator's intuition.

The Soviet concept of "commensurability" is comparable to what Westerners usually call "imitation." Imitation is a very free form of translation.

---

90. Ibid., pp. 42–43. Lefevere discusses also the pros and cons of phonemic translation, which he finds "positively harmful" (*Translating Poetry*, p. 96); "metrical" renditions ("a very rigorous straitjacket imposed on the target text," ibid., p. 37); rhymed translations ("doomed to failure from the start," *Translating Literature*, p. 49); and interlinear versions, which he finds acceptable as a pony for the semi-bilingual reader (*Translating Poetry*, p. 97).

91. Rossel's, *Voprosy teorii*, p. 7.

92. A. V. Fedorov, a former proponent of literalism, is the author of *Osnovy obshchei teorii perevoda* (Moscow, 1968).

93. V. A. Dmitrenko, "Maksimal'nost' v perevode," *Tetradi perevodchika*, no. 11 (1974): 22–23.

The writer of poetic imitations "produces, to all intents and purposes, a poem of his own, which has only title and point of departure, if those, in common with the source text."[94] In the seventeenth century the poet John Dryden remarked: "To state it fairly: imitation of an author is the most advantageous way for a translator to show himself, but the greatest wrong which can be done to the memory of the dead." Some modern American translators agree. At a conference on literary translation held in New York in 1970, Guy Daniels, an American translator of Lermontov, quoted these words of Dryden's. He then charged that Dryden's criticism of "imitation" was equally applicable to "Lowellization" (referring to "imitations" by the American poet Robert Lowell), by which he meant "distorting—very *creatively* distorting, of course—an original beyond all recognition." He also quoted Nabokov, who had said of Lowell, "I wish he would stop mutilating dead and defenseless poets." Irving Howe then suggested that the viability of imitations depends on the "imitator's" stature as a poet (Robert Lowell fulfills this requirement) and on the availability of other, more accurate translations to give us a rough sense of the standard from which Lowell deviated. Daniels also disapproved of Nabokov's very literal English rendition of Pushkin's *Eugene Onegin*, asking the rhetorical question: "Why did Nabokov's pratfall, predicted by Dryden, finish Nabokovian literalism, while the twin heresy of Lowellization has flourished?" His answer was that "Lowell's anti-translations often 'read well,' whereas Nabokov's definitely do not." Daniels concluded with a dire warning: "The present vogue for imitations is a grave—and perhaps mortal—threat to the art of poetic translation. . . . All the emphasis is on *impact*, and none on fidelity to the original. (But then, who cares about such trifles when the 'in' thing is to 'now-ify'—and 'subjectify'—the universe?)"[95]

Interestingly, analogous developments could be observed at about the same time in the Soviet Union, which was then still quite isolated from Western European and American literary fashions. Thus in 1979 in the scholarly journal *Voprosy literatury*, the Belorussian translator V. Ragoisha expressed unease at the recent vogue for "non-translations," by which he meant "free translations, versions, imitations." Ragoisha attributed this phenomenon to the widespread use of interlinear translations (cribs), which "convey only the contents of a poetic work (and even that not very fully), and least of all its poetics." He complained: "Instead of closely

---

94. Lefevere, *Translating Poetry*, p. 76.
95. Cited in *World of Translation*, pp. 72, 137, 172–73. (See Introduction, note 13.)

studying this phenomenon, we began combating it, banning it from the practice of translation, or at best just ignoring it. While that was being done, 'non-translation' began masquerading as ordinary translation—nay, as the most 'perfect' and the most 'poetic,' claiming that it alone reproduces the 'spirit' of the original. Ecstatic apologia for it began to appear in the press."[96]

In fact two of the most eminent Soviet translators of foreign poetry—Mikhail Lozinsky (1886–1955) and Boris Pasternak (1890–1960)—employed radically different methods. Pavel Antokol'sky (1896–1978), himself a poet and translator of French verse, compared the two. He described Lozinsky, essentially a literalist, as a "character actor" endowed with an unusual capacity to impersonate other poets, even mimic their mannerisms. On the other hand, Pasternak was a great poet in his own right.[97] Pasternak's free renderings of *Hamlet* and *Faust,* though at times magnificent poetry, often bore greater resemblance to his *own* verse than to Shakespeare's or Goethe's. Indeed, in the opinion of Efim Etkind, the "excessive stylistic latitude" of Pasternak's *Faust* made it "no longer a translation."[98] Curiously, one minor error by Pasternak—having the hero of *Faust* proclaim himself one of the jubilant peasants, a remark nowhere to be found in the German original—proved ideologically useful. In the introductory essay to Pasternak's Russian edition of *Faust,* this incident was presented as evidence (quite contrary to actual fact) of Goethe's militantly democratic political views.[99]

As already suggested, Pasternak's preference for very free renditions may in part have resulted from his inability for many years to publish original work. Translation was to him not only a source of livelihood, but also a sublimation of his creative impulse. Paradoxically, this apolitical poet's predilection for a method that offered him artistic latitude bore undoubted affinities with the official Soviet school of Socialist Realism. One characteristic conceit of this school was the belief that not only are there no untranslatable texts, but that translation is actually capable of *improving* upon even a major poet. Thus Andrei Voznesensky wrote in his English-language essay "A Russian Poet's Homage to Pasternak": "It occurred to me that perhaps Pasternak sounds better in translation. Marginal stuff is destroyed in translation. . . . In my earlier writing, when I had compli-

96. V. Ragoisha in *Voprosy literatury,* no. 5 (1979): 33–34.
97. Cited in *Masterstvo perevoda, 1963,* p. 7.
98. E. Etkind, *Poeziia i perevod* (Moscow and Leningrad: Sovetskii pisatel', 1963), p. 214.
99. Ibid., pp. 208–9.

cated rhymes and rhythms, translations [of my work] were unsuccessful. They were bad. In translation, the power of form is not necessary. One must have lightness. One must be able to carry the meaning of the contents."[100] Oddly, in view of his own practice, Pasternak himself believed that retaining the power of the original is the hallmark of successful translation.

A "creative" approach to original texts was clearly favored by Ivan Kashkin (1899–1963), the leading theoretician of Socialist Realist literary translation. A well-known translator of British and American writing, from Chaucer and Chesterton to Carl Sandburg and Robert Frost, Kashkin is chiefly remembered as the Russian discoverer of Hemingway. He also preached "realistic translation." As the Soviet scholar P. I. Kopanev pointed out approvingly in 1972, this actually meant applying the principles of Socialist Realism.[101] Ordinarily Kashkin preferred not to make this point quite so bluntly in his writings. But on at least one occasion he did declare it openly, saying: "Our Soviet literary translation is not at all 'a photographer's craft,' but creative assimilation, *a branch of Socialist Realist art*." Kashkin's more usual reluctance to acknowledge his Communist allegiance may have been because translation, after all, is not an entirely *independent* art; its final achievement is not wholly original. Creating Socialist Realist writing is one thing; *superimposing* it on the work of another author—and a "bourgeois" one at that—is a rather different matter.

In some respects the relationship of a literary translation to its original text resembles that of a concert to the printed musical score, or of a theatrical performance to the published version of a play. In the 1920s, "reinterpretations" of theatrical classics by avant-garde Soviet directors were very much in vogue. In the 1930s, however—when Kashkin was expounding his theories—the experimental theaters of Vsevolod Meyerhold and other modernist directors were being closed, ushering in a long period of ostensible "respect" for the classics. Henceforth, Gogol's *Inspector General* was to be performed in the traditional manner, and Stanislavsky's Moscow Art Theater attempted to produce Chekhov's plays in much the same way as he had staged them in Imperial Russia thirty years earlier.

This conservative reaction may have been another reason why Kashkin used the term "Socialist Realism" so sparingly: it was a comparatively new

---

100. Andrei Voznesensky, "A Russian Poet's Homage to Pasternak," *New York Times Magazine*, June 28, 1981, p. 34.
101. P. I. Kopanev, *Voprosy istorii i teorii khudozhestvennogo perevoda* (Minsk: Izdatel'stvo Belorusskogo gosudarstvennogo universiteta, 1972), pp. 265–66.

doctrine. In practice, however, he stubbornly and thoroughly promulgated its methods. Soviet translators, he wrote, should "view a literary work as an ideological and artistic unity and subjugate all of its parts to a correctly perceived whole." More specifically: "The Soviet translator cannot renounce his right . . . to read the original with the eyes of a contemporary of ours, in the light of his Socialist revolutionary *Weltanschauung,* the right to perceive everything not simply in its development, but in a directed, revolutionary development."

To perceive something in its "revolutionary development" was, of course, one of the ritualistic incantations of Socialist Realism. Still, Kashkin apparently wanted to be more explicit. A Soviet literary translator, he emphasized, must "perceive and reproduce the reality of the original in the light of *our world view* [and] the translator's participation in the life of our literature." The translator is responsible for "the understanding and appropriate interpretation of the original. . . . And the chief criterion of this understanding must be ideological truth, the truth of the meaning [*ideinosmyslovaia pravda*]." Moreover, Kashkin provided Soviet literary translators with concrete instructions. They must

> *first of all strive to convey to our readers everything that is progressive* [in the work being translated], *all that is living and timely for the present.* They should also preserve whatever can be retained without impeding full, clear, and correct understanding of the thought and imagery of the original. This should be accomplished without undue burdening of the text with unnecessary detail that is characteristic only of the alien linguistic structure and *sometimes should not be translated at all.*[102]

The implications of Kashkin's advice were fully in accord with the precepts of Socialist Realism then obligatory in original Soviet writing. The translator was instructed to emphasize what was "typical" (and then only in its "revolutionary development," namely, what Marxism-Leninism *wished would become typical*). He or she should take the opportunity to *magnify* whatever descriptions the foreign literary work may have contained of class struggle, implied admiration for Communism, or any incidents and situations that lent support to Communist Party teachings or current Soviet

---

102. Ivan Kashkin, *Dlia chitatelia-sovremennika: Stat'i i materialy* (Moscow: Sovetskii pisatel'), pp. 443, 447, 490, 479, 451; emphasis added.

practices. Conversely, whatever did not fit this description was to be downplayed, or in extreme cases, actually omitted. *Thus Kashkin's advice to ignore "alien linguistic structure" could easily be interpreted as sanctioning "minor" censorship of foreign literary texts, for example deletion of sexually suggestive scenes or, more important, of "casual" remarks disrespectful of the Soviet Union or of the Communist movement.*

Soviet writers occasionally raised objections to Kashkin's doctrine; but these were always timid and ultimately ineffective. Of necessity, their strictures were directed only at the less politicized aspects of his teaching. Soviet critics never confronted the most dangerous implication of Socialist Realism, namely, the sanctioning of ideological censorship of non-Soviet texts to the point of premeditated distortion. For example, Efim Etkind (then still in the Soviet Union) questioned the wisdom of advising translators to be guided by factors other than those found in the text proper. He wondered whether the translator was really *able* to reread the original "in the light of his Socialist revolutionary perception and view of reality," as advised by Kashkin.[103]

More seriously, Givi Gachechiladze, a leading Soviet theoretician of translation in the 1960s and 1970s, argued that "the original was created in its time as a reflection of its time. The originally created image cannot be changed. If one were to ascribe to it something new and characteristic of the translator's [own] epoch, this would be tantamount to a betrayal of historical truth."[104] Gachechiladze's objections were seconded by P. I. Kopanev.[105] But the reservations of individual scholars were naturally no match for the mighty (if rather strange) alliance of militant and doctrinaire proponents of Stalinist Socialist Realism with barely tolerated and sometimes persecuted nonpolitical poets like Pasternak. The two sides of the alliance pursued utterly different goals. Pasternak preferred paraphrastic translation because it offered him artistic latitude at a time when other avenues of artistic expression were closed to him. Communist ideologues viewed it as yet another method of political control over Soviet writing. In their opposition to literal translation, however, the two groups presented a united front that endured until the advent of *glasnost'* in the late 1980s.

My account of Soviet theoretical polemics concerning various aspects of literature is intentionally brief. Depressingly, until the Gorbachev era,

---

103. Etkind, *Poeziia i perevod*, pp. 137–38.
104. Givi Gachechiladze, *Vvedenie v teoriiu khudozhestvennogo perevoda: Avtorizovannyi perevod s gruzinskogo* (Tbilisi: Izdatel'stvo Tbilisskogo universiteta, 1970), p. 167.
105. Kopanev, *Voprosy istorii i teorii*, p. 270.

much of the discussion was essentially self-congratulatory, marred by obligatory lip service to the Marxist-Leninist creed and attempts to demonstrate that a given theoretical premise was a correct extrapolation from current Communist dogma. Inasmuch as this dogma was allegedly universal in its application, no attempt was made to distinguish between translation into Russian and translation into or from other Soviet languages. The hundreds of articles and scores of books written on literary translation in Soviet times, many of them by persons who themselves worked in the languages of the national minorities, failed to reveal the slightest suggestion that the principles of translation into Russian might not be applicable to other languages. Yet it stands to reason that Turkic languages like Kazakh or Kirgiz, which have a rich folklore but scant traditions of written literature, should not be handled in exactly the same way as languages having established literary traditions.

Moreover, these theoretical battles bore relatively little relationship to actual translation *practice*. My several decades of reading Soviet Russian renditions of Western writing, in addition to conversations with scores of Soviet translators, have thoroughly demonstrated this fact. Of course, as Marxist theory insisted, the general social, political, and economic situation influenced the work of translators just as it influenced Soviet literature and culture. But the endless sterile scholastic debates over the implications of official Socialist Realism were quite divorced from the hard facts of the literary process.

Furthermore, the terminology employed was often meaningless. Jiří Levý, writing in what was then Soviet-bloc Czechoslovakia, complained that the term "realistic translation" as used by some Soviet theoreticians often meant simply "a good translation"—a less than helpful designation.[106] Some support for his puzzlement may even be found in Lauren G. Leighton's 1991 book, which on the whole treats Soviet translation theory with considerable respect:

> Perhaps it is difficult for a non-Marxist to comprehend what a realist translation, as described by Kashkin and Gachechiladze, is in actual print.... Ultimately, it is not possible to distinguish between an artistic [*khudozhestvennyi*] and realist translation—which is perhaps why Gachechiladze uses the terms interchangeably. Moreover, nothing is ever said about obvious questions provoked by his discus-

---

106. Levyi, *Iskusstvo perevoda*, p. 43.

sions of reflections of reality: what of the degree to which the original *fails* to reflect reality? What of works whose basic aesthetic premise is to distort reality?[107]

What is a good translation, and who are to be the judges? Not surprisingly, opinions differ. In particular, professional translators of the paraphrastic, "free" persuasion (who are in the overwhelming majority) wish to be evaluated by their potential readers alone. As Richard Howard argued: "Translations of French writing are made for people who do not read French and are to be judged from this perspective. . . . It is not possible to read a translation, even a translation properly edited, as a *work in English* if the reader knows French and is concerned with the problems and practices of equivalents between the two languages."[108] Richard Exner seconded these views: "English readers matter, not multi-lingual scholars. . . . It can never be the goal of any translator to be judged as excellent by those who do not need his translation."[109]

The claim that translations into English should be judged as "works in English" is unconvincing. Translations, after all, are not wholly original works. Someone should represent, so to speak, the interests of the author of the original. Clearly, the general reading public is in no position to undertake that role. As Lefevere pointed out, "The unilingual reader, who does not have the ability to judge, has to be 'satisfied' with whatever is available whether it is up to standard or not."[110] I therefore agree with him that "translations can be judged only by people who have no need for them, that is, those who are bi- or multilingual."[111] Translators most certainly have a right to a degree of artistic latitude comparable to that enjoyed by performing musicians or actors on the stage. Given talent, inventiveness, and originality, ample room remains for individual interpretation of a composer's score or a playwright's text; and the performance will bear its interpreter's unmistakable imprint. At the same time, no glaring departures from the printed page can be tolerated. Adequate room to display the

---

107. Lauren G. Leighton, *Two Worlds, One Art: Literary Translation in Russia and America* (DeKalb: Northern Illinois University Press, 1991), p. 80.

108. Richard Howard, "A Professional Translator's Trade Alphabet," in Arrowsmith and Shattuck, *Craft and Context of Translation,* p. 163; original emphasis.

109. Richard Exner, "On Translating Late Rilke: Remarks on Some Recent Examples," *Chicago Review* (Winter 1978): 160.

110. Lefevere, *Translating Poetry,* p. 3.

111. Ibid.

translator's art is offered by the literary counterparts of the gesture, the facial expression, and the tone of voice.

The question of which kind of translation best satisfies the reader is more complex than may appear at first. Different types of readers will prefer different renditions. The person untrained in foreign languages will probably be happiest with a free translation that reads easily. Students of the foreign language in question can best be helped by an accurate literal translation. Someone who once knew the foreign language, but has forgotten it since, may prefer a translation that sounds like a translation; it may allow him to imagine he is reading the original. Finally, a person able to read the original work may appreciate touches of scholarship or, conversely, become irritated at the translator's errors.[112]

Gilbert Highet offered another rationale for a multiplicity of renderings. Great books, he wrote, "are so rich, so various, so deep and complex that they may mean many different things to different people. Therefore there can be—there *must* be—many different translations of them. No two actors can ever play Hamlet in the same way. . . . Similarly, no two men can ever translate Homer or Dante in the same way. It follows that, if we cannot read the original, we ought to use not one translation but several."[113]

M. P. Alekseev, then still a young scholar in the depths of Siberia, concluded in 1931 that "one cannot, apparently, judge the aesthetic merits of any translation without considering the nature of the audience for whom it is intended." The justice of this observation is yet to be widely recognized, as is Alekseev's other insight: a good translation is one that accomplishes what it sets out to do.[114]

---

112. Savory, *Art of Translation*, pp. 58–59.

113. Gilbert Highet, *People, Places, and Books* (New York: Oxford University Press, 1953), p. 224.

114. Alekseev, "Problema khudozhestvennogo perevoda," pp. 170–71, p. 4.

3

Plying the Translator's Trade

August Wilhelm Schlegel (1767–1845), the poet and critic whose translations (with Ludwig Tieck) of Shakespeare's plays made Germany in effect the bard's second homeland, observed that the only true way to test the validity of a literary or linguistic theory was to produce a translation that embodied its tenets.[1] Well and good. But what of translation theories? Here, presumably, Schlegel's advice should prove to be of even greater and more direct relevance. On closer scrutiny, however, we see that this is not the case. Certain translation theories are more suitable for some texts, while others are more so with different types of writing. Moreover, literary translators in plying their trade are understandably interested in results, not in proving or disproving a theory. They therefore tend to "adjust" theories to suit particular circumstances, much as American scholars of Russian subject matter nearly always "adjust" transliteration methods from the

---

1. André Lefevere, *Translating Literature: The German Tradition from Luther to Rosenzweig* (Amsterdam: Van Gorcum, Assen, 1977), p. 47.

Cyrillic. Yet another circumstance explains why modern translators rarely follow any one translation theory very strictly. Many of these theories proffer advice that is not merely different, but mutually exclusive. For example:

1. A translation must give the [literal sense of the] words of the original.
2. A translation must give the ideas of the original [departing from the text if necessary].
3. A translation should read like an original work.
4. A translation should read like a translation.
5. A translation should reflect the style of the original.
6. A translation should possess the style of the translator.
7. A translation [of a non-contemporary work] should read as a contemporary of the original.
8. A translation [of a non-contemporary work] should read as a contemporary of the translator [avoiding stylized or archaic language].
9. A translation may add to or omit from the original [if this would improve it].
10. A translation may never add to or omit from the original.
11. A translation of verse should be in prose.
12. A translation of verse should be in verse.[2]

Clearly, the range of choice is wide and the theories often contradict one another.

Soviet translators (at least until the rise of Stalinism) were similarly confronted by conflicting advice. In addition, they had been asked, in effect, to take vows not only of poverty (this was guaranteed by their miserly pay), but of humility and obedience as well. However, unlike Western translators, their choice of method was dictated not just by personal choice or intellectual fashion, but by overriding political considerations. Kornei Chukovsky, a leading Soviet theoretician, in 1930 could still defend literalism in translation, shortly before that creed became politically suspect: "The translator must renounce his individual peculiarities. He must learn to mimic another person's gestures, inflections of voice, man-

---

2. This list was assembled by Theodore Savory, *The Art of Translation* (London: Jonathan Cape, 1957), pp. 48–49.

nerisms, and forget his own ego. He may not attain these goals, but he must always strive toward them. This is required by our epoch, which prizes above all scientific truth, documentary quality, precision, and authenticity."[3] These recommendations harmonized with the literalist orientation of many leading translators of the time. Soon such advice would become dangerous; and Chukovsky himself would alter it.

The Bolshevik coup d'état of November 7, 1917, had affected virtually all areas of the country's life, including even the ostensibly nonpolitical activity of literary translation. As if echoing the words of the Communist "Internationale," everything was to be translated anew, *vsë zanovo*. The grandiose translation project *World Literature* was launched in 1918. The victorious Communist government appeared particularly eager to bring out new renderings of "heroic" classical plays by Schiller and Shakespeare (possibly because of their suitability for outdoor mass spectacles, similar to Vladimir Mayakovsky's *Mystery Bouffe* with its cast of thousands). However, the hunger for new translations was also a result of doctrinal considerations. In what would eventually be denounced as yet another "vulgar" Marxist aberration, fanatical new converts to the Soviet cause claimed that translated works inevitably bear the imprint not merely of the translator's political sympathies—a proposition that *might* be defended, if rather tenuously—but of his or her *social origins* as well. Similarly, the Marxist preference for all things collective, coupled with suspicion of individualism, extended also to a fashion for collectively produced translations. Nonetheless, in practice many translated literary works of the 1920s continued the Symbolist traditions that had been popular during the last two decades of Imperial Russia, including their partiality to the Tolstoyan device of *ostranenie*, making the familiar look strange.[4]

Translations began to multiply after the initial chaos of World War I and the Bolshevik Revolution. Whereas in 1918 only 134 translations were published, by 1927 their number had risen to 782, perhaps a majority of them bearing the imprint of the privately owned publishing houses that flourished briefly during the period of the New Economic Policy. This quantitative increase, however, was not an unmixed blessing. As M. P. Alekseev explained in 1931: "Demand creates supply. Haste has brought

---

3. Kornei Chukovskii and Andrei Fedorov, *Iskusstvo perevoda* (Leningrad: Academia, 1930), p. 24.
4. German Ritz, *150 Jahre russischer Heine-Übersetzung* (Bern, Frankfurt am Main, and Las Vegas: Peter Lang, 1981), pp. 14–17.

about a decline in the quality [of translations]. . . . There are loud complaints about the decline of the Russian art of translation, and about the growth of defective production that is now being dumped on the book market."[5] To be sure, this was not a uniquely Russian problem. The American poet and critic Allen Tate complained in 1972 that the modern proliferation of translations had brought with it a decline in quality. Modern renditions of verse, he noted, are often guilty of "blurring the outlines of the original by throwing over it a pastiche of contemporary fashion."[6]

After the striking increase of the 1920s, Soviet translations—at least of poetry—began by 1930 to *decline in importance*. According to Andrei Fedorov, this was allegedly due to a lack of interest in modern foreign verse, and to the fact that Soviet poets had "no special need for foreign poetic material." Therefore the only function of poetic translation, he asserted, was to introduce Soviet readers to "facts that are of no major significance to modern Russian literature or to modern readers."[7] Clearly a better explanation is available for this precipitous decline in interest since 1927, a mere three years earlier. The reason was Stalin's accession to power, which had almost immediate repercussions in literature. In the interval an organization of Stalinist zealots, the All-Russian Association of Proletarian Writers (RAPP), had gained official Communist support and unleashed a reign of ideological terror. RAPP's commissars insisted in unmistakable terms that literature should express proletarian ideology, and that writers must devote themselves to promoting the objectives of the First Five-Year Plan, inaugurated in 1929. *Writing not connected with the Plan came under a virtual ban.*[8]

By 1932 RAPP had been disbanded; and two years later a new organization, the Union of Soviet Writers, came into existence. While few authors mourned the demise of RAPP, the new Union was hardly an improvement. Although ostensibly less dogmatic, it was a rigid monopoly, which RAPP had not been. From now on, a writer—or a translator—had only the choice of joining the Writers' Union or belonging to no organization of the writer's craft at all. The latter meant in practice having virtually no access to

---

5. M. P. Alekseev, "Problema khudozhestvennogo perevoda," in *Sbornik trudov Irkutskogo gosudarstvennogo universiteta,* vol. 18, no. 1 (Irkutsk: Izdanie Irkutskogo Universiteta, 1931), p. 154.

6. Allen Tate, *The Translation of Poetry* (Washington, D.C.: The Gertrude Clarke Whittall Poetry and Literature Fund, 1972), pp. 14–15.

7. Chukovskii and Fedorov, *Iskusstvo perevoda,* p. 221.

8. William E. Harkins, *Dictionary of Russian Literature* (New York: Philosophical Library, 1956), p. 325; emphasis added.

publishing outlets, union housing, or medical care. Although the Writers' Union required that its members adhere to the heavily politicized literary doctrine of Socialist Realism, the postulates of the doctrine were never clearly defined in the thousands of books and articles devoted to the subject during the half-century when its tenets were obligatory. For that matter, neither were the attributes of Formalism, a charge that was hurled at recalcitrant writers. Everybody knew, however, that Socialist Realist writing, painting, and music were good, loyal, Soviet, and Communist, whereas Formalism was bad, disloyal, bourgeois, and alien.

In the field of translation the chief theoreticians of Socialist Realism were M. P. Alekseev and Ivan Kashkin. It was they who denounced literalism as a variety of the Formalist scourge. In its place they endorsed the type of free translation that supported a Marxist-Leninist interpretation of specific historical situations, even if doing so entailed disregarding "accidental" peculiarities and features of the original text. In certain respects, Soviet translation theory and practice in the 1930s was a revival of the eighteenth-century Russian Neoclassical translation doctrine.[9] Only after the death of Stalin in 1953 did the extremism of this position begin to be moderated, though certainly not eliminated. As one translator of Belorussian literature into Estonian complained in 1970: "Occasionally, we encounter rather strange notions of what constitutes creative translation. There are translators who take excessive liberties with the original, introduce their own interpolations, unceremoniously condense and revise literary works. This is particularly common in the translation of verse, though on occasion translators of prose also attempt to 'improve' on the author, demonstrating that they are 'smarter' than he is."[10]

Thus Kornei Chukovsky's appeal in 1930 for translations that mimicked the author's gestures, inflections of voice, and mannerisms, while forgetting the translator's own ego, fell on deaf ears. It was clearly incompatible with the spirit of free rendition that by then was being hailed as consonant with the teachings of Socialist Realism. And Chukovsky's demand that translators be modest to the point of inconspicuousness, renouncing any ambition to be artists in their own right, acquired an unintentionally cruel ring in the conditions of the mid-1930s and beyond.

The successive waves of arrests and trials during Stalin's purges of the 1930s affected translators as well as other cultural figures. This was hardly

---

9. Ritz, *150 Jahre*, pp. 14–17.
10. Olev Jygi, in *Neman*, no. 2 (1970): 166–67.

surprising: after all, translators *do* demonstrate a suspicious interest in foreign lands and cultures. Valentin Stenich, a leading translator best known for his renditions of John Dos Passos (who had only recently been declared an enemy of the Soviet Union), died in a concentration camp. Paradoxically, however, the ranks of the translators were simultaneously being replenished. A number of important poets and prose writers who for political reasons were denied the opportunity to publish original work were "mercifully" allowed to translate to earn their livelihoods. Such men and women must not be compared to those important Russian authors of the past who, for whatever personal reason, *chose* to do some translating work, or even devoted most of their energies to it, like Vasily Zhukovsky. No, these Soviet translators were engaged in literary forced labor of sorts. Theirs was *translation under duress.*

Examples of this are not hard to find. After being reduced to silence as an original writer in the 1930s, Isaak Babel produced translations and film adaptations of Sholom Aleichem's Yiddish stories until he was arrested and executed in 1940. In accordance with a resolution of the Central Committee of the Communist Party in 1946, the humorist Mikhail Zoshchenko was expelled from the Writers' Union and ostracized by Soviet publishers and literary journals; but he still was permitted to translate *To Borrow Some Matches,* a comic novel by the Finnish Communist Maiju Lassila.[11] (Apparently Zoshchenko knew no Finnish, but produced his rendition from an interlinear trot.) A happier case was that of Samuil Marshak, a "gentleman translator" also famous as a children's poet. According to his colleague Lev Ginzburg, translation to Marshak was neither "an infatuation or a hobby, *nor a source of extra income, and most certainly not a haven from the storms of his time or the vicissitudes of fate.* 'I translate not to order, but out of love,' he confessed in his autobiography."[12] A prosperous and politically conformist member of the literary establishment, Marshak translated Byron, Tennyson, Keats, Wordsworth, Kipling, Blake, and English nursery rhymes. He also can be credited with making Robert Burns widely popular in Russia.

For decades literary translation provided a refuge and some income to three great Russian poets in political disfavor, Osip Mandelshtam, Boris Pasternak, and Anna Akhmatova. In his introduction to Nadezhda Mandel-

11. Maurice Friedberg, *A Decade of Euphoria: Western Literature in Post-Stalin Russia, 1954–64* (Bloomington: Indiana University Press, 1977), pp. 238–39.
12. Lev Ginzburg, *Nad strokoi perevoda: Stat'i raznykh let* (Moscow: Sovetskaia Rossiia, 1981), p. 109; emphasis added.

shtam's memoirs, Clarence Brown noted that "her knowledge of languages was very valuable in the twenties and thirties when she and her husband, like many of the old intelligentsia, were driven into a feverish spate of translating in order to live." Presumably she was the one mainly responsible for the translations they did together, since her English was far better than his. However, when pressed on this subject, "she waved the question aside with a gesture of distaste, [saying]: 'Who knows? What *didn't* we translate?' "[13] The pair continued to translate until Mandelshtam's arrest and death in a concentration camp in the Soviet Far East in 1938.

Boris Pasternak was the most famous among the poets relegated to translation work by the State's refusal to print their original poetry. He appears to have resented translating under duress. "Mayakovsky shot himself," he is said to have declared on one occasion, "while I translate." After Stalin's death, when Pasternak became free once again to publish his own work, he refused to translate any longer. His enemies, he wrote, had wished to reduce him to the status of a professional translator.[14] Conscious of his own stature as a poet, Pasternak was not inclined to regard other writers with deference. He favored free renditions because, as his fellow translator Lev Ozerov attested, "Pasternak viewed the originals as *his own property*. Accordingly, he felt free to deal with them as he saw fit."[15]

Pasternak's range was exceptionally broad. He translated Goethe's *Faust* as well as a number of Shakespeare's plays (*Antony and Cleopatra, Hamlet, Henry IV, King Lear, Macbeth, Othello, Romeo and Juliet*), English poetry (Byron, Shelley, Keats, Swinburne), German poetry (Hans Sachs, Goethe, Herwegh, Rilke), as well as Polish, Hungarian, Czech, and Georgian verse, much of the latter from interlinear cribs. His highhanded approach to Shakespeare was actually not very different from Schiller's

---

13. Clarence Brown, Introduction to Nadezhda Mandelshtam, *Hope Against Hope: A Memoir* (New York: Atheneum, 1970), p. vii.

14. The original Russian of Pasternak's observation is "Maiakovskii zastrelilsia, a ia perevozhu."

The statement that his enemies wished him to be merely a translator comes from a letter he wrote to Mrs. Esther Markish. Several years ago while on a visit to Israel, I met Mrs. Markish, the widow of the leading Soviet Yiddish poet Peretz Markish, who was murdered on Stalin's orders in August 1952 together with a large group of other Yiddish writers and cultural figures. At that time Pasternak promised her that he would translate some of her husband's verse. After Markish's posthumous rehabilitation his work could be printed again in the USSR, and Mrs. Markish reminded Pasternak of his promise. In his letter to her, Pasternak refused to honor his promise. I personally read that letter. It was written shortly before the publication of *Doctor Zhivago* in 1957, and three years before Pasternak's death in 1960.

15. Lev Ozerov, "Iskusstvo variatsii," *Literaturnoe obozrenie*, no. 2 (1977): 109–10.

cavalier treatment of *Macbeth* nearly two centuries earlier. As the Polish scholar Jan Parandowski pointed out, Schiller's arbitrary cuts and other changes in the text of Shakespeare's drama, which were aimed at making the German *Macbeth* conform to his own taste and to current fashions, "demonstrate that a person may be a poet of genius, and yet not understand the temperament and imagination of another poet of genius."[16]

Anna Akhmatova's greatness as a poet was comparable to Pasternak's, and Mandelshtam recognized her as an equal. She was also, so to speak, Zoshchenko's co-defendant in the Central Committee's notorious decree of 1946 attacking writers, musicians, and scientists. Andrei Zhdanov, the Stalinist Savonarola who launched the campaign of vilification against Zoshchenko and Akhmatova, referred to this grand lady of Russian poetry as "half-nun and half-whore." As a translator, however, Akhmatova was the opposite of both Mandelshtam and Pasternak. Lev Ozerov quotes her as saying that in her renditions of verse: "I want to be invisible. My work should remain in the background, unnoticeable. Only the author of the original must be in the limelight. Otherwise, one should write one's own verse."[17] Akhmatova practiced what she preached. But while translating classical Korean, Hindi, Romanian, Norwegian, ancient Egyptian, and East European Slavic poets, often with the assistance of interlinear cribs, she also wrote her own poetry "for the drawer." Her "Poem Without a Hero" was written sometime between 1940 and 1962; clearly, it could not be published for many years. Her "Requiem," a dirge for the martyred nation of the Stalinist purges, could appear in her homeland only twenty years after her death, in the more open atmosphere of the late 1980s.

André Gide has been quoted to the effect that it is easy "to discredit a translation, to alert readers to obvious errors, but hard to appreciate and point out fundamental virtues."[18] American and Western European translators often complain that in the vast majority of cases, translation experts as well as book reviewers stand ready to pounce upon occasional howlers in specific renderings but offer little practical assistance. However, at least one Soviet specialist, Lauren G. Leighton, has argued (as late as 1991) that Soviet conditions were fundamentally different: "Soviet translators are less

---

16. Cited in Edward Balcerzan, ed., *Pisarze polscy o sztuce przekładu, 1440–1974: Antologia* (Poznań: Wydawnictwo Poznańskie, 1977), pp. 14–15.

17. Ozerov, "Iskusstvo variatsii," pp. 109–10.

18. William Arrowsmith and Roger Shattuck, eds., *The Craft and Context of Translation* (Austin: The University of Texas Press, 1961), p. 165.

vulnerable to arbitrary criticism because established vocabulary, methodology, and standards *have helped eliminate amateurish reviewers*. . . . Soviet translators have, above all other advantages [sic], a national platform from which to speak. . . . Soviet translators exert strong influence because [standards] are enforced.[19] This description of the status of literary translation in the former USSR is strongly idealized. Amateurish reviewing certainly flourished there; but I am not aware of any "special advantages" that Soviet translators enjoyed. On the contrary, even in the 1980s they continued to suffer from important disabilities, such as restrictions on foreign travel and residence abroad, and even lack of access to ordinary foreign reference books. Although an important "national platform," the annual *Masterstvo perevoda* containing essays on translation history and theory, did resume publication in 1990 after an interruption of several years, not one of the many translators I met in Moscow in the early 1990s considered his or her profession privileged or influential. On the contrary, many emphasized their subservient status in the Union of Writers.

If we disregard the habitual Soviet grandstanding and self-congratulation that were all but obligatory until the mid-1980s, it becomes evident that the status of translators in the Soviet Union was quite similar to that of their counterparts in Western Europe and North America. Thus Nikolai Chukovsky, son of Kornei Chukovsky and himself a novelist and translator of Robert Louis Stevenson and Mark Twain, noted in sorrow if not in anger:

> Critics write about the author of the original text while ignoring the translator. It does not occur to them that they can judge the author only if the translation is accurate and [otherwise] satisfactory. . . . Master literary translators . . . work for years side by side with hacks, with semiliterates, with wheelers and dealers. Still, nobody says—this one is a master, and that one a hack who has ruined many a book with impunity. Not a few publishers even prefer dealing with hacks. They [the hacks] stand ready to translate anything under the sun and will grind out a translation to meet a deadline.[20]

19. Lauren G. Leighton, *Two Worlds, One Art: Literary Translation in Russia and America* (DeKalb: Northern Illinois University Press, 1991), p. xv; emphasis added.

20. Nikolai Chukovskii, in *Masterstvo perevoda, 1969* (Moscow: Sovetskii pisatel', 1970), pp. 388–89.

These grievances were corroborated by Semen Lipkin, the Soviet Union's leading translator from classical Persian and from the modern Iranian and Turkic languages spoken in Central Asia and the Caucasus:

> If our criticism had been concerned with translations, a great many mistakes and blemishes might have been avoided. Our criticism, alas, pays all too little attention to our craft, unforgivably little. Translators, as a rule, are taken to task for this petty mistake or another, for "howlers," or else they are praised for avoiding them. Only in isolated cases does criticism attempt to probe the work of a translator the way it probes that of a writer. . . . [It usually ignores] the translator's style, his artistic integrity, the originality of his artistic devices, his *Weltanschauung*, his understanding of the original text, his knowledge of life, the aptness of his strategies.[21]

Certainly the translator's craft is not an easy one. In 1977 the well-known poet Boris Slutsky published the short poem "Trudnosti perevoda" ("The Difficulties of Translation"):

> While translating verse
> You crash through a wall
> And with a bloody face
> You are suddenly on the stage
> Lit up by thousands of watts
> Facing thousands of eyes
> After having made your way
> Through the bricks, like a stream.[22]

The would-be literary translator—Russian or any other—encounters pitfalls from the very outset. One might expect the difficulties to be minimal in rendering very concrete images. Not so, according to the French translator Marthe Robert: "The impossibility of translation stems from the fact that there is no exact equivalent in one language for even the most concrete

---

21. S. I. Lipkin, in *Masterstvo perevoda, 1963* (Moscow: Sovetskii pisatel', 1964), p. 51.
22. The original runs as follows: "Perevodia stikhi/prokhodish' cherez stenu/i s mordoiu v krovi/vykhodish' vdrug na stsenu/pod tysiachu svechei,/pred tysiach'iu ochei/skvoz' kladku kirpichei/probivshis', kak ruchei/Stoish' ty nalegke,/illiuzii ne stroia,/razmazav na shcheke/kirpich i slezy s krov'iu,/skvoz' steny, skvoz' beton,/skvoz' temnotu streliaia,/nashel ty vernyi ton?/Popal ty v tsel'?/Ne znaiu" (Boris Slutskii, "Trudnosti perevoda," *Zvezda*, no. 7 [1977]: 114).

words of another. The word 'bread,' for instance, cannot be translated. In another language it has not the same weight, the same age, the same semantic frame, the same degree of expressiveness; it indicates the same object but without the same social and psychological connotations."[23] Nabokov pointed out that in Russian the term "cheese" does not include cottage cheese, which is *tvorog*. In American English, as I discovered years ago, "meat" does not necessarily include poultry; and on "meatless days" during World War II, turkey and chicken were available. A single unit of measurement may signify wildly different quantities. Thus two Bulgarian translation specialists demonstrated that at different times the term "mile" has denoted *twenty-five* different distances, ranging from 580 meters to 11,293 meters.[24] Jiří Levý recommended that translators change all units of measure (feet, gallons, pounds) into metric units, but leave specific currencies (dollars, francs, rubles) alone.[25] The latter advice is not very helpful: readers are entitled to know whether fifty rubles (or francs, pesos, marks) was a lot of money or very little at the time in which the novel is set. This knowledge often colors the narrative: was it a modest dowry or an extravagant one? A serious bet or a symbolic one?

As all translators know, words in one language are not exactly comparable to their dictionary counterparts in another one. Mikhail Lozinsky, whose observations were grounded in decades of translating experience, pointed out: "Nouns embrace concepts that do not coincide, verbs denote activities and states that do not fully correspond to each other, adjectives describe different traits, and adverbs carry out dissimilar functions. One cannot even rely on numerals. Thus, 'dans huit jours' means 'within a week,' and 'loger au quatrième' means 'to live on the fifth floor.' "[26] Even among literalist translators, this lack of equivalence can lead to very different versions of the same work. An interesting case where this did not happen concerns the multiple renditions into Russian of Edgar Allan Poe's poem "The Raven." Over the years, all the Russian translations of this poem were essentially similar, because the bird's cry "Nevermore" (*nikogda*, "never") inevitably propelled translators toward traditional rhymes like

23. *World of Translation*, p. 197. (See Introduction, note 13.)
24. S. Vlakhov and S. Florin, in *Masterstvo perevoda, 1968* (Moscow: Sovetskii pisatel', 1969), p. 451; cited in Rano Faizullaeva, *Natsional'nyi kolorit i khudozhestvennyi perevod* (Tashkent: Izdatel'stvo "FAN," Uzbekskoi SSR, 1979), p. 54.
25. Irzhi Levyi [Jiří Levý], *Iskusstvo perevoda*, trans. Vl. Rossel's (Moscow: Progress, 1974), pp. 134–35.
26. M. Lozinskii, "Iskusstvo stikhotvornogo perevoda" (1936), reprinted in *Druzhba narodov*, no. 7 (1955): 161.

togda (then) or *vsegda* (always). The spell was finally broken by Vasily Betaki, who forced the stubborn raven to change his cry to *tomu ne byt'* ("that is not to be"), thus freeing the rest of the poem from the stranglehold of overused rhymes and rhythms.[27]

With all these caveats in mind, how is the conscientious translator to proceed? Viktor Koptilov, a Soviet Ukrainian translator and theoretician, suggested a three-stage process. First analyze the contents, semantics, and style of the original, as well as its rhythm and syntax. Here it is vital to determine the relationship of the details to the artistic whole. For example, in Poe's "Raven" the bird cannot be replaced with any other species. The second stage consists of "*attempts at finding* in the language and literary tradition of the translation an equivalent means of reproducing the main features of the original." This stage (as Etkind emphasized) requires a solid knowledge of comparative stylistics.[28] Third in this quasi-Hegelian sequence is the synthesis: "the blending [*sintez*] into a new artistic whole of those features that were singled out in the original and were then transformed in conformance with the peculiarities of the literary language of translation."[29]

The most basic problem encountered by all translators is how to convey the meaning of a translated text without offending the grammar and syntax of the target language. Eric Bentley's observations pertain to English, but are equally applicable to other languages:

> Accuracy must not be bought at the expense of bad English. Since we cannot have everything, we would rather surrender accuracy than style. This, I think, is the first principle of translating, though it is not yet accepted in academic circles. The clinching argument in favor of this principle is that, finally, bad English cannot be accurate translation—unless the original is in bad German, bad French, or what have you.[30]

One might test the idiomatic faithfulness of the language of translation as follows:

---

27. This story was related at a conference on literary translation in Belgrade in January 1988 by George Ben, formerly of Leningrad but then of London. Ben was himself a translator of American poetry into Russian.
28. Viktor Koptilov, in *Voprosy teorii khudozhestvennogo perevoda* (Moscow: Khudozhestvennaia literatura, 1971), pp. 154–56 and 158; original emphasis.
29. Ibid., p. 162.
30. Cited in Arrowsmith and Shattuck, *Craft and Context of Translation*, p. 106.

> Suppose that we have succeeded in writing a faithful [French] translation of a characteristic [English] page of Ruskin, and that we submit it for criticism to two well-educated French friends, one of whom has but little acquaintance with English, while the other has an intimate knowledge of our language. If the first were to say "A fine description! Who is the author?" and the second "Surely that is Ruskin, though I do not remember the passage," then we might be confident that in respect of style our translation did not fall too far short of our ideal. We should have written French that was French, while it still kept the flavor of the original.[31]

Finding an appropriate language of translation is complicated by the fact that different languages change at different rates. In 1930 Andrei Fedorov called attention to the fact that "since the eighteenth century French has not changed as rapidly as Russian, and the French reader does not perceive [eighteenth-century language] as archaic to the same degree."[32] He also advised readers to bear in mind that the language of verse ages less rapidly than the language of prose. One reason for this disparity is that verse is more abstract and stylized whereas prose is more closely linked to conversational language.[33]

A concrete case was described by Lev Ginzburg, a leading translator of German verse into Russian:

> I was once translating into Russian "Poor Heinrich," a poem by the famed twelfth-century *Minnesinger* Hartmann von Aue. Now where was I to find in modern Russian the lexical equivalents for the translation of this ancient poem written in Middle High German? How was I to convey the spiritual, almost intimate links tying the hero and the heroine, he a feudal lord stricken with leprosy, she a twelve-year-old peasant girl from Swabia who was under the spell of

---

31. Savory, *Art of Translation*, p. 55.
32. Chukovskii and Fedorov, *Iskusstvo perevoda*, pp. 196–97. I made the same point some thirty years ago in my review of Nabokov's English rendition of *Eugene Onegin* (*Novyi zhurnal* 77 [1964]: 297–300). So angered was Nabokov by the impertinence of one so young and not even a native speaker of either Russian or English, that he suggested that perhaps "Moris Fridberg" did not really exist. See Nabokov's "Reply to My Critics," *Encounter*, February 1966; reprinted in *Strong Opinions* (New York: McGraw-Hill, 1973), pp. 241–67.
33. Chukovskii and Fedorov, *Iskusstvo perevoda*, p. 203.

deeply rooted folk notions of mercy and self-denial that were tinged, moreover, with medieval mysticism?[34]

Jiří Levý suggested a possible solution to dilemmas of that kind:

> The foremost difference between a translator who is an artist and one who is a mere craftsman is that the artist, while in the process of moving from the original to the rendition, *conjures up the reality which he describes. That means that he penetrates the text and visualizes personages, situations and ideas.* The ordinary craftsman, by contrast, merely perceives the text in a mechanical manner, and then translates mere words. This implies a need for the aesthetic education of translators.[35]

Translators of old literary texts must proceed cautiously in deciding on the optimum age of the language of translation. Theodore Savory described the problem:

> Cervantes published *Don Quixote* in 1605; should that story be translated into contemporary [that is, Shakespearean] English, such as he would have used at that time had he been an Englishman, or into the English of today? There can, as a rule, be very little doubt as to the answer, and in most cases the reader is justified in expecting the kind of language that he himself is accustomed to use. If a function of translation is the product in the minds of its readers, the answer is clear. Yet there is need to notice in passing the possibility of an exception when the original author is read more for his manner than his matter. We may read the speeches of Cicero chiefly that we may have the opportunity to appreciate his eloquence. Today the most eloquent speaker of English is Sir Winston Churchill, yet Churchill's style is not Cicero's style. Should a speech by Cicero be so translated as to sound as if it had been delivered by Churchill? No.[36]

Savory mistakenly assumed that we can establish the impact of *Don Quixote* on its first readers when we clearly cannot; and he expected a unani-

---

34. Ginsburg, *Nad strokoi perevoda*, pp. 26–27.
35. Levyi, *Iskusstvo perevoda*, p. 63, emphasis added.
36. Savory, *Art of Translation*, p. 56.

mous answer to the question whether the novel should now be translated into modern English. Nabokov's English *Eugene Onegin* demonstrates that dissent is possible. Nonetheless Savory's final verdict—that Cicero should decidedly *not* be made to resemble Churchill—remains valid.

Translation techniques change with time, but this does not imply "improvement" in the results. We cannot speak of "progress" in translation any more than we can speak of "progress" in drama or poetry: Tennessee Williams is not an "improvement" over Chekhov, who in turn is not an "improvement" over Molière and Sophocles; and Pushkin does not represent progress in comparison to Homer. Lev Ginzburg observed in 1987 that whereas in the 1920s literalist renditions of great authors were written in "dusty, lifeless, antiquated language, so distant from living modern speech," the more recent practitioners of free translation needed to avoid the opposite danger, namely: "a disrespectful and offensive chumminess in dealing with the texts of great writers. This is not simply 'modernization' or 'democratization.' It is an intolerable cheapening and watering down of the lexicon of world classics."[37] Ginzburg rejected as similarly "dishonest" the frequent Western practice of rendering classical (that is, nineteenth-century) Russian poetry in free verse, without rhythm or rhymes. This, he said, "smacks of surrender" and is "really a forgery [*podlog*]." By the same token, unrhymed foreign poetry should not be translated into Russian verse, as occasionally is done. This results in losing "the inner melody, the lyrical, emotional and rhythmic structure of the original."[38]

An impassioned appeal for up-to-date renditions appeared in 1983 from the pen of Anatoly Kim, a prose writer and translator into Russian:

> A translation must be made not merely from one language into another (say, from Old French into Russian), *but without fail into modern Russian, that is, in the final analysis, into the language of modern concepts and feelings.* What does the translating of concepts and feelings into the language of modernity imply? It means that Hamlet's soliloquy should be rendered with the resources of modern language that would make Hamlet's doubts, passions and spiritual tension live and become *our own* doubts and torments.[39]

---

37. *Perevod—sredstvo vzaimnogo sblizheniia narodov: Khudozhestvennaia publitsistika* (Moscow: Progress, 1987), p. 497.

38. Ginzburg, *Nad strokoi perevoda*, p. 29.

39. Anatolii Kim, in *Literaturnoe obozrenie*, no. 4 (1983): 20; emphasis added in the first italicized passage. The words "our own" are italicized in the original.

But as Lev Ozerov pointed out, nothing can alter the fact that translations do become dated:

> While the original of Shakespeare's *Hamlet* is unique and cannot be changed, *our old renderings of Hamlet now make for difficult and occasionally painful reading*. . . .
> The obsolescence of translations is inevitable, in part because every generation wishes to see its reflection in the mirror of the classical text. Hence thirty Russian Hamlets. And even more are to come. Life is right. There is but one Hamlet, but scores of renditions.[40]

Does this mean that "obsolete" renditions become completely useless? Not necessarily. Subsequent translators may still make use of them. The Bulgarian translator Liuben Liubenov reported that in his country new renderings were allowed to incorporate segments of old ones, provided this fact was acknowledged.[41] The Soviet writer and critic Vikenty Veresaev utilized previous renditions of *The Iliad* by Gnedich and Minsky when he translated this work himself. He justified this procedure by saying: "A translator should make full use of everything that was successful in earlier renditions. Naturally, this should not be done mechanically, by simply incorporating passages into one's own translation. One should blend them with one's own style, or more precisely, with the style of the original text as perceived by the specific translator."[42]

Sometimes bits and pieces of older renditions serve the purpose of preserving a poetic allusion. Thus the title of Viktor Golyshev's Russian version of Robert Penn Warren's *All the King's Men* was not translated literally as *Vse liudi korolia*, but rather as *Vsia korolevskaia rat'*, which preserved the association with Samuil Marshak's earlier translation of *Humpty-Dumpty*. Needless to say, this stratagem works only when the older translation is sufficiently well known. For the same reason Boris Zakhoder, the translator of *Alice in Wonderland*, substituted some of the author's allusions to English nursery rhymes with more or less analogous material from Russian folklore.[43] Zakhoder presumably was unaware that

---

40. Lev Ozerov, in *Literaturnoe obozrenie,* no. 3 (1983), pp. 31–32; emphasis added.

41. Liuben Liubenov, "Osnovnye problemy poeticheskogo perevoda," *Slavica Slovaca* (Bratislava) 17, no. 14 (1982): 300–301.

42. Cited in Iu. D. Levin, "Ob istoricheskoi evoliutsii printsipov perevoda (K istorii perevodcheskoi mysli v Rossii)," in *Mezhdunarodnye sviazi russkoi literatury,* ed. M. P. Alekseev (Moscow and Leningrad: Izdatel'stvo Akademii Nauk SSSR, 1963), p. 8.

43. T. E. Nekriach, in *Teoriia i praktyka perekladu* (Kiev), no. 3 (1980): 81–82.

this was also Nabokov's solution in his Russian *Alice*, published in 1923 in Western Europe. Nabokov's translation was not available in Soviet libraries, however. N. M. Demurova, who produced yet another rendering of *Alice*, confirmed the fact in 1970: "I was not successful in locating a copy."[44]

Comparative poetics, championed by Efim Etkind for its usefulness in literary translation, can be a dependable yardstick for appraising the merits and demerits of different renderings. By combining linguistic and literary approaches to the text, a comparative method avoids undue tilting (*krenit'-sia*) in the direction of either free or literal translation. In the book they coauthored in 1979, the Soviet translators V. Ragoisha (a Belorussian) and Viktor Koptilov (a Ukrainian) likewise took a comparative approach. Koptilov warned that altering the literary form of a text (as in translation) affects the perception of its contents. Such changes are often unavoidable. Thus Polish syllabic verse is rendered in East Slavic languages as syllabotonic (the customary structure of East Slavic verse), but the monorhythm of certain kinds of Oriental poetry can be reproduced in a variety of rhythms.[45]

Renditions of verse often result in *simplification* of the original text, a problem long familiar to teachers of literature in translation. Poetic texts that are subtle in the original are somehow often transformed by translation into naive doggerel. Robert de Beaugrande warned of this danger:

> As a reader, the translator naturally tends to complete the text, filling in gaps or supplying details and responses at appropriate points. . . . It is frequently left to the readers [of poetry] to make associations between the object and other things indicated by it. A translator might well supply these associations not only in responding to the text, but also while producing the translation. The result is a text deprived of its dynamic aspect, since the reader's role has been filled by the translator.[46]

A Russian expression, *perevodchik dochityvaet* (the translator completes the reading), aptly describes the activity of explaining to the reader allusions he could not possibly understand on his own. An American reader, for instance, cannot be expected to know that in Russia 1937 was the year of a bloody purge; or that the "cult of personality" refers to one

---

44. *Masterstvo perevoda*, 1969, p. 159.
45. V. Ragoisha and V. Koptilov, in *Voprosy literatury*, no. 5 (1979): 31–32.
46. Robert de Beaugrande, *Factors in a Theory of Poetic Translating* (Amsterdam: Van Gorcum, Assen, 1978), p. 30.

particular person, Stalin; or that in Marxist parlance "idealism" is bad and "materialism" is good. In prose this can be explained in introductions or, in extreme cases, in footnotes. What Beaugrande rightly deplored are translations that provide ready-made answers to questions that were raised in the original poem merely to stimulate the reader's independent thought.

Translators often gauge the style of their work according to the audience for which it is intended. Marina Tarlinskaja recommended this policy:

> Variable degrees of closeness between O[riginal] and T[ranslation] exist not only "diachronically" (different epochs have different attitudes toward adequate closeness), but also "synchronically." First, different styles require different "distances" between O[riginal] and T[ranslation] (shorter in translating documents or scientific prose, longer in translating fiction and particularly poetry). Second, the distance between O[riginal] and T[ranslation] depends on the kind of reader the translator has in mind: closer ("text-oriented") translations are aimed at sophisticated readers, while freer ("audience-oriented") translations are meant for a broader audience.[47]

In the work of translation, as in other areas of the Soviet literary process, practical considerations occasionally forced *de facto* acquiescence to approaches that in theory were denied *de jure* recognition. Thus the Lithuanian poet and translator Eduardas Mezhelaitis defended "philological translations," namely, prose renditions of verse, though only for very limited use. Some works, he argued, simply cannot be rendered in any other way; and "philological translations" are better than no translation at all.[48] Yuri Mineralov accepted the legitimacy of paraphrase as a method for another reason: namely, its venerable history. Paraphrase, he reminded his Soviet readers, had been popular in Russia in the late eighteenth century. Lomonosov, Sumarokov, and Tred'iakovsky, the three leading Neoclassical poets of that time, had competed to produce the best "paraphrastic ode"; and in 1752 Tred'iakovsky had written "Ode XVI, Paraphrase of Psalm 143." The poet Derzhavin had often paraphrased the Psalms, as well as Horace and Pindar in "all of his more important odes." Accordingly,

---

47. Marina Tarlinskaja, "On Equivalence in Translation: Shakespeare's Sonnet 66 and Ten Translations into Russian," *International Journal of Slavic Linguistics and Poetics* 30 (1984): 89.

48. Lev A. Anninskii, comp., *Khudozhestvennyi perevod: Problemy i suzhdeniia* (Moscow: Izvestiia, 1986), pp. 9–10.

Mineralov declared, "paraphrase is but a pseudonym for artistic imitation." In an effort to prove that it deserved recognition as legitimate *modern* art, he appealed to the authority of recent as well as modish scholarship. "Semiotics," he explained, "views every artistic imitation as a *translation* 'from language to language.' . . . This is not a play on words, but a modern scientific truth."[49]

While Mezhelaitis and Mineralov sought to rehabilitate venerable translation practices, V. A. Dmitrenko attempted to demonstrate the nonthreatening nature of the new comparative, or as he called it, "maximal" (*maksimal'nyi*) method:

> What does it mean in practice? It implies taking into consideration the weaknesses of earlier concepts, and the *divergences* and the *convergences* of the languages involved in the translation. These are revealed by means of a semantic-stylistic and artistic analysis of the original, and are reproduced accordingly in the translation. All of this implies translation of the convergences and interpretation of the divergences. It also implies reaching the limits of translatability, allowing for the grammatical-stylistic norms and possibilities of the target language. In other words, it implies producing a translation in which all departures from the original can be "blamed" either on the source language or the target language, and not on the translator.[50]

Literary translators periodically are warned to avoid the dangers of "translationese." E. G. Etkind defined this as outwardly literate speech, quite acceptable from a pedagogical point of view, but insidious in the manner in which it robs the original of its literary allure. As a case in point he cited a recent French translation of Nikolai Leskov. The author's highly idiosyncratic prose had been "cleaned up" and "corrected," thus becoming bland "translationese." What the translator should have done, according to Etkind's, was

> to find counterparts in French stylistics to Leskov's linguistic resources. These may be of a different nature, from other areas of life and shaped in dissimilar ways, but their function should be the same. They should be *analogous functionally*. Translation theory

---

49. Ibid., pp. 158–59.
50. V. A. Dmitrenko, "Maksimal'nost' v perevode," *Tetradi perevodchika*, no. 11 (1974): 24; emphasis in the original.

must identify the inner resources of such "functional similarities" in languages that are being compared, and the discipline identifying those resources should be called *comparative stylistics*.[51]

This is not to say that Etkind's "comparative systems" are the only way to successful translation. Lauren Leighton rightly pointed out that

> If the translator searches long enough and carefully enough, he will find the "key" to conveying any style. For Kipling, Chukovsky found the key in swiftly shifting cadences and an emphasis on "jingoistic" [?] masculine line endings. For Burns, he used (as did Samuil Marshak) a "signal" device—the adroit and sparing use of Church Slavonicisms and eighteenth-century morphology to "signal" the reader that this poetry is rustic, quaint and vexedly colloquial. . . . [For Whitman], recognition that the rhetorical and declamatory effects of the "singer of freedom" are based on intonational devices.[52]

A paper presented at an international symposium in 1982 emphasized that "translationese," while ostensibly correct, is in fact contaminated with features of the source language the translator has subconsciously retained. While formally acceptable in the target language, these traits of the source language betray their foreign origin readily enough. "Translationese" is also quite common among foreign students of a language. It affects their lexicon, syntax, and grammar. These non-native speakers are generally unaware that locutions of "translationese" that are *preferred* in their native language are only *tolerated* in the foreign tongue.[53] "Translationese" is spoken by a number of Tolstoy's protagonists in *War and Peace* and *Anna Karenina*, who are forced to use Russian even though they are more at home with French; by many characters in Isaak Babel's short stories, whose Russian bears a strong imprint of Yiddish; by Nabokov's Pnin, whose English is very Russian. Certain words are to be found almost exclusively in translations, such as *kroshka*, the usual Russian rendition of the American "baby," meaning a young woman; *prepodobnyi*, "Reverend," and so on. The older English

---

51. E. G. Etkind, in *Teoriia i kritika perevoda* (Izdatel'stvo Leningradskogo universiteta, 1962), pp. 26–28; original emphasis.
52. Lauren G. Leighton, trans. and ed., *Kornei Chukovsky's "A High Art"* (Knoxville: University of Tennessee Press, 1984), p. xxii.
53. *Khudozhestvennyi perevod: Voprosy teorii i praktiki* (Erevan: Izdatel'stvo Erevanskogo universiteta, 1982), pp. 132–34.

translations of Russian novels rendered *batiushka* incongruously as "little father." Newer ones have been using "amortization" in lieu of "depreciation," "demobilized" instead of "discharged," "responsible workers" rather than "senior officials," and "social worker" instead of "public figure."

A nation's literature, particularly its poetry, is not simply shaped arbitrarily by a code of rules called prosody. These rules do not merely reflect the preferences of writers, poets, translators, and critics but also mirror some basic features of the language. Thus Andrei Fedorov attempted to explain to his countrymen why French poetry is so unlike the Russian, and why French writers, for instance, cannot produce garden variety four-foot iambic verse. Because French, unlike Russian, has a fixed stress on the last syllable, a French poet would have to restrict himself entirely to two- or three-syllable words in order to create trochaic, iambic, or dactylic stress. Not only would this be too artificial: most likely the French would not even regard it as verse. Moreover, the characteristics of a source language affect the manner in which verse in that language is translated into French. Finally, many Frenchmen view the preservation of a foreign poem's meter or rhyme as an impediment in reproducing its precise meaning.[54]

Translators of Spanish poetry into Russian must contend with the fact that Spanish verse is syllabic, while Russian verse is syllabo-accentual. In addition, Spanish poetry uses both consonantal rhymes (that is, full rhymes, including stressed vowels and all the sounds that follow) and assonantic rhymes (with an identical stressed vowel, but with different sounds following). Both may occur in masculine, feminine, and dactylic rhymes. By contrast, until the twentieth century assonantic rhymes in Russian were found predominantly in folk poetry, and therefore were considered a feature of inferior versification. For this reason Russian renderings of Spanish assonantic verse have been written almost exclusively in blank verse ever since the time of Zhukovsky and Pushkin.[55]

Long sentences are not unknown in Russian writing; suffice it to recall the seemingly endless sentence at the beginning of Gogol's "The Overcoat." Nevertheless, Russian translators tend to chop up analogous sentences found in other languages. Maria Lor'e divided a 227–word sentence in Hemingway's "The Short Happy Life of Francis Macomber" into three; and N. Volzhina, another leading translator of Anglo-American prose, similarly split up an 81-word sentence in the same author's *The Snows of*

54. Chukovskii and Fedorov, *Iskusstvo perevoda*, pp. 94–95.
55. A. A. Mishustina, in *Teoriia i praktyka perekladu* (Kiev), no. 3 (1980): 113–14.

Kilmanjaro.[56] Occasionally German and French sentences are overly long as well; Chukovsky and Fedorov recommended chopping them up unless their excessive length was intentional, as in Goethe's *Werther* or the works of Marcel Proust.[57] Nora Gal', another translator of English and American writing, believed that in Russian "It is nearly always advisable to *eliminate auxiliary verbs which are all but obligatory in Western languages*" because in Russian "an auxiliary verb plus an infinitive render a sentence clumsy and unwieldy."[58] Another translator of British and American literature, Vladimir Rossel's, called upon his fellows to beware of English participles and gerunds. A profusion of these would cause a literal Russian translation to teem with *shchii* and *vshi* endings of verbs. Such words are not only unwieldy, but funny as well. *Shchi* is the Russian word for "cabbage soup," while *vshi* means "lice."[59]

Another pitfall to be avoided is that of making a translation sound *overly* Russian. In 1842 Vissarion Belinsky faulted M. P. Pogodin for having the German protagonists of Goethe's *Götz von Berlichingen* "speak Russian in the manner of bearded shopkeepers and coachmen."[60] Likewise in 1975 Nora Gal' warned against using words in translations that are too exclusively Russian.[61] The linguist T. R. Levitskaia registered a similar caveat when she recommended translating fixed expressions in the source language by set expressions of similar meaning in the target language "as long as the latter are not specifically ethnic in nature."[62] Jiří Levý noted that "the psychological makeup of a nation," real or imagined, is reflected in its language. Accordingly, English understatements (such as, "I am afraid I cannot") should be augmented to full size ("unfortunately I cannot"); and analogous allowances should be made for the Spanish predilection for grandiloquence.[63]

At a 1973–74 seminar on literary translation at the University of Louvain in Belgium, a local teacher of Russian, Vera Fosty, presented a lengthy

---

56. V. A. Kucharenko et al., "Kliuchevye i tematicheskie slova v originale i perevode khudozhestvennogo proizvedeniia," *Filologicheskie nauki* 4 (1983): 68.

57. Chukovskii and Fedorov, *Iskusstvo perevoda,* pp. 189–93.

58. Nora Gal', *Slovo zhivoe i mertvoe,* 4th enlarged edition (Moscow: Kniga, 1987), p. 93; emphasis in the original.

59. V. Rossel's, *Estafeta slova: Iskusstvo khudozhestvennogo perevoda* (Moscow: Znanie, 1972), p. 28.

60. V. M. Zhirmunskii, *Gete v russkoi literature* (Leningrad: Nauka, 1981), p. 138.

61. Nora Gal', *Slovo zhivoe i mertvoe,* 2d ed. (Moscow: Kniga, 1975), pp. 93–96.

62. T. R. Levitskaia and A. M. Fiterman, *Problemy perevoda: Na materiale sovremennogo angliiskogo iazyka* (Moscow: Mezhdunarodnye otnosheniia, 1976), pp. 185–86.

63. Levyi, *Iskusstvo perevoda,* pp. 128–29.

paper comparing the French and Russian languages. The French lexicon, she noted, contains 80,000 words; Russian has more than twice that number. Typically, Russian speakers know more words having to do with weather or with flora and fauna; this reflects their greater proximity to nature. (The same appears to be true of Russians as compared with speakers of American English, though the English lexicon is much larger than the Russian.) In Fosty's judgment Russian is a *concrete* language, emphasizing objects that one can see or touch. It is less prone to the *abstractions* that are favored in French. Moreover, "Russian is a rather synthetic language, while French is an analytical one. It is undoubtedly the tendency to compensate [for these attributes] that causes the first to be repetitious and redundant, while the latter strives for conciseness and abhors all repetition." Fosty also observed that Russian contains many maxims and sayings (principally derived from the fabulist Krylov), as well as aphorisms from Griboedov's *Woe from Wit* and other literary sources. This is less common in French, where similar material often verges on the cliché. (Here too, American English is closer to Russian in its propensity to cite or paraphrase the Bible, Shakespeare, or *Alice in Wonderland*.) Russian is an "emotional" language, according to Fosty, whereas French is restrained and intellectual.

She then proceeded to list Russian literary texts in ascending order of difficulty of translation into French. By far the easiest are Pushkin's *Tales of Belkin:* "One might think they were translations from the French." (*The Tales of Belkin* and Chekhov's short stories are also among the first Russian texts read by American students of the language.) Then come nineteenth- and twentieth-century Russian authors who eschew archaic forms and dialect and favor a simple, straightforward style, for example Konstantin Paustovsky. Soviet authors of village prose of the 1960s and 1970s, such as Shukshin, Nosov, Belov, and Astaf'ev are hard to render into French because they use regional and peasant dialects as well as Soviet neologisms. Sholokhov is harder still. Most difficult of all are Zoshchenko, Leskov, and the Russian poets.[64] (By and large, the same order of difficulty prevails in translation from Russian into English.)

One feature of the Russian language which constitutes a serious impediment in the translation of English verse is its very high percentage of polysyllabic words (especially when compared with English). The contrast

---

64. In *Problèmes littéraires de la traduction* (Leiden: E. J. Brill, 1975), pp. 113–15, 117–20. (See Introduction, note 12.)

is particularly striking because the length of Russian words is further augmented in the conjugation of verbs and the declension of nouns, adjectives, and participles. This difference is not merely an impression, but a statistically verified fact. The average length of words in English prose texts is 1.4 syllables, but in Czech it is 2.4, in French 2.47, and in Russian 3.0.[65] While in Russian long words are more common in prose than in verse, very long words are not uncommon. Four-syllable words account for 9.6 percent of all words in Russian prose texts and 4.6 percent in verse; five-syllable words amount to 3.6 and 0.8 percent, and six-syllable words, 1.9 and 0.1 percent.[66] For every thousand words of an English literary text, 824 are monosyllabic; the analogous figure for Russian is only 328. The problem this creates for translators is only too obvious. Chukovsky gave as an instructive example the case of Anna Radlova, who in translating Shakespeare made a desperate effort to retain the original number of lines in each poem. In so doing she resorted to mutilation of Shakespearean imagery as well as syntax, and her Russian is full of monosyllabic stumps (*obrubki*).[67] On the other hand, one might argue that Radlova had little choice. Consider Chukovsky's observation three decades earlier:

> As is known, in English (particularly in its later varieties) the vast [*ogromnoe*] majority of words consist of a single syllable. On the average, every English word is barely half the length of the Russian. This brevity imparts to English speech a special kind of conciseness and vigor. Translation into Russian invariably replaces a seven-line paragraph with a flabby one of eleven or twelve lines. This is deadly in a language in which "crime" is *prestuplenie*, "bus" is *omnibus*, "wee" is *malen'kii*, where sentences often make do without conjunctions, and so on. For that reason an English novel which requires 1,600,000 printer's letters requires 2,200,000 in Russian, even in a condensed translation. This proportion is unavoidable.[68]

Ivan Bunin, Russia's first winner of the Nobel Prize for literature, recalled that while translating Longfellow's *The Song of Hiawatha* he was

---

65. Levyi, *Iskusstvo perevoda*, p. 247.
66. T. A. Ledovskaia and F. I. Mauler, "Nekotorye sposoby dostizheniia ekvilinearnosti v poeticheskoi stroke," *Tetradi perevodchika*, no. 18 (1981): pp. 26–27.
67. Kornei Chukovskii, *Vysokoe iskusstvo: O printsipakh khudozhestvennogo perevoda* (Moscow: Iskusstvo, 1964), pp. 193–94.
68. Chukovskii and Fedorov, *Iskusstvo perevoda*, pp. 53–54.

tempted, because of the brevity of English words, to have a single line of the original correspond to several lines of Russian. Ultimately he abandoned the idea, but at the cost of "lightening" (that is, compressing) the Russian text.[69] Even so, his 1896 rendition of the poem, which preserves the rhythm of the original, remains unsurpassed a century later. According to the Soviet translator Ia. A. Khelemsky, "Had Ivan Alekseevich Bunin done nothing in his life other than translate *Hiawatha*, he would still be remembered in the annals of Russian writing; he would still have left a strong imprint on Russian poetry."[70]

L. S. Barkhudarov illustrated the effect of transforming a taut English verse into a flabby Russian stanza by citing four lines from Byron's "The Chain I Gave" side by side with his own interlinear rendition:

> The chain I gave was fair to view
> The lute I added sweet in sound.
> The heart that offer'd both was true,
> And ill deserved the fate it found.

In Russian:

> Tsepochka, kotoruiu ia podaril, byla krasivoi na vid,
> Liutnia, kotoruiu ia dobavil—priiatnoi na slukh,
> Serdtse, kotoroe podarilo ikh oboikh, bylo vernym,
> No nezasluzhennoi byla sud'ba, kotoraia byla emu ugotovana.

Barkhudarov commented: "Beyond any doubt, one of the fundamental difficulties faced by the translator of English verse into Russian is the necessity of verbal compression of the poetic text, of reducing its lexical volume."[71]

When the venerable Soviet poet and translator Samuil Marshak was taken to task by the much younger poetess Iunna Morits for taking liberties with English poetry, Vil'gel'm Levik, an eminent translator of nineteenth-century French and German poetry, came to his defense: "The enormous difference between the length of English words (most of them short, monosyllabic) and Russian words (mostly long, trisyllabic) occasionally

---

69. L. S. Barkhudarov, "Nekotorye problemy perevoda angliiskoi poezii na ruskii iazyk," *Tetradi perevodchika*, no. 28 (1984): 39–40.
70. *Perevod—sredstvo vzaimnogo sblizheniia narodov*, pp. 196–97.
71. Barkhudarov, "Nekotorye problemy," p. 40, emphasis in the original.

necessitates longer stanzas. And should this prove impossible (in a sonnet, for instance), then one must sacrifice a somewhat larger number of details than we do when translating, say, from the German or from the French."[72]

Nearly any student of a foreign language will attest that the grammatical gender of nouns is quite arbitrary, and occasionally defies common sense. Consider the following passage from Mark Twain's "The Awful German Language":

> In the German it is true that by some oversight of the inventor of the language, a Woman is a female; but a Wife ("Weib") is not—which is unfortunate. A Wife, here, has no sex; she is neuter; so, according to the grammar, a fish is "he," his scales are "she," but a fishwife is neither. To describe a wife as sexless may be called under-description.[73]

Since the gender of nouns differs from one language to another, the shift occasionally creates a serious obstacle in translation. Roman Jakobson related in *Linguistic Aspects* that the Czech poet Josef Hora was "reduced to despair" because Boris Pasternak's *My Sister Life* (*Sestra moia zhizn'*) simply could not be translated into Czech, in which the word for "life" (*zivot*) is masculine. This shift may also prove a hindrance in translation from one semiotic system into another. Thus the Russian painter Il'ia Repin could not understand why German artists depicted sin as a female; the reason was that the Russian word for "sin" (*grekh*) is masculine, while the German (*die Sünde*) is feminine. Similarly, Russian children are baffled by German fairy tales in which death is a male figure (*der Tod*); in Russian death is female (*smert'*).[74] In his rendition of Heine's "Die Lotesblume ängstigt," in which the lotus is in love with the moon, the nineteenth-century translator M. L. Mikhailov failed to consider the fact that in German "lotus" is feminine and "moon" masculine; the reverse is the case in Russian. Pointing this out, his colleague Petr Veinberg suggested that to retain the sense of the original Mikhailov should have substituted the feminine flower *liliia*, "lily," for the masculine Russian *lotos*, and the

---

72. Vil'gel'm Levik, in *Voprosy literatury*, no. 5 (1979): 59.
73. Mark Twain [Samuel L. Clemens], "The Awful German Language," from *A Tramp Abroad* (1880), appendix to Volume I.
74. Reuben A. Brower, ed., *On Translation* (New York: Oxford University Press, 1966), p. 237.

masculine Russian *mesiats,* "moon," for its feminine synonym *luna.*[75] Two years afterward, Veinberg produced a translation that incorporated his own advice. Unfortunately, it was marred by clichés, prosaic locutions, and cheap diminutives.[76]

The best known incident involving careless substitution of grammatical genders in a translation involves a great Russian poet's rendering of a famous German's verse. In Lermontov's translation of Heine's "Ein Fichtenbaum steht einsam," the love of the masculine pine tree (*der Fichtenbaum*) for the feminine palm tree (*die Palme*) was "destroyed." Substitution of the Russian *sosna* (pine) and *pal'ma* (palm), both of which are feminine, "transformed lovesickness into melancholy loneliness."[77] By desexualizing the male's yearning for the distant female in Heine, Lermontov produced instead a Romantic poem about "a dream of something distant and beautiful, but altogether and by definition unattainable." Not surprisingly, other translators hastened to correct Lermontov's oversight.[78] By 1936 thirty-nine different Russian renditions of Heine's poem had been published, plus several parodies. Tiutchev, Maikov, Gippius, Engel'ke, Zagul', and the Soviet poet Pervomaisky rendered *der Fichtenbaum* as *kedr* (cedar), which is masculine, while Fet, Veinberg, and Meisner preferred *dub* (oak), likewise masculine.[79]

In her reminiscences of Anna Akhmatova, Lidiia Chukovskaia reported that Akhmatova criticized Marshak's renderings of Shakespeare's sonnets because in the original many of them are dedicated to a man, whereas Marshak's are addressed to a woman.[80] It is unlikely that Marshak failed to notice that fact. Some of the sonnets (e.g., Sonnet XX) are very ostentatiously addressed to a young man whose beauty outshines that of women. Quite possibly Marshak wanted to avoid any intimation of homoerotic attraction—a subject then quite unmentionable in Russia, where

---

75. Iu. D. Levin, *Russkie perevodchiki XIX veka i razvitie khudozhestvennogo perevoda* (Leningrad: Nauka, 1985), p. 278.

76. Ibid., pp. 281–82.

77. V. D. Radchuk, in *Teoriia i praktyka perekladu* (Kiev), no. 3 (1980): 11.

78. L. V. Shcherba, " 'Sosna' Lermontova v sravnenii s ee nemetskim prototipom," in *Izbrannye raboty po russkomu iazyku* (Moscow: Uchpedgiz, 1957), pp. 97–109. That it might have been simply an oversight on Lermontov's part is suggested by his confusion of the English "kindly" with the German *das Kind.* In the Russian poet's rendition, Byron's "Had We Never Loved so Kindly" became *"Esli b my ne deti byli"* [Were we not children] (K. I. Chukovskii, *Iskusstvo perevoda* [Moscow and Leningrad: Academia, 1936], p. 27).

79. V. D. Radchuk, in *Teoriia i praktyka perekladu,* no. 3 (1980): 11.

80. Lidiia Chukovskaia, *Zapiski ob Anne Akhmatovoi,* vol. 2, 1952–62 (Paris: YMCA Press, 1980), pp. 15–16.

homosexuality was indeed a criminal offense. But perhaps in the future Lermontov's "faulty" rendition of Heine's poem will be accepted in Russia as simply another poem about lesbian love.

Until censorship was relaxed in the late 1980s, the principle of the Orwellian "memory hole" was apparently as obligatory in historical accounts of literary translation as it was in other Soviet records of the past. Because literalism stood condemned, hardly any data on it was available, either in Soviet or émigré sources, in spite of the fact that until the 1930s many translators had followed its tenets. Valery Briusov's *Aeneid* was essentially literalist, as were V. D. Merkureva's Shelley; Georgi Shengeli's *Don Juan*, "Childe Harold," Baudelaire, and Verhaeren; I. A. Aksenov's Anatole France; M. L. Lozinsky's *Tartuffe* and *Hamlet;* and above all, the Dickens of Evgeny Lann and Aleksandra Krivtsova. In keeping with Soviet customs of those years, defeated literalists could only be criticized or ridiculed. Their side of the story was not publicly available, even if somewhere recorded.[81]

Typical of the antiliteralist polemics of that era was Starinkevich's observation in 1953 that Evgeny Lann's fanatical devotion to faithful reproduction of Dickens's English prompted him to have "characters of the novel he translated use [the formal Russian] 'vy' not only when addressing a child, but even when addressing a dog." Starinkevich suggested sarcastically that by the same logic, Russian translations from the French should avoid using neuter nouns because French ones can only be masculine or feminine.[82] Vladimir Rossel's' critique of literalism in 1984 was more polite, as befitted a scholar; in any case, more latitude was permitted in 1984, the dawn of Gorbachev's *glasnost'*, than in 1953, the year of Stalin's death. Nevertheless Rossel's too, by and large, failed to present the literalist point of view, though he tried to show why so many gifted translators had remained under its spell for years. According to his explanation, people like Georgi Shengeli and the husband and wife team of Evgeny Lann and Aleksandra Krivtsova had made virtues into shortcomings. Precision had become pedantry, so that attempts to retain the specific formal features of an original work resulted in disregard of good Russian usage. Rossel's found this to be true of Shengeli's rendition of Byron, as well as of Lann and Krivtsova's *David Copperfield, The Pickwick Papers,* and *Nicholas Nickleby.* Most unfor-

---

81. M. L. Gasparov, "Briusov i bukvalizm," in *Poetika perevoda: Sbornik statei* (Moscow: Raduga, 1988), pp. 29–61.

82. E. Starinkevich, "Masterstvo perevodchika," *Druzhba narodov*, no. 5 (1953): 193. In Russian, as in German or French, children and animals are addressed by the informal *ty*.

tunately, in his opinion, when Dickens was treated in this way he stopped being funny, particularly in *Pickwick Papers*. Rossel's therefore considered it unforgivable that Lann's *Pickwick* was included in a recently published multivolume set of Dickens. He did concede that a number of literalist renderings (such as Adrian Frankovsky's Swift, Defoe, and Fielding) had become classics and continued to be reprinted.[83] Clearly, in 1984 literalism no longer represented a danger to the reigning school of Soviet translation, which ostentatiously claimed to be "free." As the poet and translator Arseny Tarkovsky already had warned fifteen years before, by that time translation was threatened by the contrary tendency to stray too far from the original. Levon Mkrtchian, a leading student of the subject, seconded this concern in 1973.[84]

The existence of both literal and free translations of a literary work provides certain advantages, as various scholars have recognized. Wilhelm von Humboldt (1767–1835) welcomed a variety of independent translations of a single literary work in the belief that a "cumulative approximation to the original" would result.[85] A contrary problem bedeviled the Soviet literary establishment: translation by different hands of a poet's *collection* of verse and publication of the product in one volume. Apparently this practice was launched soon after the Bolshevik Revolution, perhaps in the Marxist belief that collective effort is preferable to individual endeavor. In one exceptional case, four poets working together—Georgy Adamovich, Nikolai Gumilev, Georgy Ivanov, and Mikhail Lozinsky—turned a single work into Russian: Voltaire's *The Maid of Orleans*. According to Yuri D. Levin, they actually succeeded in preserving the stylistic uniformity of the French original.[86] (Of the four, Gumilev was soon to be executed by a Soviet firing squad on charges of military conspiracy, while Adamovich and Ivanov emigrated to Western Europe. Only Lozinsky remained in the USSR, where he became a leading translator of Western European poetry.)

I know of no other instance of truly collective translation, in which several translators collaborated on the final product, and none in which translations by different hands did *not* affect the stylistic uniformity of the book in question. But bowing to the then fashionable collectivism, the typical Soviet

---

83. Vladimir Rossel's, *Skol'ko vesit slovo: Stat'i raznykh let* (Moscow: Sovetskii pisatel', 1984), pp. 33–34.
84. Arsenii Tarkovskii, in *Literaturnaia gazeta*, September 10, 1969; cited in Levon Mkrtchian, *Cherty rodstva* (Erevan: Izdatel'stvo Aiastan, 1973), p. 79.
85. Lefevere, *Translating Literature*, p. 40.
86. Levin, "Ob istoricheskoi evoliutsii," pp. 6–7.

procedure was to assign several persons to translate a single volume of a foreign poet's verse. The quality of the renditions produced by this method was necessarily uneven. Even more damaging was the loss of the foreign poet's unity of style, which rarely survived collective translation. Andrei Fedorov in 1930 decried this mode of operation; but 1930 was prior to the apogee of Stalinism.[87] The peculiarly Soviet predilection for crash programs, known as *shturmovshchina* (storming), aggravated this editorial problem. Thirty-two years after Fedorov's lament, a speaker at a national Soviet conference on literary translation reported that in some cases a volume of verse by a single foreign poet was parceled out among as many as *forty* translators. As the speaker noted, this practice totally eliminated any likelihood that the resulting Russian book might convey some sense of the flavor of the original.[88]

Presumably the forty translators represented an extreme case. Nevertheless, the fact remains that translation by several individuals of a volume of verse by a single foreign poet was standard Soviet practice. According to Efim Etkind, this procedure created two hazards. Either the various translators muffled their individuality, producing a reasonably consistent common style that was colorless and bland (an effect that might also result from overly thorough editing)—or they defiantly flaunted their individuality. In the latter case the foreign poet—whether Byron, Goethe, Rimbaud, or someone else—assumed a multiplicity of guises that produced an equally bland overall effect.[89] Soviet critics periodically denounced the practice of farming out sections of a single poet's collection of verse to different translators. (For example, Marshak observed that "truly poetic renditions must be accumulated rather than manufactured.") Such criticism was apparently to no avail.[90]

---

87. Chukovskii and Fedorov, *Iskusstvo perevoda*, pp. 223–24. I have some firsthand experience with this problem. About twenty-five years ago, Doubleday publishers asked me to edit a translation of Leon Trotsky's biography of the young Lenin by the recently deceased radical American journalist, Max Eastman. When the manuscript arrived, I discovered that different chapters had been translated into several varieties of English, presumably by Eastman's lady friends. Their various prose styles ranged from British to American, and from finishing-school composition to working-class immigrant prose. To edit them in a way that made them appear like the work of a single translator, allegedly Eastman himself, was no easy task. See Leon Trotsky, *The Young Lenin*, trans. Max Eastman, ed. Maurice Friedberg (Garden City, N.Y.: Doubleday, 1972).

88. *Ot znakomstva k rodstvu: Materialy Vserossiiskogo soveshchaniia po khudozhestvennomu perevodu, Kazan', ianvar' 1962 g.* (Kazan': Tatarskoe Knizhnoe Izdatel'stvo, 1963), p. 282.

89. Efim Etkind, *Poeziia i perevod* (Moscow and Leningrad: Sovetskii pisatel', 1963), pp. 428–29.

90. See, for example, Evgenii Eliseev, "Perevodchik ili soavtor," *Druzhba narodov*, no. 6 (1952): 237; V. Dmitriev, "Praktika, kotoruiu ne sleduet podderzhivat'," *Voprosy literatury,*

Until controls were relaxed in the late 1980s, Soviet censorship was fairly consistent, treating foreign writing no more leniently than domestic literary production. An outright, though unofficial, prohibition affected not only unfriendly politicized foreign literature (such as Orwell's *1984* and *Animal Farm*, Huxley's *Brave New World*, Koestler's *Darkness at Noon*, and Ionesco's *Rhinoceros*) but also *apolitical* writing by objectionable authors like Saul Bellow, Isaac Bashevis Singer, André Gide, Albert Camus, and scores of others. The works of Soviet émigrés were similarly banned, with rare exceptions made for authors already deceased—as if following the maxim: the only good émigré is a dead one. In the late 1980s and early 1990s most of the objectionable authors' works were finally printed in Russia, including books by émigrés like Nabokov and Solzhenitsyn. During the preceding seventy years, however, translations had been routinely censored. Affected were occasional unfavorable remarks in foreign books about the USSR or Communism, whether in authorial speech or voiced by literary characters. Thus in Hemingway's *For Whom the Bell Tolls* all derogatory quips about Communists during the Spanish Civil War disappeared. Soviet editors or censors did a thorough job of removing all flippant comments about the USSR from Kurt Vonnegut's antimilitaristic novel *Slaughterhouse Five* and Gore Vidal's *Washington, D.C.*, even though the latter book was above all an attack on McCarthyism in America. In John Steinbeck's *Travels with Charlie* the censors got rid of a funny scene describing Khrushchev pounding the table with his shoe at the United Nations, even though by that time Khrushchev had already been deposed. In Truman Capote's *In Cold Blood* most of the information suggesting that American farmers are reasonably prosperous people was removed because, one suspects, it would have invited invidious comparison with Soviet collectivized agriculture. Soviet censors suppressed the entire narrator's part in Arthur Miller's play *The Crucible*—the section attacking intolerance and witch hunts and extolling freedom of speech—again, presumably, because this might have suggested undesirable parallels with Soviet conditions. It is worth emphasizing that none of these changes were authorized by the American writers concerned, at least those still alive at the time. I wrote to all of them, and each one assured me that permission to censor their books had not been sought and certainly had not been granted.

---

no. 5 (1960): 134–43; and S. Ia. Marshak, in *Perevod—sredstvo vzaimnogo sblizheniia narodov,* p. 134.

While politically motivated censorship of American and Western European literary texts was as a rule unacknowledged, Soviet writers and editors occasionally conceded that overly blunt language and excessively frank portrayals of sex were toned down in the translation of foreign literary texts. They were indeed, and several offenders had their mouths washed out with soap in the late 1970s: James Baldwin (*If Beale Street Could Talk*), John Updike (*Marry Me*), and Kurt Vonnegut (this time for *Breakfast of Champions*). Vonnegut's book was also cleansed of its dirty drawings, the kind associated in juvenile America with *Mad* magazine.[91] Both kinds of censorship—the political as well as the "moral"—were largely abandoned in the late 1980s.

Politicized translation, including censorship, has a venerable history in Russia, antedating the Soviet regime by nearly a century. Ivan Kashkin's advice to Soviet translators to simply omit those passages considered unsuitable for a Soviet audience (his euphemism was: texts that "merely reflected an alien culture") had its forerunner in Belinsky's observations of 1838. In his review of M. P. Pogodin's recent rendition of *Hamlet* Belinsky wrote:

> *When translating Shakespeare for public performance he* [the translator] *not only has the right, but is duty-bound to omit everything that cannot be understood without commentaries, that is really a reflection of the author's age,* in short, whatever requires special study to be understood. . . . Moreover, something which may be read in the seclusion of one's study is not always suitable for girls, or for that matter for women. This rule must be law for plays performed on the stage.

Radical in literature as well as in politics, Belinsky followed up this expression of concern for female sensitivities with some far-reaching advice:

> If the only way to introduce Shakespeare to the public is by disfiguring his texts, well, then, have no qualms. Go right ahead, distort the text, as long as you achieve your goal, as long as the two or three or even a single Shakespearean play—however disfigured [*iskazhenie*]

---

91. Examples of censored passages in Soviet translations of foreign writing may be found in Friedberg, *Decade of Euphoria*, pp. 16–57. For general information on Soviet censorship, see Martin Dewhirst and Robert Farrell, eds., *The Soviet Censorship* (Metuchen, N.J.: The Scarecrow Press, 1973), and Marianna Tax Choldin and Maurice Friedberg, eds., *The Red Pencil: Artists, Scholars, and Censors in the USSR* (Boston: Unwin Hyman, 1989).

by you—have instilled in the public respect for Shakespeare. As long as they have paved the way for better, fuller, and more faithful renditions of the same play, you have accomplished a noble task. Your mutilation or initiation are a thousand times worthier of respect than the most faithful and accurate rendition, if the latter, its merits notwithstanding, hurts the advancement of Shakespeare's fame instead of spreading that fame.[92]

Belinsky sanctioned textual changes in Shakespeare's plays in order to advance a cause he regarded as noble. In so doing, he unwittingly set a precedent that in years to come would be used to serve causes less worthy.

By the mid-nineteenth century the practice of exploiting literary translation to benefit a political agenda was already well established. This was confirmed in his memoirs by Count P. I. Kapnist, an official of the Imperial Ministry of the Interior, who wrote that a number of Russian poets "have turned to translating from foreign languages precisely those lyric works which portray unsatisfactory aspects of public life in the West, including the open wounds of the proletariat. In these translations they endeavor (by resorting to appropriate verse forms, idioms or manipulation of the contents) to suggest parallels with certain aspects of our [Russian] life."[93] Mikhail L. Mikhailov (1829–65) headed Kapnist's list of poets who engaged in this activity, and deservedly so. While in Siberian exile, Mikhailov translated revolutionary poetry from several languages. Many of his renditions were mutilated by the censors or banned from publication altogether because they contained blasphemy or preached hatred of the upper classes. Indeed, a number of them were printed for the first time only after the establishment of Soviet rule.

A later poet and translator, Dmitry Mikhailovsky (1828–1905), emulated Mikhailov's example. It is likely that his renditions of foreign verse contributed to the dissemination of radical ideas in Russia. The same can be said of the translating and publishing activities of Petr Veinberg (1831–1908), a leading continuator of the traditions of the so-called revolutionary democrats of the 1860s. The specific foreign authors and works that he chose to translate reflected the causes he sought to advance. From Lessing, of course, he took *Nathan the Wise,* a drama that champions religious tolerance and the social

---

92. Cited in *Perevod—sredstvo vzaimnogo sblizheniia narodov,* pp. 40–41; emphasis added.
93. P. I. Kapnist, *Sochineniia* (Moscow, 1901), 2:419; cited in Levin, *Russkie perevodchiki,* p. 198.

and legal equality of the Jews. From among Shelley's writings he selected *The Cenci,* a tragedy denouncing feudal despotism and political tyranny. Populist revolutionaries often used this play for readings aimed at peasant audiences. Veinberg's translation of Karl Gutzkow's tragedy *Uriel Acosta,* which was performed in the prestigious Aleksandrinsky Theater, elicited a review by A. N. Pleshcheev describing it as a play that "nurture[s] in the public humane feelings and sympathy for free thought which have always been persecuted by forces of evil, obscurantism and violence."[94]

Occasionally the Imperial censorship intervened. Passages that, in the censor's opinion, showed a lack of respect for the authority of Church or state ("blasphemy" or *lèse majesté*) were mercilessly blotted out, sometimes literally with black ink. (The same was true of imported reference works and general nonfiction.)[95] For example, entire sections of Heine's poetry in Veinberg's translation were replaced by dots. However, Veinberg was an experienced man of letters. Often he could persuade the censor to retain a word here and there among the dots, thus salvaging a hint of the censored material and leaving the reader frustrated and angry at a political system that prescribed what he could and could not read.[96]

Not all Russian translators of the nineteenth century were political liberals or radicals. Some were exemplary patriotic citizens, like Irinarkh Vvedensky (1813–55), a towering figure in Russian translation in that period. On his own authority Vvedensky suppressed offending terms or passages in the works he translated. For example, where Thackeray's *Vanity Fair* contained derogatory references to Russia Vvedensky simply left them out (for example, mentions of "knouts" and "brutal Cossacks," or the claim that Rebecca, after her visit to St. Petersburg, became a Russian spy). In one instance he unceremoniously "corrected" Thackeray's Russophobic text. In the English original a French servant remarks, à propos of Napoleon's invasion of Russia, "The Russians, bah! the Russians will withdraw." Vvedensky clearly found this intolerable. In his Russian version of the novel the servant states, "Only the Russian Emperor can defeat Napoleon. But the distance from Moscow to Brussels is quite considerable, sir."[97]

---

94. Levin, *Russkie perevodchiki,* pp. 198, 260, 274.
95. The workings of Russian censorship are described in Marianna Tax Choldin's excellent study *A Fence Around an Empire: Russian Censorship of Western Ideas under the Tsars* (Durham, N.C.: Duke University Press, 1985).
96. Levin, *Russkie perevodchiki,* pp. 275–76.
97. Ibid., p. 134.

Another staunch conservative was Alexander Druzhinin (1824–64), though as a firm believer in making great literature accessible to everyone he was quite willing to have his renditions of Shakespeare printed in Nekrasov's left-leaning journal *The Contemporary* (*Sovremennik*). Indeed, Druzhinin's predilection for Shakespeare was at least partly inspired by a belief that the English bard and other "world geniuses" might wean Russian readers away from "didactic" leftist books.[98] His favorite Shakespearean plays were *King Lear* and *Coriolanus*. In rendering the former, he emphasized the loyalty of Lear's subjects to their monarch; accordingly, his favorite character in the play was the Earl of Kent. (Druzhinin's monarchist sympathies were less extreme than those of Nikolai Gnedich, whose 1808 rendering of the play actually suppressed Lear's insanity, the better to highlight the moral injustice of robbing him of his lawful throne.)[99] However, Shakespeare's text offended Druzhinin's sense of propriety, leading him to make a number of excisions ranging in length from two words to ten lines. For example, he cut out many of the Fool's songs, Gloucester's ribald jokes about Edmund's illegitimate ancestry, Edmund's own reflections about the circumstances of his birth, Lear's monologue on the subject of adultery, and many of the insults that Shakespeare's characters hurl at each other.[100] Druzhinin's decision in the 1850s to translate *Coriolanus* may well have been politically motivated, since the drama lends itself to an antidemocratic interpretation. At a time when criticism of Russia's autocratic political system was on the rise, the angry speeches of the Roman patrician Coriolanus against rebellious plebians would obviously have pleased Russian conservatives.[101]

Most people today view politicized renditions of foreign writing much as they regard newspaper editorials and cartoons. They enjoy those that agree with their personal opinions. On rare occasions, they may even express admiration for the skills of their political opponents. Unlike old newspapers, however, politicized translations live on. Some readers—unfortunately including sophisticated ones—like or dislike specific renderings because of their ideological tendentiousness. One celebrated Soviet translator who shared this attitude was Samuil Marshak, who apparently

---

98. Ibid., pp. 151, 161.
99. Chukovskii, *Vysokoe iskusstvo*, pp. 34–36.
100. Levin, *Russkie perevodchiki*, pp. 153–54.
101. Ibid., p. 160. See also Chukovskii, *Iskusstvo perevoda*, pp. 30–31. Both Levin and Chukovskii believed that with this translation of *Coriolanus* Druzhinin sought to get even with the radical writer Chernyshevskii and his allies.

attached much importance to translators' political views. Thus he prized very highly the renderings of Heine by Mikhailov and of Béranger by Kurochkin.[102]

Vasily Kurochkin (1831–75), poet, translator, and journalist, was known as a fiery radical. Therefore it is hardly surprising that he "politicized" his renditions of the rebellious Pierre-Jean de Béranger, the "poet of the people," who was probably the most widely read French poet in prerevolutionary Russia. Kurochkin's versions of Béranger cannot be regarded as translations, but rather as efforts to *adapt* the French poet to Russian conditions. For instance, Kurochkin replaced Béranger's allusion to phony military heros by a reference to graft, which was a greater problem in Russia. Where Béranger wrote of drums, Kurochkin referred to sticks. He even inserted a reference to the reactionary Russian journal *Northern Bee* (*Severnaia pchela*), which the French poet probably did not even know existed. Béranger's poems in Russian guise included references to the Russian Orthodox faith and to the Imperial Russian double-headed eagle. In short, Kurochkin's Béranger was really Kurochkin.[103]

According to a Soviet study of this nineteenth-century Russian translator, "For Kurochkin, the most important thing was not precision in translation, but incorporating Russian conditions into the rendition of political satire."[104] Kurochkin's politicized versions of Béranger continued to be reprinted in the Soviet period. They are not merely inaccurate representations of their French originals, but quite incomprehensible to readers of the late twentieth century who no longer understand Kurochkin's century-old Russian allusions. In a 1979 Russian volume of Béranger's verse, translations by Kurochkin and his "progressive" contemporaries account for over half the contents.[105] Samuil Marshak's partiality for ideological kindred spirits among translators is at least partly to blame.

One oblique result of political influences on Soviet publishing—in particular, the unavailability of Bibles in the USSR prior to the late 1980s—was the difficulty Soviet translators experienced in dealing with even vaguely

---

102. Lev Ginzburg, cited in *Khudozhestvennyi perevod: Vzaimodeistvie i vzaimoobogashchenie literatur* (Erevan: Izdatel'stvo Erevanskogo universiteta, 1973), pp. 231–32.

103. Dmitriev, "Praktika," pp. 134–43.

104. Valentin Dmitriev, "Izderzhki perevoda," *Tetradi perevodchika*, no. 19 (1982): 46.

105. Ibid., pp. 43–45. In both of the articles cited here, Dmitriev takes strong exception to the common Soviet editorial practice of assigning to several translators a foreign poet's verse to be published in a single volume. He argues that this procedure prevents the Russian reader from even guessing what the foreign poet is like.

religious references in Western texts. One translator did not know that John the Baptist is *Ioann,* not *Ivan* Krestitel'.[106] The translators of Joseph Heller's *Catch-22* could not recognize the biblical commandment, "Honor thy father and thy mother." This was only one among many such examples of religious illiteracy in their rendition of the novel, or indeed in Soviet translations of English and American writing generally. Commenting in 1970 on the faulty rendering of *Catch-22,* Maria Lor'e recognized that familiarity with religion and the Church was essential in the translation of Anglo-American literature—regardless of the translator's own religious convictions (or lack of same).[107] Nora Gal', who in 1975 regarded knowledge of the Bible as superfluous for translators, had modified her opinion by 1987 to the point of conceding that Soviet translators must at least be able to *recognize* biblical imagery, names, and citations and know where to find information about such matters.[108]

With the increased availability in Russia of religious materials and even instruction since the late 1980s, this problem has been somewhat alleviated. To be sure, ignorance of the Bible is not just a Soviet characteristic. It is widespread even in the United States, the most church-going country in the West, where Bibles are still routinely provided in motel rooms. Helen Wolff, a leading publisher of foreign writing, has complained that "in a century as completely laicized as ours, translators frequently fail to catch Biblical phrasing and thus miss not only reverberations but sometimes plain sense as well."[109]

A rather amusing instance of politicized translation (in this case, for the purpose of dubbing a motion picture) involved a Russian version of Francis Ford Coppola's *The Outsiders* (in Russian, *Izgoi*). The Soviet translator mistook the term "Greasers," the name of a youth gang in the film, for "Greeks," and was duly taken to task for her ignorance. The reviewer, however, saw nothing wrong with the political "improvements" occasioned

---

106. Gal', *Slovo zhivoe i mertvoe* (1975), p. 118.
107. Mariia Lor'e, in *Masterstvo perevoda, 1969* (Moscow: Sovetskii pisatel', 1970), p. 340. If *Catch-22* caused Soviet translators such difficulty, one wonders how they would cope with Heller's *God Knows,* in which an aging King David complains to Bathsheba about that upstart Solomon. The novel is replete with biblical allusions.
108. Nora Gal', in *Slovo zhivoe i mertvoe* (1975), reacted to the inability of Heller's translators (M. Vilenskii and V. Titov) to recognize the name of John the Baptist by saying, "So what if the translator never read the Bible; he could have seen a canvas in a museum"—not a very convincing argument. In 1987 the political climate was different. See Gal', *Slovo zhivoe i mertvoe* (1987), p. 132; emphasis in the original.
109. Helen Wolff, "Translation and the Editor," *Delos,* no. 2 (1968): 161.

by her lack of knowledge, such as comments on the "hard life of immigrant workers in America," and "in spite of everything, life was better at home in Greece."[110] Needless to say, these remarks did not appear in the original sound track of the film.

In a general sense, the history of literary translation in Russia reveals a pendulum-like movement from literalist to paraphrastic phases, with each supplanting the other when the established approach seemed to have become intolerable. Assuming that this cyclic pattern will continue, we can expect that some variety of literalism will reemerge in Russia in the foreseeable future. Precisely this idea was suggested in 1988 by the appearance of an erudite and brilliantly argued essay by M. L. Gasparov, a Soviet classicist and specialist in poetics. His essay traced the gradual conversion *to* literalism of Valery Briusov (1873–1924), a leading Symbolist poet and translator of the *Aeneid*. After the 1905 Revolution in Russia, Briusov became disenchanted with his earlier belief in the universality of European civilization, which (he formerly had thought) differed only "in costume and in the manner of speech." Having replaced this conviction with a new creed that held every civilization to be unique, he now believed that only a literalist rendering could express this uniqueness. Briusov now *wanted* his rendition of the *Aeneid* "to strike the Russian reader as strange and foreign."

Furthermore, Gasparov advanced two theses that obliquely predicted a revival of literalism in Russia. First, he argued that periods of free translation follow periods of literalism, and "the Soviet era is one of reaction to the literalism of the Modernists." Second, he divided Russian cultural history into periods of expansion, when large numbers of people are initially introduced to culture (nobility in the eighteenth century; the bourgeoisie in the latter part of the nineteenth; workers and peasants in Soviet times); and periods of "deepening" of culture (Romanticism and Symbolism in Russia). An era of cultural expansion favors free translation, whereas a "deepening" culture is conducive to literalism. In Gasparov's view, Russia was entering the latter phase as of 1988.[111]

It is obvious that successive translations of a foreign literary work by a variety of hands will differ to a greater or lesser extent. But how "original" are these different versions? A Soviet court in 1963 considered a case of alleged plagiarism of the Russian translation of a foreign novel. To establish

---

110. S. F. Beliaev, "Zamechaniia iz zritel'nogo zala," *Tetradi perevodchika*, no. 21 (1984): 104.

111. See Gasparov, "Briusov i bukvalizm," pp. 29–61. The quotations are from pp. 49 and 56.

the "normal" level of coincidences between alternate versions of a single text, the court ordered a comparison among several five-page samples of different Russian translations of Graham Greene's *The Quiet American* and Thackeray's *Vanity Fair*. It turned out that between 40 and 62 percent of the words (exclusive of proper names and personal pronouns) were the same in all samples. Interestingly, the greatest lexical overlap was found among the best translations.[112]

Let us now consider briefly the artistic creeds and working habits of five prominent Russian translators. Vasily Zhukovsky (1783–1852) and Irinarkh Vvedensky (1813–55) were Russia's foremost translators of verse and prose, respectively, in the nineteenth century. The other three belong to the twentieth century. Vladimir Nabokov (1899–1977), who translated both into and from Russian, evolved from a conventional adherent of free rendition into a highly rigid proponent of literalism. Ivan Elagin (1918–87), like Nabokov an émigré, was a moderately paraphrastic translator of American verse into Russian. Finally, Nikolai Liubimov (1912–   ) was an exponent of very free translation. Arguably the most inventive Soviet translator of drama and prose, he is best known for his renditions of French writing and of *Don Quixote*.

Zhukovsky's translations are so free that they are difficult to distinguish from his original poetry. Indeed, Zhukovsky himself cheerfully admitted that this was the case. However, it is not entirely fair to accuse him of concealing the fact that his verse consisted largely of translations—for which the younger and more gifted contemporary poet Mikhail Lermontov is said to have denounced him. It is true that Zhukovsky did not bother to group his translations by author. Instead he published them chronologically, that is, in the order in which he had produced them (occasionally without indication of the original). However, this was perfectly normal procedure among Russian translators of that period, including those who were themselves major poets. Baratynsky, Batiushkov, and Tiutchev behaved in the same way. Tiutchev especially had no need to present his own work falsely under a famous foreign name.

The liberties Zhukovsky took with his texts may have reflected the fact that some of the authors he translated, like Schiller and Goethe, were merely his older contemporaries. Accordingly, "he felt free to remold them in his own image." Indeed, he knew Goethe personally. Zhukovsky's

---

112. Ia. Retsker, "Plagiat ili samostoiatel'nyi perevod," *Tetradi perevodchika*, no. 11 (1974): 24; original emphasis.

methods also had some influential defenders. Thus Alexander Druzhinin, then a famous writer, critic, and fellow translator, insisted that "Zhukovsky never departed from the letter of the original unless absolutely necessary. He never sacrificed the letter of the original without good reason. At the same time he never imposed on his native language forms and idioms that were alien to it. His manner of work should be studied by all translators for generations to come."[113]

In the opinion of some Soviet scholars, such as A. Fiterman and N. N. Vil'mont, a number of Soviet translation principles (such as *adekvatnost'*, or "commensurability") merely perpetuated those followed by Zhukovsky. Especially intriguing are the similarities between an anonymous French essay translated by Zhukovsky in 1810 and a central principle of Socialist Realist translation theory, which by implication sanctioned ideologically motivated censorship. The French essay suggested that translators forgo reproducing the kind of "information [that] is of interest only to that nation." This advice is nearly identical to that proffered in 1954 by Ivan Kashkin, the advocate of Socialist Realism: "The [translated] text must not be submerged in superfluous details. *Those that are merely associated with foreign lexical structure should often be simply left untranslated.*"[114]

The same essay advised aspiring translators to visit the native regions of the poets whose works they translated.[115] Strange as this advice may appear nowadays, the anonymous author's views were not considered outlandish at the time. The great poet Goethe himself asserted that anyone wishing to understand verse must visit the realm of poetry, and anyone aspiring to understand a poet must visit the poet's habitat. As he wrote in 1819 in "Noten und Abhandlungen zu besserem Verständnis des West-östlichen Diwans":

> Wer das Dichten will verstehen
> Muss ins Land der Dichtung gehen
> Wer den Dichter will verstehen
> Muss in Dichters Lande gehen.

Occasionally such counsel is interpreted literally. Thus prior to undertaking his Polish rendition of Homer's *Odyssey*, Józef Wittlin personally

---

113. Levin, *Russkie perevodchiki*, pp. 24, 18, 17.
114. Ivan Kashkin, in *Voprosy perevoda* (1954); cited in *Perevod—sredstvo vzaimnogo sblizheniia narodov*, p. 340; emphasis added.
115. Michael R. Katz, *The Literary Ballad in Early Nineteenth-Century Russian Literature* (Oxford: Oxford University Press, 1976), p. 44.

retraced the journey of Odysseus. More often Goethe's advice is understood to mean that the translator should be steeped in the thought-world of the original, namely, its culture, values, and beliefs. Nabokov did exactly that when he read virtually every book referred to in Pushkin's verse novel *Eugene Onegin* prior to actually translating the poem. As Justin O'Brien remarked: "Is it too much to ask that the translator possess a somewhat similar cultural background to that of the author he is translating? If he does not have it, at least he should be willing and readily able to make up for this deficiency. In other words, he ought to have read most of the books his author has read, heard the same music (if music matters to that author), seen the same works of art (if works of art matter), *and been in the same places*."[116]

One other feature of Zhukovsky's translation method that links him to Soviet modernity is his reliance (in one case) on an interlinear crib (*podstrochnik*). Zhukovsky knew several modern European languages (as many Soviet translators did not), but not classical Greek. Yet, as he wrote in 1849, he undertook to translate the *Odyssey* because in his old age (he was not quite sixty!) and as a family man, he wanted to savor some primordial (*pervobytnaia*) poetry. In his second childhood, he declared, he longed to hear some ancient Greek tales. To get around his language handicap, he enlisted the help of a German scholar:

> In his own very legible handwriting he [the scholar] copied for me the original text of the entire *Odyssey*. Under every Greek word he wrote a German word, and under every German word the grammatical sense of the original. Thus I could have in front of me the entire literal meaning of the *Odyssey* and could see the entire word order. This chaotically faithful rendition that made no sense to the reader contained the entire material of the edifice. All that was lacking was beauty, harmony, and grace. And that was, in essence, my task [to supply]. I had to seek out the graceful that was concealed in the ungraceful: to search, by means of poetic intuition, for beauty that was contained in deformity; and to create harmony from sounds that wounded the ear.[117]

---

116. Brower, *On Translation*, p. 85, emphasis added.
117. *Perevod—sredstvo vzaimnogo sblizheniia narodov*, pp. 399–401.

Boris Pasternak used interlinear cribs (*podstrochniki*) when he translated the Georgian poets Baratashvili, Yashvili, and Tabidze. Yet he sought scholarly assistance even when translating from English, a language he knew quite well. The Shakespeare specialist Mikhail Morozov evaluated Pasternak's *Romeo and Juliet* for him and recommended some thirty-five changes, of which Pasternak accepted (often under protest) seventeen. Morozov suggested an even greater number of changes in the translation of *Hamlet*. Nonetheless, he considered Pasternak not merely a "mature" poet, but a genius. Morozov did insist that while free renditions of such minor Elizabethan poets as Decker and Haywood might be tolerated, efforts to "improve" on Shakespeare (as some Frenchmen had attempted) only expose the translator to ridicule. Pasternak, on the other hand, believed that Shakespeare's less successful scenes could only gain from being rendered "less transparently and less clearly."[118]

Irinarkh Vvedensky also sought outside assistance. In a letter to Charles Dickens, which he wrote in 1849 and inserted in his translation of *Dombey and Son*, he admitted:

> I consulted educated Englishmen regarding passages the meaning of which was totally obscured by local color which a foreigner who has never been to England could not understand. I understood you as an Englishman and at the same time, in my thoughts, I had you move to Russian soil, and made you express your ideas as you would if you lived under Russian skies. Accordingly, it goes without saying that my translation could not be a literal one, an absolute copy.

Vvedensky's rejection of literalism reflected his belief that even the simplest of terms have different connotations in various languages, and every language has a syntax of its own. Hence, an overly close translation would distort the flavor of the original. Besides, he observed, "A gifted translator should focus his attention first and foremost on the author's spirit, on the essence of his ideas, and only then on his manner of expressing these ideas. . . . You must [mentally] relocate the writer to your country, to the society in which you live, and then ask yourself the following: how would he express his ideas if he had lived in your circumstances?"

Characteristic of the chaos that reigned in nineteenth-century Russian publishing was the appearance of another Russian rendition of *Vanity Fair*

---

118. Ibid., pp. 377–87.

almost simultaneously with Vvedensky's. A thirteen-page review by Vvedensky of the anonymous competitor's version and the latter's rejoinder are quite revealing. The competitor, Vvedensky wrote, is unfamiliar with much of the English lexicon, grammar, usage, and—most important—with British customs and mores. Moreover, the rival's rendering "systematically *omits* the most difficult passages of the original which are also its *best*." Vvedensky's conclusions were merciless: "*In the final analysis, who needs a translation in which one does not recognize the original?*" The nameless competitor, in turn, charged Vvedensky with "expanding" Thackeray's text "by means of insertions composed by the translator which are nowhere to be found in the original."[119] The latter charge persuaded subsequent Russian critics. Vvedensky's rendition was declared to be his own original work, which was merely *inspired* by Thackeray's *Vanity Fair*—a description that echoed similar estimates of Zhukovsky's very free renditions of foreign verse.

Arbitrary insertions (*otsebiatina*) by a translator into a text have remained firmly associated with Vvedensky's name down to the present time. He freely added details and circumstances lacking in the original text, though in a manner he claimed was "attuned" to the author's own style. For instance, in Thackeray the parents of a marriageable daughter spend a *fifth* of their annual income on balls and champagne; Vvedensky explains that they spend their *last kopeck*. In Thackeray a certain character "could knock off forty Latin verses in an hour"; in Vvedensky he "can shower you with quotations from Horace and Seneca, and moreover, can write Greek hexameters."[120] Moreover, at the end of a passage he liked to add his own summary of the preceding text, often in the form of a Russian proverb or saying. Presumably these explanatory devices were suggested to Vvedensky, a schoolmaster by trade, by textbooks of that time (and later years as well) in which such summaries, reviews, and paraphrases were commonly used.

Vladimir Nabokov was likewise a teacher: while working on his English translation of *Eugene Onegin* he was a professor of Russian literature at Cornell University. He was also famous as a novelist both in Russian and in

---

119. Levin, *Russkie perevodchiki*, pp. 124–27.
120. Ibid., p. 131. Vvedenskii's traditions lived on in the USSR. A number of years ago a student of mine, Andrea Lee Williams, compared Tennessee Williams's *A Streetcar Named Desire* (New York: New Directions, 1980) with V. Nedelin's Russian version (*Tramvai Zhelanie*, in *Stekliannyi zverinets i eshche deviat' p'es,* ed. Ia. Bereznitskii and V. Nedelin, [Moscow, Iskusstvo, 1967], pp. 156–273). In the Russian text, Nedelin added a substantial amount of his own explanatory material by "weaving it" into the text, a technique favored by Vvedenskii.

English. Unlike the plebeian Vvedensky, however, Nabokov was of aristocratic Russian origin. Always politically aloof, late in life he became uncompromisingly literalist in his allegiances as a translator, thus continuing the elitist traditions of the well-known Russian poet and country squire Afanasy Fet (1820–92). In the course of Nabokov's long career, his translation practices ran the gamut from the very free version of *Alice in Wonderland*—in which the story is transposed into a Russian setting—and the rigidly literalist *Eugene Onegin,* in which all explanations are reserved for the footnotes. Interestingly, in translating his own work Nabokov avoided both extremes. He did not anglicize a Russian narrative or russify an English one; in many cases he inserted explanations into the translated text or substituted a reference from the culture of the target language for the original reference.[121] It is possible, of course, that Nabokov regarded his self-translations not as translations at all, but as *similar* works by the same author, which he thus felt free to rewrite. Still, the contrast between these and his earlier free renditions of Lewis Carroll and Pushkin is quite striking.

Nabokov's translation of *Eugene Onegin* stirred up great controversy because of the stature of both translator and author, and the defiantly rigorous application of a method then definitely unpopular. In a programmatic essay, Nabokov mapped out a strategy for his English rendition of Pushkin's masterpiece: "I want translation with copious footnotes, footnotes reaching up like skyscrapers to the top of this or that page so as to leave only the gleam of one textual line between commentary and eternity."[122] He kept his promise. The four-volume Bollingen edition of his *Eugene Onegin* numbers 256 pages of text and 1,175 pages of introduction and commentary. The latter were exceptionally informative and often brilliantly written. Yet it was primarily the literal rendition itself that became the object of critical attention, most of it disapproving. Nabokov's own description of his work was modest to the point of self-deprecation. He wrote: "In my translation [of *Eugene Onegin*] I have sacrificed to total accuracy and completeness of meaning every element of form save the iambic rhythm, the retention of which assisted rather than impaired fidelity."[123]

---

121. Jane Grayson, *Nabokov Translated: A Comparison of Nabokov's Russian and English Prose* (Oxford: Oxford University Press, 1977), p. 168.

122. Vladimir Nabokov, "Problems of Translation: *Onegin* in English," *Partisan Review*, no. 22 (1955): 512.

123. Cited in Brower, *On Translation*, p. 97.

At the time this translation appeared (1964), Nabokov was neither published nor reviewed in the USSR. Since hardly any of the Western reviewers knew Russian (Nabokov ridiculed Edmund Wilson's quite serviceable command of the language), most of the serious criticism was directed less at the translation itself than at the general principles of literalism, using Nabokov's work as an instructive specimen. Perhaps the most closely reasoned critique was that of André Lefevere:

> Nabokov not only insists on literalness, he also attempts to carry this literalness to its final consequence: what cannot be rendered through mere sense equivalence must be painstakingly explained in footnotes. . . . Surely, if one translates word for word, that is, matches sense with sense, there should, if translation can be based on the principle of sense equivalence, be no need for footnotes? If there is [such a need], we shall be forced to conclude that a "literal" translation on its own cannot cope with the source text it is supposed to translate. The footnote, in this case, amounts to the literal translator's admission of defeat.[124]

Dudley Fitts likewise took a dim view of Nabokov's annotations, but for different reasons:

> [Nabokov] contemplates a line or two of translation accompanied by notes of every conceivable kind—exegetical, semantic, aesthetic, metrical, historical, sociological. . . . A tireless writer of footnotes [myself], I find this concept endearing; but I am not sure that it is anything more. The trouble is that such a translation, though it might give the prose "sense" of the original together with an explanation of whatever goes to lift the prose above itself and transmute it into a form of art, might also provide no evidence beyond the saying so that the art was art in the first place. . . . The translation of a poem should be a poem, viable as a poem, and, as a poem, weighable.[125]

---

124. André Lefevere, *Translating Poetry: Seven Strategies and a Blueprint* (Amsterdam: Van Gorcum, Assen, 1975), p. 27.

125. Brower, *On Translation*, pp. 33–34.

These criticisms of Nabokov's extensive annotation had been anticipated over a century earlier by August Wilhelm Schlegel, perhaps the most important German translator of all time:

> What is the aim of poetic re-creation? I think it should provide those who have no access to the original with as pure and *uninterrupted* an appreciation of it as possible. *The translator should therefore not resuscitate in the notes the difficulties he has already solved in the text.* What use does the natural friend of poetry have for the laboriousness of textual criticism, variants, conjectures, emendations? The few learned readers who are able to compare will see at once which reading the translator has followed.[126]

Nabokov's literal rendition of *Eugene Onegin* abounds in archaic locutions, strange syntax, and other tell-tale signs of extreme efforts at achieving "accuracy." This particular aspect of the work has attracted relatively little criticism because, according to G. S. Fraser, "to sound strange and odd, to sound rather foreign, is thought a merit in modern verse translations, where it would have been thought a fault in the older translators."[127] Indeed, Edward J. Brown suggested that this consideration may have prompted Nabokov consciously to impart an opaque quality to his *Eugene Onegin*.[128]

Owing to the Soviet authorities' ban on publishing literary work by émigrés, there was little hope when Nabokov's Russian version of *Alice in Wonderland* was published in the early 1920s in Western Europe that the book would ever reach a Soviet audience. However, a substantial Russian reading public existed at that time in East Central and Western Europe and in North America. Scores of émigré journals appeared in Paris, Berlin, and other cities in the 1920s and 1930s, including for a time even an impressive illustrated journal for children. Hence until World War II, translations into Russian could find some readers and modest publishing outlets beyond the Soviet Union. Nabokov (then using the pseudonym "Sirin") was not the only important émigré author to translate foreign works into Russian at that time. The poet Marina Tsvetaeva (1892–1941) was another. Tsvetaeva was a reasonably prolific translator. Like her contemporary Pasternak, she favored rather free renderings that often showed scant concern for many

---

126. Lefevere, *Translating Literature*, pp. 50–51; emphasis added.
127. G. S. Fraser, "On Translating Poetry," *Arion* 4 (Summer 1966): 130–31.
128. Edward J. Brown, "Round Two: Nabokov vs. Pushkin," *Slavic Review* 36 (March 1977): 101–5.

features of the original text.[129] At least this was her approach before she returned to Russia.

Tsvetaeva and Nabokov belonged to the illustrious First Emigration of persons who left Russia during or soon after the Bolshevik Revolution of 1917. Many novelists, poets, and translators were among those who fled the new Bolshevik regime, including the future Nobel Prize winner Ivan Bunin. The Second Emigration consisted of former Soviet citizens who remained in the West at the conclusion of World War II. Although on the whole far less impressive intellectually and artistically than its predecessors, this second group nevertheless included several gifted prose writers and poets. Among the latter was Ivan Elagin (pseudonym of I. V. Matveyev), whom I met in the early 1950s when we were both graduate students at Columbia University. Subsequently Elagin transferred to New York University, in part because in lieu of a conventional doctoral dissertation N.Y.U. was willing to accept an annotated Russian verse translation of a major work of American literature. The result, a Russian version of Stephen Vincent Benét's *John Brown's Body*, established Elagin as a major translator of American poetry. This poem, together with Elagin's many later Russian renderings of American verse, appeared in *Amerika*, an illustrated State Department magazine published for distribution in the Soviet Union.

Predictably, some of the problems Elagin encountered in translating *John Brown's Body* were the result of the relative length of English and Russian words. Thus the first line of Benét's Invocation ("American Muse, whose strong and diverse heart . . .") could not be translated because the five syllables of the first two English words become eight in Russian. Moreover, retention of the rhythmic pattern necessitated speaking of the American Muse in the third person. Elagin was adamant on that point. "Rhythm," he insisted, "is the basis of Russian verse." Since adherence to this principle required him to introduce some rhythm into Benét's arhythmical poem, he chose to rename the Invocation, calling it "Invocation to the American Muse."[130] In this roundabout way he disposed of the five-syllable Russian adjective (*amerikanskoi*) that would have lengthened

---

129. At an international colloquium on Tsvetaeva in 1982 several presentations were devoted to her translations. See, e.g., Simon Markish, " 'Le Voyage' Bodlera v perevode Mariny Tsvetaevoi," in *Marina Tsvetaeva: Actes du 1.er colloque international*, Lausanne, 30 June–3 July 1982 (Bern: Peter Lang, n.d.), pp. 431–35.

130. Ivan Elagin, "Nekotorye problemy poeticheskogo perevoda," *Dialog—S.Sh.A.* (Washington, D.C.), no. 1 (1977): 111.

the opening line, and at the same time retained the form of direct address. As he explained:

> In translating rhymed poetry it is sometimes necessary to make certain sacrifices, but when the poetry is rhymeless I always prefer to add an extra line to the Russian translation if such an addition enables me to convey the sense and style of the original more fully to the Russian reader. If this is to be considered an evil, it is yet the least of evils. I think it much worse, again using Chukovsky's words, to transform "a smoothly flowing narrative into a sequence of convulsed short exclamations and sobs." A rigid adherence to the equilinear principle inevitably brings about such convulsions in the language.[131]

According to Elagin, one of the foremost obstacles in translating from English to Russian is the fact that English contains concepts and things that are simply not present in Russian life. Translators often encounter this stumbling block in dealing with the alien cultures described in foreign language texts.[132] In such cases, Elagin wrote, "One must very often resort to replacements and descriptive devices instead of lexical equivalents. Instead of naming the object, one describes it." In explaining an object that had a proper name, he occasionally would retain the name ("jack-in-the-pulpit") and add an "internal footnote" in the text proper: *Dzhek-propovednik-dikii tsvetok*, "Jack-the-preacher—a wild flower."[133]

A more troublesome issue in translating *John Brown's Body* was what to do about black English. Elagin recalled: "I was very much tempted at first to translate all the peculiarities of Negro speech by means of Russian peasant idioms. I have managed to resist this temptation, realizing that it would be as incongruous to represent nineteenth-century black slaves conversing in Nizhnii Novgorod accents as it would be to describe peasants in some northern Russian village eating soul food." He also avoided having black American slaves make Russian grammatical mistakes to call attention to the fact that their speech was nonstandard. Instead, he had them use slang and colloquialisms.[134] Elagin was not the only person to be perplexed by the problem of how

---

131. *World of Translation*, p. 177.
132. This is described with respect to Yiddish, for example, by Irving Howe in *The World of Translation*.
133. Elagin, "Nekotorye problemy poeticheskogo perevoda," pp. 101–2.
134. *World of Translation*, pp. 184–85.

to put black English into Russian. Professionals in the USSR were grappling with the same difficulty. Rita Rait-Kovaleva, a translator of American writing famous for her renditions of J. D. Salinger and Kurt Vonnegut, explained: "One can really comprehend the language of Faulkner's protagonists only if one knows the pretentious Southern speech of scions of 'noble' families, and the inconsistent (both simplified and intricate) speech of 'poor whites' and Negro farmhands and sharecroppers in which—side by side with the biblical lexicon and in the rhythm of the spirituals—one hears underworld slang with Anglo-Saxon four-letter words."[135]

For obvious reasons, one cannot really conjure up any satisfactory manner of rendering black English in Russian. Even the Yiddish-flavored speech of the protagonists in the novels of Philip Roth, Bernard Malamud, and Saul Bellow can cause a Russian translator some difficulty. Russian prose lacks a tradition of subtle Jewish inflection, and the translator must be on guard against exaggerating it to the point of grotesqueness in the manner of Isaak Babel's Jewish characters.[136] Viktor Golyshev, the translator of Robert Penn Warren's *All the King's Men*, Faulkner's *As I Lay Dying* and *Light in August*, and Thornton Wilder's *The Bridge of San Luis Rey*, together with his younger colleague Vladimir Kharitonov, the translator of Saul Bellow's *Herzog*, discussed this issue in 1978 in an appreciative article about Maria Lor'e, a distinguished critic and editor also known for her translations of Mark Twain and John Galsworthy. According to Golyshev and Kharitonov, even the most gifted translator will be unable to find adequate Russian equivalents for certain words. Lor'e's rendition of Thomas Wolfe's "Only the Dead Know Brooklyn" is a case in point: "Any translation of that story into Russian is doomed to partial failure. There is no Brooklyn in Moscow and accordingly no equivalent of the 'Brooklynese' spoken by the narrator. The peculiarities of his speech are conveyed through spelling. Compounding the difficulty is the fact that the storyteller speaks in the vernacular."

Wolfe's stratagem of conveying colloquial speech through spelling cannot be reproduced in Russian. Maria Lor'e herself explained why:

> In English, writers garble the pronunciation. To do the same in Russian doesn't get you anywhere. And then, if you press too much

---

135. *Redaktor i perevod: Sbornik statei* (Moscow: Kniga, 1965), p. 8.
136. This was demonstrated in New York in October 1991 at a conference of Soviet and American literary translators held under the auspices of P.E.N., Hunter College, and the Soros Foundation. In her otherwise fine translation of a story by Grace Paley, Maria Kan could not, in the opinion of some people in the audience, capture its *mildly* Jewish flavor.

you immediately hear [folksy provincial] Ryazan or Orel idiom. Of all the layers of language, the speech of the common people has the most national flavor. So the more liberties you take with it in Russian, the more you turn Englishmen into Russians, which is also wrong. In syntax, the best one can do is to try to be more colloquial and less bookish. So far, no one has come up with anything more ingenious.

Golyshev and Kharitonov commented:

> How did Lorye proceed in the face of such heavy odds? She chose the vocabulary carefully, avoiding the slightest hint of transatlantic strangeness and phrases too closely associated with purely Russian phenomena. The syntax has been simplified and the frequency of subordinate and participial phrases has been reduced. Inversion—with the verb at the end of the sentence—is used so sparingly so that it is not lost on the reader, while at the same time it never clutters up the text with facile stylization. . . . The reader has a distinct feeling that the characters are not Russian, not even English but American, speaking the way urban Americans speak, in the rhythm peculiar to them. How the translator [Lor′e] achieves that effect is difficult to say. Most probably she draws intuitively on the many associations the Russian reader has. After all, we all have our idea of America.[137]

The Soviet translators' extensive discussions concerning ways and means of rendering in Russian such varieties of American speech as Brooklynese, black English, or Yiddish-tinged English naturally reflect the fact that in the several decades prior to the collapse of the USSR, American writing was the single most important component of literary translation in that country. However, in the nineteenth century and down to 1917, continental European literature occupied that position, particularly French literature. Early in the twentieth century the poet Nikolai Minsky (pseudonym of N. M. Vilenkin, 1855–1937) translated Molière's comedy *Monsieur de Pourceaugnac*, in which the central protagonist's two alleged wives speak respectively in the Picard and the Gascon dialects of standard French. Since at that time Ukrainian and Belorussian were widely perceived by Russians not as distinct Slavic languages but as dialects of Russian, Minsky

---

137. Viktor Golyshev and Vladimir Kharitonov, "Maria Lorye, the Translator," *Soviet Literature*, no. 6 (1978): 146–47.

had the wives speak Ukrainian and Belorussian. This stratagem backfired, presumably because the use of all three Slavic languages on the stage created the illusion that Molière's comedy was actually *set in Russia*. Minsky's unfortunate experience served as a warning: subsequent translators no longer used such devices.[138]

In his essay "Seven Agamemnons," Reuben A. Brower identified "the first condition of all translating" as "the necessity for the translator to find within *his own language and civilization* some equivalents for what he has experienced through the language of the original."[139] This advice was seconded by André Lefevere, who declared that a translator should possess "the ability to select, within the literary tradition of the target language, a form that will most closely match the position the source text occupies in the literary tradition of the source language."[140]

Two leading contemporary Russian translators are on record as following that rule in their work. Maria Lor'e recalled:

> When I worked on nineteenth-century [British] writers, mainly Thackeray, I read a lot of our [Russian] nineteenth-century literature, and not only the first-raters but also some of the second-raters, for example, Pisemsky and Veltman, Odoyevsky, Dahl and Pavlov. . . . I made copious notes as I went along, things I felt could come in handy, things that have been forgotten but are not antiquated and could still be used, and are still in the language, and not just words but turns of phrase and word order. I could only use a small portion of what I had dug up. Still, it enabled me to become imbued with the language of the epoch and to be alert to the immense possibilities of the Russian language which we fail to use.[141]

In their article on Lor'e, Golyshev and Kharitonov commented:

> [She] convey[s] with virtuoso skill the involved syntax of Dickens. In Lorye's translation his cumbrous periods are almost ideally balanced and are instantly readable and understandable. This is all the more of a triumph since with Dickens (and, by the way, with

---

138. N. G. Elina, "O perevode na russkii iazyk stilisticheski okrashennykh plastov ital'ianskogo iazyka," *Tetradi perevodchika*, no. 21 (1984): 89.
139. Brower, *On Translation*, p. 187, emphasis added.
140. Lefevere, *Translating Literature*, p. 102.
141. Cited in Golyshev and Kharitonov, "Maria Lorye, the Translator," p. 146.

Thackeray) the intricately structured sentence is often designed to give a comic effect.[142]

Nikolai Liubimov, modern Russia's foremost translator of French literature (and also of *Don Quixote*), was unequivocal in his endorsement of Maria Lor'e's practice of total immersion in Russian writing:

> Those translating into Russian must read Russian authors whenever they have any free time. However, they should not imitate readers who "skip nature descriptions and look for the love scenes." They should read with pencil in hand. They should gather honey from various flowers like bees. This does wonders for broadening the translator's lexical range. It helps him save for the Russian reader the original's linguistic wealth.[143]

Liubimov certainly practiced what he preached:

> When I translate a specific author, I always attempt to find something analogous to him in Russian literature. That does not mean at all that I am trying to mimic somebody. What I am trying to do is to gain a foothold. . . . When I translated Maupassant's novel *Bel Ami*, I reread all of Chekhov. I did not "steal" a single one of Chekhov's expressions. What I was learning from Chekhov was the conciseness which he shares with Maupassant. When I translated Schiller's *Kabale und Liebe*, I reread Lermontov's plays as well as selected chapters from [Dostoevsky's] *Insulted and Injured*, *The Idiot*, and *Brothers Karamazov* (the encounters of Katia and Grushen'ka). . . . We must, however, be mindful of the following. We can and we should ingest the overall lexical atmosphere of a specific author of a particular period, but we must not borrow expressions that are characteristic of that author and which have gained literary currency through his work.[144]

He offered additional specific examples:

---

142. Ibid.
143. Viktor Golyshev and Vladimir Kharitonov, in *Perevod—sredstvo vzaimnogo sblizheniia narodov*, p. 144.
144. Ibid., p. 143. Also Nikolai Liubimov, *Perevod-iskusstvo* (Moscow: Sovetskaia Rossiia, 1977), pp. 42–43.

> When translating those parts of *Don Quixote* that deal with hunting, I reread not only the famous hunting scene in *War and Peace*, not only Nekrasov's *Bear Hunt* and *Dog Hunt*, but also Mei's [second-rate] stories of hunting.[145]

Liubimov recalled that before undertaking the translation of Marcel Proust's *À l'ombre des jeunes filles en fleurs*, in which an artist muses about his art, he immersed himself in Russian art histories and memoirs of individual Russian painters.[146] He attended peasant weddings and feasts, where he listened carefully to the proverbs and sayings that pepper peasant speech. This proved invaluable when he worked on the Russian rendition of *Gargantua and Pantagruel*.[147] While translating the *Decameron*, Liubimov noticed that the more risqué or downright crude the scenes in the text were, the more courtly, lofty, and sentimental was Boccaccio's lexicon. "In this way," Liubimov explained, Boccaccio "deflected accusations of obscenity; and simultaneously, by contrasting his lofty style with the earthiness of the situations, heightened the comic effect." In quest of Russian literary models for his rendering of the *Decameron*, Liubimov reread much of eighteenth- and early nineteenth-century Russian writing, including Sumarokov, Kheraskov, Bogdanovich, Kniazhnin, Kapnist, Murav'ëv, Vasily Maikov, Karamzin, Dmitriev, Vasily Pushkin, and early Zhukovsky.[148]

The translation of regional dialects presented special problems. Liubimov wrote:

> What kinds of regional speech did I, a translator of Rabelais, resort to? Only those that a modern reader understands without footnotes and without having to consult Dal' [a dictionary]. By the same token, in my renditions of *Don Quixote* as well as *Gargantua* I used only those archaic locutions that can be understood without explanatory notes and without Sreznevsky [another dictionary]. . . . Strange as it may seem, I employ regional dialect in my rendering of Flaubert's *Madame Bovary*. After all, it is essentially a "regional" novel. It is for that reason that Flaubert's subtitle to the novel reads "Provincial Mores." . . .

---

145. Liubimov, *Perevod—sredstvo vzaimnogo sblizheniia narodov*, p. 144.
146. Nikolai Liubimov, *Perevod-iskusstvo*, 2d enlarged edition (Moscow: Sovetskaia Rossiia, 1982), p. 45.
147. Ibid., p. 31.
148. Ibid., pp. 68–69.

Regional speech seeps through in it not only into the dialogue, but into authorial speech as well.[149]

Readers of Liubimov's masterful (and very free) rendering of Rabelais's exceptionally intricate comic novel are invariably struck by the translator's highly inventive manner of reproducing the original's idiosyncratic legal, culinary, and other specialized terminology, and most particularly, proper names. Nora Gal' recommended that in the "translation" of foreign names that contain a meaning (such as Mrs. Charity or Mademoiselle Petite) an attempt should be made to create words that sound foreign but at the same time suggest Russian ideas. She cited a number of examples from a Russian rendering of *Parkinson's Law,* such as *Vash de Nash, Episkop Nerazberiisky* (which suggests "Yours and Ours," "Bishop of Can't-Make-It-Out," the latter word rhyming with "of Canterbury"), and *Tëk Oil da Vytek* (literally, "the Oil [sic] flowed until it all ran out"), a translation of "The Trickle and Dried Up Oil Corporation."[150]

Liubimov believed that untranslated foreign words were undesirable, though occasionally he had to tolerate their presence, as in his rendering of Marcel Proust. On the other hand, he did believe in the usefulness of "translated" names, roughly along the lines suggested by Nora Gal'. He cited the Spanish-sounding *Ograbil'o* (which suggests "was robbed") and four French-sounding names: *Zhru* ("I am gorging myself on"), *Grabezhi* ("robberies"), *de Lizobliud* ("plate licker"), and the most clever of them all, *Zhuivusnedui* ("chew on and don't worry").

How to render foreign terms and names is a perennial issue for translators. Jiří Levý believed that replacing an unfamiliar term by an analogy in the target language is appropriate when the *general* picture is adequately clear, whereas repetition by transcription is preferable whenever the notion would otherwise make no sense. He also thought that dialectical speech should be rendered in the idiom of some indeterminate province—not very useful advice for dealing with the distinct forms of language used by ethnic minorities and special social groups living side by side with the majority population. As for proper names that contain a meaning, he held that these may be "translated" when their function is purely cognitive, as in Neoclassical drama or in *commedia dell'arte*.[151]

---

149. Liubimov, *Perevod—sredstvo vzaimnogo sblizheniia narodov,* p. 149.
150. Gal', *Slovo zhivoe i mertvoe* (1975), pp. 142–49.
151. Levyi, *Iskusstvo perevoda,* pp. 123 and 193–240.

Translation is "re-creation," Levý wrote. Closest to it is the art of acting on the stage.[152] That is to say, translation is subjective interpretation. Another comparison suggesting itself is the performance of a musical score. Clearly, renditions of drama intended for the theater must satisfy a number of requirements that are not obligatory in texts designed for sight reading.[153] Apparently with that distinction in mind, Anna Akhmatova deplored the tendency of critics to single out a specific translation as being allegedly superior to all of its forerunners: "It is a pity that nowadays Pasternak's translation [of *Hamlet*] is being praised as superior to Lozinsky's. Lozinsky's rendition is very good, too, though quite different. Lozinsky's should be read like a book, while Pasternak's should be heard from the stage. Neither should be praised at the expense of the other. We should instead be happy for Russian culture's gain."[154]

What characteristics distinguish translations intended for the stage? Robert W. Corrigan explained:

> The first law in translating for the theater is that everything must be speakable. It is necessary at all times for the translator to hear the actor speaking in his mind's ear. He must be conscious of the gestures of the voice that speaks—the rhythm, the cadence, the interval. He must also be conscious of the look, the feel, and the movement of the actor while he is speaking. . . . I suppose what I am saying is that it is almost necessary to direct the play, act the play, and see the play while translating it.[155]

As the Polish scholar Jerzy Zawieyski put it: "The translator of drama must always be concerned with the dialogue, with liveliness of speech, with simplicity and spontaneity of language. . . . The criteria that decide which is a successful translation of a play are oral. They are: reading it aloud, and

---

152. Ibid., p. 90.

153. Curiously, there exist "intermediate" renderings, so to speak. Thus J. M. Cohen explains: "The Elizabethans seem to have designed their translations for reading aloud on winter evenings; their habit of repetition, often so foreign to the original, makes for drowsiness, and at the same time guarantees that the listener will not have dropped far behind if for a moment he closes his eyes" (*English Translators and Translation* [London: Longmans, Green, 1962], p. 14).

154. Lidiia Chukovskaia, *Zapiski ob Anne Akhmatovoi*, vol. 1 (Paris: YMCA Press, 1976), p. 90.

155. Arrowsmith and Shattuck, *Craft and Context of Translation*, p. 101.

the ease and spontaneity of delivery in dialogue."[156] Henry Keupler also discussed the special demands made on the translator of plays:

> Drama is a communal experience which transcends the realm of written material. A play needs "Nachdichtung"; not "straight" translation, but an "equivalent effect"; the translator will often keep faith with the original by departing from it in judicious fashion.[157]

To complicate matters further, the translator is further enjoined to consider the theatrical customs of individual countries (*façon de jouer*); the use of gesture and the emotional aspects of languages (*façon de parler*); and more broadly, a country's intellectual traditions. Thus French audiences display greater tolerance than do theatergoers in other nations for "stylized" drama, while the English tend to avoid maxims and quotations. In short, a modern stage play when translated "is transferred to become a play in another environment."[158] Different national theatrical traditions are reflected even in the actual length of the performances. A Shakespearean play is shortest on an English stage, longest in Germany, and somewhere in between in Italy. Styles of acting differ as well:

> British classical acting requires the actor to physicalize the text, to reinforce possible textual obscurities with kinesic signs, to push forward through the language of the text, even at times *against* the text. The German tradition, which is more intensely intellectual, tends to the opposite extreme—the text acquires a weightiness that the spatial context reinforces, and it is the text that carries the actor rather than the reverse. The Italian tradition of virtuosity on the part of the individual actor creates yet another type of performance style. The text of the play becomes the actor's instrument and the performance of that play is an orchestration of many different instruments playing together.[159]

---

156. Michał Rusinek, ed., *O sztuce tłumaczenia* (Wrocław: Zakład imienia Ossolinskich, 1955), pp. 434–35.
157. Henry Kuepler, "Translation vs. Adaptation in the Contemporary Drama," in *Langue et Littérature: Actes du VIIIe Congrès de la Federation Internationale des Langues et Littératures Modernes* (Paris: Les Belles Lettres, 1961), pp. 199–200.
158. Ibid.
159. Susan Bassnet-McGuire in Theo Hermans, ed., *The Manipulation of Literature: Studies in Literary Translation* (London: Croom Helm, 1985), pp. 91–92; original emphasis.

It is clear that several renditions of one play may also facilitate the task of theatrical directors who wish to stage different interpretations of the drama as appropriate for a specific audience, such as children, intellectuals, or traditionalist retirees.[160] Jiří Levý proposed an original strategy: a literal translation of the most important passages, plus an approximate rendition of the rest.[161] However, this procedure may itself create new difficulties. For example, an Azeri translator of Gorky's plays failed to appreciate the fact that the original texts contain a number of *kliuchevye,* "key" words (such as *tovarishch,* "comrade"; *pravda,* "truth"; *mat',* "mother"; *zhalost',* "pity"; *delo,* "cause"). Instead of choosing a *single* synonym for each of these terms and using it throughout, the Azeri translator employed several. As a Soviet critic complained, this destroyed the emotional effect of Gorky's "key" words.[162]

Translating dialect for the stage is a pesky problem because the need is for oral delivery of the words, not reproduction on the printed page. This difficulty has been compounded in the postwar period by the virtual disappearance of dialect in many parts of Europe, for instance in large German cities, where many people are no longer sensitive to the associations and stereotypes connected with a particular dialect.[163] Furthermore, translators tend to render several dialects of the source language in a single dialect of the target language; to use lexicon and expressions that were current when the translator was young (which is one reason why translations "age" more rapidly than originals); or simply to disregard the dialectical subtleties of the original, making the rendering conform to the translator's notion of good writing.[164] Accordingly, a good translator will visualize the performance of the play on the stage and select an appropriate form of speech:

> A good playwright describes his personages *from the inside*. Their character dictates their manner of speech, not vice versa. Therefore

---

160. Levyi, *Iskusstvo perevoda,* p. 216; cited by A. A. Mishustina, in *Teoriia i praktyka perekladu* (Kiev), no. 1 (1979): 70.

161. Levyi, *Iskusstvo perevoda,* p. 21.

162. Ia. Sadovskii, in *Voprosy literatury,* no. 5 (1979): 23–24.

163. Karl-Richard Bausch and Hans-Martin Gauger, eds., *Interlinguistica. Sprachvergleich und Übersetzung: Festschrift zum 60. Geburtstag von Mario Wandruszka* (Tübingen: Max Niemeyer Verlag, 1971), p. 448.

164. Levyi, *Iskusstvo perevoda,* pp. 86–87. Levyi cites G. Boiadzhiev (in *Poeziia teatra* [Moscow, 1960], pp. 81–82), whose other examples of poor acting (cheap pseudo-poetic sentimentality; overemphasis on linguistic characterization of personages, such as an overabundance of diminutives in renditions of children's literature; and disregard for the original text) in his view have close parallels in poor literary translation.

a translator must not become addicted to collecting the linguistic peculiarities of the personages. . . . Their speeches are rooted in the translator's notion of their characters and the evolution of these characters.[165]

At one time opera in Russia was usually performed in the original language, as was also the practice in most other countries. That custom has changed, so that most operas are now sung in Russian. It stands to reason that the task of translating an opera libretto requires competence in music as well as literature. Joseph Machlis, who translated into English such classics as *Rigoletto, La Traviata, La Bohème, Cavalleria Rusticana,* and *Fidelio* as well as three modern works, Poulenc's *Dialogues of the Carmelites* and Prokofiev's *War and Peace* and *The Flaming Angel,* offered the following observations on the technique:

> In general, operatic translation can be done either by a musician who is literary or by a writer who has studied music. The dangers in either case are many. On the one hand, a translation that is too powerful in its own right tends to distract the listener from the music. . . . On the other hand, one that is too slavish may very well fall flat. To guide him the translator has only his ear, his taste, his common sense, his sense of language, and what others have achieved in this field.[166]

Machlis recalled his procedure in translating the libretto of Sergei Prokofiev's opera *The Flaming Angel:*[167]

> In this work the verbal accent had to coincide absolutely with the musical accent so that the overall effect would not be of a translation but as if the music had originally been written to the English words.

---

165. Levyi, *Iskusstvo perevoda,* pp. 205–6; original emphasis.
166. Joseph Machlis, "Opera in Translation," *Music Journal* 36, no. 1 (1978): 20.
167. According to a Soviet operatic dictionary published in 1965, Prokofiev's *The Flaming Angel* (*Ognennyi angel*) had its premiere in Venice on September 14, 1955. It is based on a novel of the same name by Valerii Briusov, a leading Russian Symbolist. Set in sixteenth-century Germany, it relates "a very confusing tale" at the center of which lies the "all-consuming and painful love of Ruprecht, a knight, for Renata, a girl possessed by feverish visions and convinced that she sees either a bright spirit or the devil." The opera's *dramatis personae* include Faust and Mephistopheles. Ultimately the heroine is burned at the stake. See A. Gozenpud, *Opernyi slovar'* (Moscow and Leningrad: Muzyka, 1965), pp. 281–82. Clearly this was not an easy libretto to translate.

I had to be careful to place bright open vowels like "ah" on the high notes, never an "ee" that constricts the singer's throat (although Puccini himself, interestingly enough, did not always follow this rule); also to avoid percussive consonants in legato passages. I soon learned to think in terms not of the individual measure but of the entire phrase, working to the melodic curve rather than to its segments. Once I learned to do that I was able to make the key word sail in on the crest of the musical phrase. In this kind of translation it was not necessary to hear the subsidiary words—prepositions, conjunctions and the like. All the listener had to do was to absorb the key word; and working by phrase instead of by measure made it much easier for him to do so.[168]

Translating operatic libretti is of course a highly restricted activity involving several individuals at most. Cinematic translation, by contrast, is a minor industry. In a long essay published in 1981, G. Zargar'ian pointed out that films produced by Soviet studios with the original sound track in a minority language (such as Georgian, Armenian, or Uzbek) were regularly "translated" into nearly a hundred other Soviet languages by means of subtitles. At the same time, more than 160 minority and foreign films were dubbed annually with a Russian sound track, while about 700 Russian films were provided with sound tracks in various other languages spoken in the country. However, in contrast to literary works, motion pictures are usually "translated" only once; and the subtitles and dubbing must be done in a hurry.

Soviet studios used several different methods to "translate" films: subtitles, dubbing, commentary, or an announcer's "retelling" of the story. (The latter two techniques, in which the commentator's voice is superimposed over the original sound track, are rarely used in the West except in newsreels, documentaries, or nature films.) Subtitles have the disadvantage that they obscure the screen; and in languages containing verbs and adjectives that lack masculine and feminine endings, they obscure the meaning as well. Moreover, subtitles are quite distracting for the viewer: to read the five to seven hundred subtitles of the average motion picture can require ten to fifteen minutes altogether. Dubbing a film with a new sound track is generally considered the most satisfying method of "translation," and

---

168. Machlis, "Opera in Translation," p. 19.

narrator's commentary the next best. Fully forty percent of Soviet cinemagoers claim to prefer dubbed films.

Producing a dubbed sound track requires not just one or two translators, as would a purely literary text, but several actors who must coordinate their speech with the visual part of the motion picture. Hence the dubbing into a new language is actually a collective effort. On the other hand, having no more than two or three performers replace all of the voice parts, thus drowning out the original sound track, produces an unsatisfactory uniformity in the spoken text. Furthermore, in presenting a film to a foreign audience, ways must also be found to "translate" gestures that are incomprehensible outside the source culture. For instance, in the film *Glinka* the composer is seen bowing to birch trees upon his return to Russia from abroad. Foreigners cannot be expected to know that the birch tree is a symbol of Russia; and this must somehow be explained.

Zagar'ian pointed out that the process of dubbing foreign films provided Soviet censors with an opportunity to tone down excessively blunt language (for example, in Russian sound tracks Italian whores sound like debutantes from finishing schools) and to eliminate "pornographic" scenes altogether.[169] Apparently this censorship was abandoned in the late 1980s when Soviet studios began to release such films as *Little Vera,* which portray sex with a level of frankness quite comparable to scenes in American and European R-rated productions.

Over the years Soviet translators accumulated considerable experience working with languages at both ends of the linguistic spectrum, from the kindred East Slavic tongues (Russian, Ukrainian, Belorussian) to the very different (non-Indo-European) Ural-Altaic languages such as Uzbek, Azeri, Tatar, or Kazakh. All of these were spoken within the Soviet Union and thus presented a problem more immediate than, say, occasional renderings of Chinese or Japanese texts.

As might be expected, conventional wisdom inclines to the belief that kindred languages are the easiest to translate into each other. For example, Jean Paris claimed that a translated text is better able to retain the flavor of the original when "both tongues have in common a certain syntax, climate and resonance," such as Danish and Norwegian or Czech and Serbo-Croatian.[170] The Polish poet Mieczysław Jastrun also preferred working

---

169. G. Zagar'ian, "Iskusstvo perevoda fil'ma," in *Masterstvo perevoda, Sbornik dvenadtsatyi, 1979* (Moscow: Sovetskii pisatel', 1981), pp. 110, 112–13, 115, 123–24, 126–27.

170. Arrowsmith and Shattuck, *Craft and Context of Translation,* p. 58.

with related languages. He found it easier to translate into Polish from Russian than from non-Slavic languages, and also easier from French than from German, apparently because the influence of Latin on Polish brought it somewhat closer to the Romance languages than to Germanic ones.[171] C. Rajagopalachari, governor general of multilingual India from 1948 to 1950 and author of over thirty books on a variety of subjects, was rather uncompromising (as befitted a man of his rank) in making similar pronouncements on this issue. In his opinion, translations of classic literary works cannot "bring out the art and beauty of the original in proper measure, except in cases where the two languages are very closely allied to one another and the people speaking them have grown up together in civilization."[172]

The contrary opinion is also widely held. Efim Etkind took the German scholar H. Seidler to task for advancing the argument that the "closer" two languages are, the easier they are to translate into each other. Seidler's thesis, as summarized by Etkind, was that "the spiritual makeup of a nation is expressed in a specific linguistic form and cannot be adequately expressed with the resources of another language."[173] Not so, Etkind retorted: actually the reverse is true. Translation from one Slavic tongue into another is more rather than less difficult; so is rendering a Yiddish text into German.[174] Theodore Savory shared that opinion—to my knowledge, the only Western scholar who has written about the problems of translation to do so. His view was that German is relatively easy to translate into English, and vice versa, while French is more difficult because of the "deceptive resemblance" of French and English words.[175]

Apparently Etkind spoke for the majority of his Soviet compatriots. In expressing their views on this subject in personal conversations with me, a dozen or so Russian and Ukrainian prose writers, poets, and translators were unanimous in their insistence that translation involving kindred languages, far from being easier, presented additional obstacles.[176] This belief

---

171. Balcerzan, *Pisarze polscy o sztuce przekładu*, pp. 363–64.

172. *The Art of Translation*. A Symposium. (New Delhi: Ministry of Scientific Research and Cultural Affairs, 1962), p. 5.

173. H. Seidler's thesis appears in his *Die Dichtung: Wesen, Form, Dasein* (Stuttgart, 1959), summarized in E. G. Etkind, "Khudozhestvennyi perevod i iskusstvo i nauka," *Voprosy iazykoznaniia*, no. 4 (1970): 23–24.

174. Ibid.

175. Savory, *Art of Translation*, p. 99.

176. I have not come across any Belorussian pronouncements on the subject. However, the Belorussian literary tradition is both more recent and far less developed than the Ukrainian, and that is also true of Belorussian literary translation.

has a long tradition in Russia. In the nineteenth-century the Russian poet Nikolai Nekrasov (1821–78) pointed out that special difficulties are involved in translating into Russian from Slavic languages like Polish or Ukrainian. Vladimir Korolenko (1853–1921), a Russian writer of mixed Polish-Ukrainian descent and an experienced translator fluent in all three languages, elucidated some of the specific problems. Russian and Ukrainian, he warned, share many words that sound identical but actually differ in shades of meaning. As a result, Russian renditions of Ukrainian texts abound in imperfect rhymes, incorrect stresses, and imprecise connotations of individual words.[177] In human speech, the substitution of certain sounds for approximately similar ones is at the root of what we call a foreign accent. By analogy, translation between kindred languages may be viewed as susceptible to "foreign accents," or if a metaphor from optics is preferred, to blurred vision. Neither should be tolerated in any art, including the verbal art of translation.

In an interesting discussion of this problem, the Soviet scholar A. M. Finkel' analyzed the self-translations done by the nineteenth-century Ukrainian novelist G. F. Kvitko-Osnov'ianenko into Russian. The results, Finkel' observed, demonstrate that Wilhelm von Humboldt was right to reject the then (and still!) popular belief that an ideal rendering is the one the author would have produced if he had written the text in the target language. Kvitko-Osnov'ianenko's own translations abound in the kind of defects typically associated with renditions into kindred languages, such as treating words that sound alike as if they were identical in meaning, whereas actually their significance is quite different. As if following Neoclassical rules of translation, Kvitko-Osnov'ianenko was rigidly literalist when satisfied with his own Ukrainian text, but highly paraphrastic when trying to "improve" it for a Russian audience. That was his right, of course, but it *did* destroy the original composition.[178]

Translations from Ukrainian into Russian and vice versa continue to be plagued by the inevitable difficulties of dealing with closely related languages. Maksim Ryl'sky, who was arguably the foremost Ukrainian poet and translator of the twentieth century, expanded upon some of the pitfalls. Interlingual homonyms (identical sounding words with different

---

177. Z. M. Kholonina, "K probleme perevoda poeticheskikh proizvedenii na blizkorodstvennye iazyki," in *Slavianskaia filologiia*, 8th ed., ed. S. B. Bernshtein and E. A. Tsybenko (Moscow: Izdatel'stvo Moskovskogo universiteta, 1973), pp. 178–79.

178. *Teoriia i kritika perevoda* (Izdatel'stvo Leningradskogo universiteta, 1962), pp. 104–25.

meanings) are the most serious trap, according to Ryl'sky. Another danger is the tendency to exaggerate ethnic coloration by imparting to the rendition too much of the ethnic flavor of *either* the source *or* the target language.[179] Interlingual homonyms are apparently very insidious. Another difficulty arises from the fact that the same word may be folksy in one language and bookish in another, "positive" in one and "negative" in the other. For example, in Russian *baba* is a generally "friendly" term which may be used to refer to a young woman, while in Ukrainian it is only derisive.[180] Vladimir Rossel's, who translated Jiří Levý from Czech into Russian, thought that "the chief obstacle in translating from a kindred language is the increasingly powerful hypnotic quality of the original, which acquires enormous potency." He too blamed interlingual homonyms for the problem.[181]

In a broader sense, the problem is the "omnipresent mutual penetration of the norms of one language into the other."[182] Translators must resist the allure of deceptively familiar words. They must avoid literal meanings in order better to reproduce the imagery and associations of the original text. The Russian translator Pavel Toper believed that fidelity could be achieved by what he called "transexpression [*perevyrazheniia*] of the original." However, "while transexpressing the original with the resources of his own language [the translator] must not stray beyond the line where personal arbitrariness begins."[183] Apparently all such warnings had little effect. A group of Soviet scholars who reported in 1971 on the current state of translations from Ukrainian into Russian declared: "*All of the translations we have examined carried into the Russian text Ukrainian words, expressions, and syntax.* At the same time, every so often translators, as if bored with their work, would simply omit from the rendition entire sentences, utterances or even large chunks of the text."[184] Such sloppiness was particularly common in translations from and into the minority languages. It reflected their low status compared with renditions into Russian of Western European and American texts.

---

179. Maksim Ryl'skii, "Zametki o khudozhestvennom perevode stikhov," *Druzhba narodov*, no. 1 (1952): 147.

180. Aleksei Kundzich, "O perevodakh proizvedenii L. N. Tolstogo na ukrainskii iazyk," *Druzhba narodov*, no. 5 (1953): 222.

181. Vl. Rossel's, "Zametki o perevode s 'blizkikh' iazykov," *Druzhba narodov*, no. 8 (1959): 219.

182. Nikolai Ushakov, *Sostiazanie v poezii* (Kiev: Dnipro, 1969), p. 225.

183. *Voprosy literatury*, no. 5 (1979): 13–14; original emphasis.

184. *Voprosy teorii khudozhestvennogo perevoda*, p. 211; emphasis added.

Finally, the translation of certain texts *into* Ukrainian raises some very specialized problems, which translators have solved in a variety of ways. A "rural" Ukrainian lexicon was appropriate for Irina Stashenko's rendition of Mark Twain, while "bookish" ornate Ukrainian was the right choice for F. Havrysh's *Brothers Karamazov*. Encountering quotations of Schiller's poetry in a novel by Dostoevsky, V. Strutinsky rightly translated them into Ukrainian from Zhukovsky's Russian Schiller rather than from the German original, since he knew that Zhukovsky's version was the one most familiar to Soviet readers. (V. V. Koptilov observed in an aside that this may have been the only case in which it made better sense to translate from a translation than from the original.) On the other hand, Strutinsky left unchanged the Old Church Slavonic words and passages in Dostoevsky's novel because Ukrainian and Russian share that same liturgical language.[185]

The use of interlinear cribs was common practice in translations into Russian from the Soviet minority languages—even from languages with many millions of speakers like Uzbek or Tatar. For example, of the 119 books by Tatar authors translated into Russian between 1969 and 1973, only eight or nine were direct translations. The rest, or over 90 percent, used interlinear trots.[186] This procedure evoked some critical comments from Lev Ginzburg, who translated from German—namely, from a major language. Obviously in the mood for some grandstanding, or perhaps trying to please a special audience, Ginzburg wrote in 1981:

> It is my profound conviction that there should be no fundamental distinction between translating from foreign languages and from the languages of the peoples of the USSR. For some reason, people continue to believe that interlinear "trots" may not be resorted to in translations from the English, where that would be in bad taste, but are quite all right in translating from the Kazakh. They are convinced that [trots] are out of the question in translations from the French, but just fine for Armenian. Indeed, in the latter case translations with the aid of such interlinear "ponies" have become the norm, even though Armenian is the language of some of the world's great literary masterpieces. I won't even mention the literatures of the small ethnic groups in the Russian Republic. Only a handful of

---

185. V. V. Koptilov, *Aktual'ny pytannia ukrains'koho khudozhn'oho perekladu* (Kiev: Vydavnytstvo Kyivs'koho universytetu, 1971), pp. 31–36.
186. Rafael' Mustafin, "Kak nam pokonchit' s prokliatym voprosom?" *Druzhba narodov*, no. 12 (1976): 229.

enthusiasts undertake the study of Chuvash, Kalmyk, Avar, and similar languages.[187]

Ginzburg argued from his own experience that a real translation is impossible without command of the original language. But he was certainly aware of the reasons for the use of "trots" and "ponies" in translations from Kazakh, Avar, Kalmyk, and Armenian. It is simply that these languages are rarely taught outside the regions where they are spoken, and therefore very few non-natives know them well enough to translate works from those languages into their own tongues. Moreover, there simply is not enough steady translating work in these "minor" languages to justify professional interest. Ginzburg surely knew that until quite recently, translations from even such major foreign languages as Chinese and Japanese, which have long literary traditions, were made from English renditions. Similarly, translations from lesser-known Slavic languages like Czech were made from the more widely spoken Polish, while Swedish or Norwegian texts were re-translated from German.[188] Even so prominent a dramatist as Ibsen (all of whose plays have been staged in Poland since early in the twentieth century) has never been translated directly into Polish from Norwegian, but only from rather inferior German versions of his original texts. Analogous procedures continue to be employed in rendering Persian, Hindi, Chinese, and Japanese verse into Polish. All are carried out with the help either of interlinear "cribs" or intermediate translations of the originals into other languages.[189]

This widely accepted use of cribs led to a curious incident reported in 1979 in the scholarly journal *Voprosy literatury*. It seems that the well-known poet Nikolai Tikhonov once found an "interlinear" crib which he proceeded to fashion into a Russian poem. The truth then came out that the crib was an invention, that there was no *original*. Did this make Tikhonov's poem an original? Not quite, because he had used the imagery of the crib. Was it a translation? Once more the answer is "no," because no original existed.[190]

Apparently this was not an isolated instance. The Soviet policy of systematic publication in Russian of token samples of poetry by members of the ethnic minorities (the more exotic the language, the better) created a

187. Ginzburg, *Nad strokoi perevoda*, pp. 7–8.
188. Levyi, *Iskusstvo perevoda*, p. 218.
189. Rusinek, *O sztuce tłumaczenia*, pp. 17–18.
190. *Voprosy literatury*, no. 5 (1979): 8–9.

small but steady demand for interlinear cribs. A year after the Tikhonov incident, Radio Liberty broadcast a talk by the émigré Russian novelist Sergei Dovlatov, in which he recalled a visit to the Kalmyk city of Elista. During his visit a local poet presented him with what he said was an interlinear translation of one of his poems. The text was simple: "I love my steppes. I love the sun. I love my collective farm's sheep. But most of all I love the Communist Party." The Kalmyk poet wanted Dovlatov to fashion these lines into a Russian poem. But when Dovlatov asked to *hear* the original in order to get a sense of the poem's sound, it turned out that there *was* no original, just the interlinear crib.[191]

Uzbek was the third largest language in the USSR (after Russian and Ukrainian) in terms of the number of its native speakers. Yet in the 1970s, translations of Western European literature into Uzbek were still being made from Russian intermediaries. Mirkarim Asim's Uzbek version of Heinrich Mann's *Man of Straw* (*Der Untertan*) was a translation of I. Gorkina's Russian *Vernopoddannyi,* while E. Vakhidov's rendering of Goethe's *Faust* into Uzbek used Boris Pasternak's Russian text. The Uzbek scholar Rano Faizullaeva noted with satisfaction that "the Uzbek translation [of Goethe] was a success—it reads like an original work." However, she also pointed out that Russian translators' frequent departures from original texts are then compounded by the shortcomings of their Uzbek colleagues. To be sure, a certain "reciprocity" existed in this respect: translations of Uzbek fiction and folklore into German were also made from Russian versions, and similarly perpetuated the defects of the latter. Despite all this, the more recent translators' additions to original texts represented an improvement over earlier emendations. For example, in a 1939 edition of Schiller translated into Uzbek from the Russian of M. Mikhailov, where Mikhailov had substituted Russian realia for Schiller's German ones, this new translation replaced them with references to Uzbek objects and customs.[192]

Translations from Western languages *into* the less commonly spoken languages of the Soviet Union did not ordinarily present major difficulties. If no qualified person could be found to translate a text directly, an indirect version could be made through Russian (or some other language). The situation was far more difficult with respect to translations *from* the minor-

---

191. Radio Liberty broadcast of November 28–29, 1980.
192. Faizullaeva, *Natsional'nyi kolorit,* pp. 7, 9–10, 12, 5. The Uzbek translator's use of Pasternak's rendition of *Faust* also means that the latter's references to revolutionary peasant wars that are nowhere to be found in Goethe's text have now migrated to Central Asia.

ity languages into Western ones like French or German, particularly since where modern literary works were concerned these were often the very first translations of any kind. Translations into Russian from the languages of the Caucasus, Siberia, and Central Asia were usually made with the aid of interlinear trots provided by native speakers of the source language. As a rule such persons had sufficient command of Russian to prepare trots in that language, but lacked native fluency, not to mention literary gifts. Exceptions existed, of course (thus Herold Bel'ger, actually an ethnic German, translated directly from Kazakh into Russian without the use of trots). However, most renderings of Uzbek verse as well as long Uzbek novels were produced from interlinear versions.[193] Even books clearly identified on the title page as "translated from the Uzbek" by a specific individual were usually based on cribs employed by someone who knew no Uzbek at all.[194] The same was true of other minority languages, as a Tadzhik translator reported.

The same practices prevailed in translations from one minority language into another. Either a Russian rendition served as intermediary, or interlinear cribs were utilized.[195] Critics periodically complained that these interlinear texts (*podstrochniki*) resulted in unsatisfactory renderings because the translator himself could not judge the extent to which his final version captured the letter and spirit of the original.[196] Commentators likewise voiced their suspicions that interlinear trots symptomized a disrespectful attitude toward the minority literatures. In response, promises were dutifully made that at some point in the future all translations would be made directly from the original texts.[197]

For the foreseeable future, however, purely practical reasons dictate that interlinear trots will doubtless continue to be used. Since Russian literary celebrities are often asked to translate from languages they do not know, they have no alternative but to rely on such aids. That being the case, they may as well be provided with good ones.[198] An apt illustration of how an original work in a minority language might evolve into a polished transla-

---

193. Gul'nara Gafurova in *Khudozhestvennyi perevod* (Erevan, 1973), pp. 223–24.
194. Soiuz Pisatelei SSSR, Sovet po khudozhestvennomu perevodu, *Aktual'nye problemy teorii khudozhestvennogo perevoda* (Moscow: Sovetskii pisatel', 1967), 2:89.
195. Ibid., 1:304–5.
196. See, for example, P. Tartakovskii, "Chernyi khleb masterstva," *Druzhba narodov*, no. 12 (1973): 260–61.
197. For instance, by Elizbar Ananiashvili, in *Khudozhestvennyi perevod* (Erevan, 1973), pp. 66–68.
198. Anninskii, *Khudozhestvennyi perevod* (Moscow, 1986), pp. 58–76.

tion was provided in 1975 by the publishers "Ayastan," who brought out a volume of Naapet Kuchak's Armenian verse with both interlinear trots and an "artistic rendering" in Russian by the well-known scholar and translator Levon Mkrtchian.[199]

It is not true, by the way, that translators into Russian from Western languages never resorted to interlinear cribs, although the practice was uncommon in the eighteenth and nineteenth centuries. A case in point is Zhukovsky's translation of Homer's *Odyssey* from Greek, a language he did not know. The reason why interlinear aids were rarely employed in those days is twofold. First, most translations into Russian in the nineteenth century were made from French or German, that is, from languages widely known in Russia among the educated classes; and second, translations from languages less well known, such as Spanish or even English, were often made from their French versions. In that respect Russia differed little from Western Europe, where ever since the end of the nineteenth century poetry in rare languages has often been translated from English cribs.

A translation based on interlinear trots is naturally quite different from one that is made directly from the source language. As L. G. Kelly emphasized, "*The essential act here is not one of translation, but one of literary creation from an unpolished original. It is doubtful whether this is translation in the full sense.*"[200] His point is well taken. Trots, cribs, and ponies are to be considered semi-finished products or precooked frozen meals of sorts. Purists will never accept them as satisfactory or authentic, but themselves are in no position to offer a substitute; and millions of consumers continue using them. Doctrinaire opposition to any and all interlinear aids is as futile as the similar dismissals of all translation once were. The slogan, "Let them learn foreign languages!" is but a variant, so to speak, of "Let them eat cake," and just as unrealistic.

The Georgian translator Elizbar Ananiashvili cautioned his colleagues who made use of trots that efforts to retain the prosody of the original could backfire. A meter that is natural to Georgian verse may sound forced in Russian.[201] That point is worth emphasizing, but the peril is no greater when trots are used than when they are not. Herold Bel'ger emphasized that Kazakh prose favors a florid, grandiloquent style that sounds strange to

---

199. For a review of the volume, see *Druzhba narodov*, no. 10 (1976): 270–72.
200. L. G. Kelly, *The True Interpreter: A History of Translation Theory and Practice in the West* (New York: St. Martin's Press, 1979), p. 112; emphasis added.
201. Elizbar Ananiashvili, "Ot remesla k iskusstvu: arifmetika i algebra perevoda," *Literaturnaia gazeta*, February 16, 1977, p. 4.

Russians, who are accustomed to a relatively lean and taut narrative. On the other hand, adjusting the original text to Russian tastes often results in distortion. Stripped of its decorative florid ornamentation, the Kazakh prose of Mukhtar Auezov's modern novel *The Path of Abai* would be reduced to conveying purely factual information.

Bel'ger offered some practical advice to translators from minority languages. He noted that some translators from Kazakh, intent on imparting a degree of local color to a text, resort all too often to exotic-sounding Kazakh words in the Russian text. Instead, he suggested, they should rely "on unusual intonation, idiosyncratic syntax, and [striking] figures of speech," just as the better translators from English or German literature do. At the same time, they should avoid expressions that strike the reader as *overly* Russian. In his opinion, the best way for translators unfamiliar with Kazakh to accomplish these goals is to resort to a *heavily annotated* interlinear trot. An aid of this kind serves as a guide to the author of the polished translation, while also warning him against specific pitfalls in the particular text.[202] Bel'ger elaborated:

> An interlinear translation [*podstrochnik*] is very much in need of all kinds of annotation, explanations, and footnotes. For instance, "familiar usage," "archaic," "dialect." Or else—literally, it means such-and-such, and figuratively this and that. Or else—"this is an idiom," or "a reference to such-and-such event," or else that it's an echo of this or of that. Or that this particular word has two meanings. Geographic terms should be deciphered, as should historical terms. Synonyms should be suggested whenever these are especially apposite—on condition that the extra bunch of synonyms should not be translated bodily into the text of the rendition, as sometimes happens. These are the charms of the interlinear trot, its true attributes which richly compensate for "gracefulness" and "poetic quality."[203]

Written interlinear trots are used rather rarely in the English-speaking world, but their partly oral equivalents (that is, a written crib supplemented by oral discussion) were much in vogue in the 1960s and 1970s. This process was known as "team translation." Since most translations are made

---

202. Gerol'd Bel'ger, "Perevod—khudozhestvennyi i podstrochnyi," *Prostor* (Alma Ata), no. 10 (1971): 103–7.
203. Anninskii, *Khudozhestvennyi perevod* (Moscow, 1986), p. 196.

into the translator's native language, the assistance provided by "native informants" or scholars with expertise in the source language is welcome. Max Hayward, the best and most prolific translator of Russian prose into English since Constance Garnett, served as a native assistant of sorts to several leading American poets who translated Russian verse. In part orally, he provided them with the information normally contained in interlinear trots, while the poets produced the final polished versions. Hayward himself is best remembered for his renditions of *Doctor Zhivago, One Day in the Life of Ivan Denisovich,* and Nadezhda Mandelshtam's memoirs. Ironically, the verses he assisted others in translating were by several celebrated Russian poets who themselves were translators of verse from languages of the Soviet minorities (with the help of trots or "ponies").

At a seminar held in May 1970 at Columbia University, the participants had an opportunity to observe how team translation works. Donald Keene, an eminent translator from Japanese into English, performed together with Mark Strand, an English-language poet who knew no Japanese but had translated from the Spanish. Keene was primarily concerned with fidelity to the Japanese original, while Strand sought to shape the translation into an English poem. The gap between their respective versions was rather wide. At another session Stanley Kunitz, who knew no Russian, described his experience working with Max Hayward on translating verse by Anna Akhmatova and Andrei Voznesensky. Hayward first provided Kunitz with a written word-by-word correspondence unrelated to syntax, and afterward with a literal version in which each word was heavily annotated for subtleties of meaning and literary significance. The two men continued to consult on the translation until the final, publishable version was achieved.[204]

Richard Wilbur, who likewise knew no Russian, related how Hayward had helped him translate three poems by Voznesensky:

> He [Hayward] read over the poems to me in Russian, and he gave me, with admirable restraint, strictly prosaic translations of them, not pushing me toward one or another word choice, and I asked him questions about the appropriateness of the meters to the subject, and I asked questions about the individual Russian words—what their flavors were, whether they were high or low—that sort of thing. I took notes all the time about what he told me. By the time I was

---

204. *World of Translation,* p. 236.

through, I really had done about as much thinking (though not in the same order) as I would do in producing a poem of my own.[205]

It appears that Voznesensky was not entirely happy with the result. However, in light of his own translation methods, he was hardly entitled to complain. In rendering poems of Hemingway into Russian, he disregarded their original sequence and broke up their stanzaic structure. His translations also contain much slang and vulgarity that do not appear in the English original, and omit Hemingway's tenderness.[206]

While "team translation" in the United States is as much a fact of literary life as interlinear trots in Russia, each has its detractors. Guy Daniels, the American translator of Lermontov and other Russian poets, disapproved of "team translation" on the ground that a poet who does not understand the original lacks "the prime mover of most good translations: the compelling desire to re-create, in one's own language, a beautiful thing one has come by *via* a foreign tongue." Moreover, he wrote, authors of polished renditions written in collaboration with "native informants" are in no position to recognize the "subtle rhythmic and other echoes of earlier poets of that particular culture"—a very astute observation indeed. Daniels also charged that "team translation" contributes to a general decline of translation standards generally: "Critical criteria are accordingly relaxed." Finally, "The growing popularity of team translation militates against the acquisition of linguistic culture on the part of the poets." If Stanley Kunitz or a dozen others can become famous translators of Russian verse without bothering to learn the language, why should *anybody* bother to learn it?[207]

Needless to say, all of Daniels's strictures are fully applicable to translation from interlinear trots as practiced in the former Soviet Union. Nonetheless, closer scrutiny reveals that the most serious defects of Soviet translation by this method are to be sought elsewhere, namely, in the cavalier attitude of translators toward the original texts. This disrespect was a consequence of the subservient position of the minority languages and literatures from which such renditions were made, that is to say, their

---

205. Edwin Honig, *The Poet's Other Voice: Conversations on Literary Translation* (Amherst: University of Massachusetts Press, 1985), pp. 92–93.

206. The Soviet scholar V. A. Kukharenko took Voznesenskii to task for his translations of Hemingway's poems, concluding that the translations were much more Voznesenskii than they were Hemingway. See V. A. Kukharenko, "E. Kheminguei v perevode A. Voznesenskogo," *Filologicheskie nauki*, no. 6 (1968): 40–49.

207. *World of Translation*, pp. 170–71.

implied inferiority vis-à-vis Russian. Translation determines the destiny of a given author in another culture; and this is doubly important for writers of "recently literate" (*mladopis'mennye*) ethnic groups.[208] Even more decisive than the length of a literary tradition is its current relative prestige and social standing. Cynthia Ozick movingly described this phenomenon in her 1971 novella *Envy; or Yiddish in America*, in which the main characters are two Yiddish authors residing in New York. One, clearly modeled on the great poet Jacob Glatstein, is known only to Yiddish readers and lived in relative obscurity. The other bears a striking resemblance to Isaac Bashevis Singer, the subsequent Nobel Prize winner. Widely translated into English, Singer enjoyed both critical and popular acclaim. Much credit for his fame clearly belongs to his translator.[209]

A number of Soviet minority authors were *almost* bilingual, *almost* able to write as well in Russian as in their native tongue. Indeed, some of them occasionally wrote in Russian for publication. Nevertheless, a discerning reader could recognize that whereas Olzhas Suleimenov, though a Kazakh by birth, was a bona fide Russian author, Timur Pulatov was really an Uzbek, while Rustam and Maksud Ibragimbekov were Azeris. Moreover, self-translations, as a rule, are anemic and colorless. Recognizing that fact, authors writing in the Soviet minority languages were eager to be *professionally* translated into Russian, especially since only those writings appearing in Russian really reached a wide audience. Accordingly, it was in the minority author's self-interest to provide a potential translator with a good interlinear trot that would call attention to various nuances of the original.[210]

Herold Bel'ger proferred the same advice, adding that the individuals preparing heavily annotated interlinear cribs should be acknowledged as co-translators of the text. Understandably, people who translate from minority languages into polished Russian often balk at such suggestions, preferring instead an imperfect rough interlinear trot. Not only do they not wish to share the credit (and the money) for the work. An additional consideration is that a heavily annotated interlinear trot restricts the translator's artistic latitude.[211] This is known among translators as the "theory of moist clay." Its adherents

---

208. Mykola Bazhan, "Sovetskaia shkola perevoda," *Druzhba narodov*, no. 8 (1977): 242–43.

209. First published in *Commentary*, the novella was subsequently reprinted in Cynthia Ozick, *The Pagan Rabbi and Other Stories* (New York: Knopf, 1971), pp. 39–100.

210. Anar, "Chto takoe 'perevod avtora'?" *Druzhba narodov*, no. 5 (1980): 239–40.

211. Bel'ger, "*Perevod*," p. 107.

actually prefer poor interlinear trots because then the "clay" will be more malleable. As Bel'ger explained: "Just as an actor finds it easiest to impersonate himself, so the translator finds it easiest to write as he writes himself, without any dependence on the material [to be translated]."[212]

From the 1930s onward, Soviet translation practice was strongly influenced by the then official approval of free translation and an ongoing struggle against the sin of literalism. Allegedly "excessive" fidelity to original texts became ideologically suspect. Distrust of translators was further strengthened by the fact that many were themselves poets and prose writers unable to publish original work of their own. For such people translation was not just a source of livelihood, but also a sublimation of the creative impulse. Writers of the stature of Pasternak were not the only ones affected. As Andrei Sinyavsky (Abram Tertz) shrewdly observed in his short story "The Graphomaniacs," under conditions of Soviet censorship nearly every unpublished author regarded himself as a victim of totalitarian thought control. Hence the complaint voiced by the poet Arseny Tarkovsky in 1973 about self-centered Russian poets who resented being relegated to the humble role of translators:

> Alas, I am not at all convinced that verse translation in our country is improving with time. The ranks of the old translators are getting thin, and we have not seen to it that adequate replacements are trained. Many young people with some literary connections have turned to translation of verse. They had thought, mistakenly, that our work affords an easy livelihood. *Some young lyric poets who have entered the field are gifted enough, but they suffer from a bloated need to assert their individuality.* And translation, by contrast, requires modesty. The translator must be content to remain in the background; the limelight belongs to the author of the original. *Nowadays translations all too often resemble the translator's original work and no longer resemble the translated text.* The author of the original is flattered to have his book embellished with famous names [of translators]. Too many of us believe that a translation need not exactly reproduce the letter and the spirit of the original. *And so a poor poem is turned into a good one and vice versa, and poems written in one stylistic manner, into a manner that is its direct opposite.*

---

212. Gerol'd Bel'ger, in *Druzhba narodov*, no. 12 (1976): 234.

A concrete example was cited by the Armenian poet Silva Kuputikian, whose native language can take pride in a literary tradition much older than the Russian one. Her verse was translated into Russian by the then still youngish poet Bella Akhmadulina who, in Kaputikian's view,

> frequently departs way too much from the original. Her inexhaustible imagination conjures up imagery, metaphors, and epithets to the point that sometimes one regrets that she gives it all away too generously to translations instead of saving it for her own verse. At the same time you feel sorry for yourself. Here you are, writing verse, suffering, carrying for days some image that is dear to you, happy over such poetic finds—and not a trace of this remains in translation. Some may object—look, the translation is now part of Russian poetry, this is delightful Russian verse! My answer is: I am very fond of lovely Russian or Ukrainian children, fair, plump and blue-eyed. But I want to come to Moscow or to Kiev with my own child—swarthy, dark-haired, with somewhat sad eyes, a bit skinny, perhaps, but all mine.

Georgia is a country with a literary tradition nearly as ancient as Armenia's, but its writers make the same complaint about translation of their original work. Thus the Georgian translator Elizbar Ananiashvili was appropriately offended at some remarks by Yuri Libedinsky, one of the founding fathers of Soviet literature, who is chiefly remembered for his Communist-inspired novel, *A Week* (published in 1922). Not only did Libedinsky find nothing wrong with translators ignorant of the language of the work they translated. He also claimed that all was well as long as the rendition "sounds well in Russian" and the translator "gets rid of everything jarring to the Russian ear."[213]

This cavalier attitude toward the literatures of two major Soviet nationalities, Georgian and Armenian, was even more blatant where smaller or more disadvantaged ethnic groups were concerned. The Leningrad poet and translator Lev Druskin related a pathetic incident involving Moishe Teif, a Soviet Yiddish poet. It appears that a poem of Teif's was translated into Russian by the poet Iunna Morits. In the process, Teif's eight Yiddish lines underwent a metamorphosis into sixteen Russian ones. "The other

---

213. *Khodozhestvennyi perevod* (Erevan, 1973), pp. 267–68; 163–64, 55; emphasis added.

half," Teif explained, "she just did on her own. But what a beautiful job she did!" He then wrote to Druskin, "Should *you* wish to translate a poem of mine, I give you *carte blanche,* but on one condition: the rendition must be better than the original." Druskin was dumbfounded by this offer: "How can one subject oneself to such humiliation!" However, it can safely be assumed that Teif, who died in 1966, was a frightened man. He was a survivor of Stalin's violent attack on Yiddish culture, which culminated in August 1952 in the mass murder of scores of Yiddish writers and poets. Moreover, state-sponsored anti-Semitism was still rife in Brezhnev's Russia.

Somewhat surprising is the fact that two relatively unknown Russian translators, Grebnev and Kozlovsky, showed so little deference toward the minority poet Rasul Gamzatov, a recognized member of the Soviet literary establishment. Gamzatov wrote in Avar, the language of a small ethnic group in the Caucasus. Although Avar verse is unrhymed, the two translators produced a smooth, though lackluster, rhymed Russian version. Whether for this or other reasons, they eventually had a falling out with the Avar poet; and in due time a new Russian version of his verse made Gamzatov sound very different. By that time Grebnev and Kozlovsky had begun to publish Russian translations of other minority poets, such as Kaisyn Kuliev. Like Gamzatov, Kuliev hailed from the Caucasus, but wrote in quite another language, Balkar. Interestingly, in the hands of Grebnev and Kozlovsky the Balkar poet began miraculously to resemble their own older renditions of the Avar poet Rasul Gamzatov.

The wonders of Soviet translation practice did not cease here. Gania Kurilov, a writer of an even smaller nationality, the Yukagir, became known as a poet under the name of Uluro Ado, which means "Son of the Lake." *Uluro Ado never wrote any poetry whatsoever,* explaining to one and all that the Yukagir people were illiterate. Instead *he produced only Russian interlinear trots* which he then presented to Lev Druskin or to German Plisetsky. These two Russian translators then shaped the trots into serviceable Russian verse. In a book published in London in 1984, Druskin explained that in addition to the literalist and paraphrastic schools of translation, a third type existed in the Soviet Union, namely, *writing instead of a poet.* He condemned this as "an embarrassment to the poetry of small ethnic groups; the reader never knows what is the author's and what is the translator's."[214]

---

214. Lev Druskin, *Spasennaia kniga: Vospominaniia leningradskogo poeta* (London: Overseas Publications Exchange, 1984), pp. 352-55.

Apparently the bizarre tale of Uluro Ado was not an isolated case. Analogous practices are described in Feliks Roziner's novel *Nekto Finkel'maier* (*A Certain Finkel'maier*), which appeared in Russian in London in 1981. Roziner's narrator is a young dissident poet who becomes an apprentice of a seasoned professional translator:

> The *maître* translated a lot. At times, he had so many commissions that he would run behind schedule and pass on some of them to me. These were, for the most part, poetry from the Caucasus and from Central Asia, supplied in advance with interlinear trots [*podstrochniki*]. Without wasting much effort, I would embellish these lines with rhythms and rhymes. As a rule, however, it seemed that this was not enough contribution on my part, that it just would not do. What was really required was "improving" this poetry, most of it mediocre. Now I had no idea how one goes about "improving" somebody else's writing, but the *maître* knew how to do it. He would patch it up here and there, and before long the poem would undergo a metamorphosis. After that, the authors of these poems would call the *maître* on the phone [to thank him]. Indeed, while discussing in print the problems of translation, they would occasionally naively confess with much enthusiasm that the Russian versions of their poems were even superior to the originals. They would write that this gave their poems a new lease on life, and endowed them with the lofty right to merge their own modest stream of verse with the mighty river of Russian poetry.[215]

Yet another kind of evidence exists for the self-demeaning, servile posture of Soviet minority authors toward the literature of the Russian Big Brother. At a time when no manifestations of obsequious literalism were tolerated in translations *into* Russian, that same literalism was actually *encouraged* in translations *from* Russian into the languages of the minorities. Thus a 1980 study by Klara Dzhideeva revealed that in the 1950s "nearly all" Kirgiz literary translators "followed the word and not the sense." The results, Dzhideeva wrote disapprovingly, were terrible. Kirgiz

---

215. Feliks Roziner, *Nekto Finkel'maier, Roman* (London: Overseas Publications Interchange, 1981), p. 117.

poets who translated Russian classics "went through a period of deceptively maintaining the illusion of literal fidelity to the original."[216]

Literalism was also *de rigueur* in the translation of Russian writing into Kazakh. Mukhtar Auezov, then the leading Kazakh novelist, provided the following account of his work on a translation of Turgenev's *A Nest of Gentlefolk*:

> Insofar as possible, I tried to translate the novel literally. Only this kind of translation can reproduce the author's language, his style, the peculiarities of his sentence structure. As I understood it, literal rendition implies translating every sentence with a separate sentence. Thus most of the punctuation marks of the Russian text would also appear in the Kazakh text. In this way the volume of Turgenev's sentences was successfully preserved in Kazakh. There were good reasons for our choice of these devices. A literal rendering of a classic of Russian literature allowed me to understand the nuances of Turgenev's art both as a translator and as a writer in my own right. And most importantly, a literal translation enabled me to present our readers with a real Turgenev, with all the peculiarities and idiosyncracies of his art.[217]

Auezov wrote these lines in 1952, shortly before Stalin's death, at the height of the official campaign of vilification of things foreign and glorification of the Russian national genius by means fair and foul. Hence this Kazakh novelist's worshipful attitude toward *A Nest of Gentlefolk* was not merely a tribute to a literary masterpiece and its creator, but also a genuflection to the culture of Russia, the first among ostensibly equal Soviet nations.

What is curious is that deprecatory attitudes toward non-Russian writing apparently still endured in the far more benign Brezhnev era, twenty years after Stalin's death. This mind set existed not only in the steppes of Central Asia, but in Ukraine—the most populous and (apart from the three small Baltic republics) culturally most advanced Soviet republic after Russia itself. A Ukrainian scholar complained in 1973 that after years of hard struggle against literalism, the practice had still not been completely uprooted. In particular, it seemed to have wormed its way into Ukrainian translations of Russian literature. This choice seems not to have been

---

216. K. Dzhideeva, *Poeticheskii perevod i istoriko-literaturnyi protsess: Iz istorii poeticheskogo perevoda russkoi klassiki v Kirgizii* (Frunze: Kyrgyzstan, 1980), p. 97.

217. Mukhtar Auezov, in *Prostor* (Alma Ata), no. 11 (1968): 105.

accidental. The literalist Ukrainian translators argued that playing games with "spirit" and "meaning"—in other words, free, paraphrastic translation—might be tolerated in renderings of French or English or other foreign writing into Ukrainian. In translating *Russian* literature, however, one must take care to treat it "lovingly and literally."[218]

---

218. Aleksyi Kundzich, *Tvorchy problemy perekladu* (Kiev: Dnipro, 1973), p. 98; emphasis added.

4

Translators and the Literary Process

In the fifth century A.D. Armenian translators were likened to saints, and a special prayer assumed that divine grace had inspired them to translate holy books for the edification of the nation.[1] That Golden Age of the profession is now but a legend. More than a thousand years later, a German theologian who was also an important translator bore witness to his colleagues' plight. In his "Circular Letter on Translating" (1530), Martin Luther described translators as poorly paid, always in danger of having their work plagiarized, and to add insult to injury, hounded by malicious critics.[2] The situation was apparently no better in eighteenth-century England. As Alexander Pope wrote to the earl of Burlington in 1716:

> Pray, Mr. *Lintott* (said I) now you talk of Translators, what is your method of managing them? "Sir (reply'd he) those are the saddest

---

1. Levon Mkrtchian, *Cherty rodstva* (Erevan: Izdatel'stvo Aiastan, 1973), p. 85; cited from N. Emin's translation from the Old Armenian of *Sharakan* (Moscow, 1914), p. 314.
2. André Lefevere, *Translating Literature: The German Tradition from Luther to Rosenzweig* (Amsterdam: Van Gorcum, Assen, 1977), p. 7.

pack of rogues in the world: In a hungry fit, they'll swear they understand all the languages of the universe: I have known one of them take down a *Greek* book upon my counter and cry, Ay this is *Hebrew,* I must read it from the latter end. By G-d I can never be sure in these fellows, for I neither understand *Greek, Latin, French* nor *Italian* myself. But this is my way: I agree with them for ten shillings per sheet, with a proviso, that I will have their doings corrected by whom I please; so by one other they are led at last to the true sense of the author; my judgment giving the negative to all my Translators." But how are you secure that those correctors may not impose upon you? "Why, I get any civil gentleman, (especially a *Scotchman*) that comes into my shop, to read the original to me in *English;* by this I know whether my first Translator be deficient or whether my corrector merits his money or no?"[3]

Ten shillings per sheet may not have been much of an income for desperate translators (note their "hungry fit"!); but clearly it was an expense much resented by Mr. Lintott, Alexander Pope's interlocutor. That it continues to be resented in our times has been attested by American publishers: "It is a thankless problem for the publisher to attempt to have the bookseller understand why it should be in order for him to charge one or two dollars more for a novel by Günter Grass than he may charge for a novel by Saul Bellow. If it is difficult to get the bookseller to comprehend the reason for this, you can imagine why it is even more difficult to get the reader to do so."[4] Indeed, there is even the old anecdote about the French Communist who complained that *L'Humanité* (the official newspaper of the French Communist Party) costs so much more than *Pravda* (the organ of the Soviet Party) because translation is overly expensive.

As late as the eighteenth century, translators labored in anonymity. Their names went unmentioned, a reflection of the lack of respect for their profession. In an effort to remedy this situation, the International Berne Convention of September 9, 1885, recognized translation as an intellectual activity, required that the translator's name be indicated on the book, and established copyright protection for translations for a period of ten years— the same length of time as for the original work. In practice, however, these requirements were often overlooked. Publishers frequently failed to print

---

3. Reuben A. Brower, ed., *On Translation* (New York: Oxford University Press, 1966), p. 2.
4. *World of Translation,* p. 155. (See Introduction, note 13.)

the translator's name, and reviewers periodically ignored his or her contribution. Only those translators who were also original authors could count on better treatment.[5]

"No one wants to be a professional translator," Justin O'Brien declared. What he meant, according to the successful American translator Richard Howard, was "that no one wants the drudgery of having to accept almost any assignment." Howard believed that in the United States "one can become a professional translator and still translate, almost without exception, only books one enjoys putting into English."[6] However, most translators would probably agree with O'Brien's view of their profession. The publisher Helen Wolff also inclined toward a negative judgment:

> Translators by and large are defensive, and understandably so. They are rarely given their due. Reviewers tend to slight them. Either they are not mentioned at all, or they may be accorded a doubtful prominence. Knowledgeable reviewers will pounce on the chance of showing how they would have done it, more subtly and intelligently, of course. And it is always easy to single out, from hundreds of pages, the passage where the translator, in his choice of idiom, has not hit the bull's eye though he still remained on the face of the target.[7]

The other side of the coin is that reviewers often find the translators' skills a bit irrelevant. Thus Burton Raffel pretty much dismissed the need for a translator to have any serious degree of competence in the source language: "Given a certain minimal [!] standard of linguistic accuracy in the translation, I would suppose that a critic . . . *would not be drastically hampered by even total ignorance of the [source] language. . . . [L]inguistic knowledge is not the best nor even a good road toward successful translation.*" Raffel proposed instead that "an informal council" of linguists, critics, and publishers issue certificates attesting that a given rendition is "reasonably close to what the original said."[8] Incidentally, he himself was the compiler of an anthology of Russian verse that teems with mistranslations.

---

5. George Mounin, *Les problèmes théoriques de la traduction* (Paris: Gallimard, 1963), pp. 186–87.
6. William Arrowsmith and Roger Shattuck, eds., *The Craft and Context of Translation* (Austin: The University of Texas Press, 1961), p. 167.
7. Helen Wolff, "Translation and the Editor," *Delos*, ser. 1, no. 2 (1968): 165.
8. Burton Raffel, *The Forked Tongue: A Study of the Translation Process* (The Hague: Mouton, 1971), pp. 104–5; emphasis added. Raffel's anthology is *Russian Poetry under the Tsars* (Albany: State University of New York Press, 1971).

The position of literary translators in modern Canada is illustrative. There in the early 1980s the number of translations doubled every five years.⁹ Nevertheless, the introduction to a bibliography of translated Canadian books could state as a fact that literary translation in that country was "looked upon as a marginal activity, slightly frivolous, and economically uninteresting."¹⁰ The world of Canadian translators was small and inbred. Literary translators refused to evaluate their colleagues' manuscripts, "because they either know the translator personally or are likely to meet him soon." The very close relationships of authors and translators in Canada produced animosities and sometimes even wrecked marriages.¹¹ On the other hand, examples of true devotion to literature have not been unknown among twentieth-century translators. Thus when the German poet Rilke "became convinced that Valéry was the greatest [living] poet, he dropped everything and proceeded to translate [his works]." This admiration was reciprocated: "Valéry himself . . . used his prestige to introduce this new *French* poet Rilke."¹²

Assuming the accuracy of the folk belief that all things are done either for love or for money, translation must be undertaken at least partly for love. Money can hardly serve as its complete reward. The 1991 edition of P.E.N. American Center's *Handbook for Literary Translators* reported that the average remuneration for translators that year was fifty dollars per thousand words.¹³ Moreover, the occupation of translator apparently exacts yet another price. Like coal miners or workers exposed to radiation, translators suffer from occupational disorders of their own. Some evidence suggests that persons who always translate from language A to language B ultimately lose the ability to converse in language A. Additionally, after working for many years, such individuals develop direct associations between units of language A and language B, which then become ossified into clichés. These habits sometimes impede recognition of stylistic differences in the original texts.¹⁴

---

9. Camille R. La Bossière, ed., *Translation in Canadian Literature: Symposium 1982* (Ottawa: University of Ottawa Press, 1983), p. 64.

10. Ibid., p. 62. Philip Stratford's observation originally appeared in his introduction to *Bibliography of Canadian Books in Translation* (1977).

11. La Bossière, *Translation in Canadian Literature*, p. 77.

12. Arrowsmith and Shattuck, *Craft and Context of Translation*, pp. 49, 55, emphasis original. The second statement is quoted from Norbert Fuerst, *Phases of Rilke* (Bloomington: Indiana University Press, 1958), no page indicated.

13. *A Handbook for Literary Translators*, 2d ed., 1991, prepared by the Translation Committee of P.E.N. American Center (New York, 1991), p. 11.

14. These points are made in an American textbook, *Psycholinguistics* (Baltimore, 1954), pp. 144–45); cited by Irzhi Levyi [Jiři Levý], *Iskusstvo perevoda*, trans. Vl. Rossel's (Moscow: Progress, 1974), p. 88.

In Russia ever since the dawn of literary translation in the eighteenth century, the status of this occupation has remained rather low. True, the prestige even of creative writing was not much higher until the next century; and Pushkin (d. 1837) was the first truly professional author able to earn a living from his craft. But later during the nineteenth century Russian writers acquired unprecedented influence. They were admired not only as artists, but also as thinkers, spiritual guides, and almost as folk heroes, much like twentieth-century American sports champions and movie stars. Suffice it to recall that in Gogol's *Inspector General*, still the greatest play in the Russian repertory, gullible provincials are dumbfounded when the impostor Khlestakov declares that he knows Pushkin personally. This was not necessarily an indication of the popularity of Pushkin's writings—most of Gogol's characters had never read a line of his—but of Pushkin's *status*. It was an obligatory genuflection, so to speak. This metaphor was realized in the strictest sense in Alexander Kuprin's *The Duel* (1905), in which one of the characters literally prays to Pushkin's bust. Except for Voltaire and Goethe, hardly any other modern authors have exerted a moral, social, and political influence equal to that of Turgenev, Dostoevsky, and Tolstoy in Russia.

The opposite was true of Russian translators. In fact, few could subsist on their earnings, notwithstanding the rapid expansion of translating activity beginning in the 1820s. Journals that wished to publish the latest works in foreign literature employed many translators. Pushkin, for example, refers ironically in *Eugene Onegin* to a stream of "wild renditions" produced by "hungry translators." The anonymous journeymen who earned their living in this way were underpaid, obliged to work quickly in order to meet deadlines, and naturally lacked time to polish their work. Irinarkh Vvedensky, later a famous translator of foreign prose, was one of these drudges in his youth.[15]

Journeymen and hacks aside, the leading Russian literary translators of the nineteenth and early twentieth centuries devoted only part of their time to the craft. They earned their livelihood as educators, civil servants, or journalists. Some were financially independent; others were professional men and women of letters. Translation as an occupation began only after the 1917 Revolution; and the beginning was decidedly inauspicious. The initially very ambitous *World Literature* series, however praiseworthy in intent, benefited in practice mainly such alien if not hostile groups as the

---

15. Iu. D. Levin, *Russkie perevodchiki XIX veka i razvitie khudozhestvennogo perevoda* (Leningrad: Nauka, 1985), p. 122.

déclassé aristocracy and "bourgeois" intelligentsia. Indeed, their hostility to the Bolshevik state was soon attested by the emigration of most of them; after all, as Lenin himself had remarked, people vote with their feet. The *World Literature* project cast an ominous shadow on the later fortunes of the translating profession, which always included disproportionate numbers of politically unreliable men and women, former (and future!) inmates of Soviet prisons, and Jews. Translation also provided a haven and a quasi-literary livelihood for politically disgraced writers, a number of them very prominent, whose ideological transgressions were being punished by a ban on the appearance of their original writings in print. This state of affairs endured virtually until the collapse of the Soviet state in 1991.

Literary translators in the USSR were professionally somewhat suspect for displaying an unhealthy interest in foreign writing. Some spent years in prison. Valentin Stenich, the translator of Dos Passos, died in a concentration camp. Ivan Likhachev, the translator of Melville and Dickinson, returned from prison but died shortly thereafter. Tat'iana Gnedich, who conducted a poetry translation seminar in Leningrad in the late 1950s, was arrested in 1945. While in prison, she began translating Byron's *Don Juan*, one of the longest poems in world literature. Of its approximately 17,000 lines, she rendered about 2,000 into Russian and committed them to memory. (Some years ago Efim Etkind showed me a page of Gnedich's manuscript of this translation, which she was eventually able to write down on the blank sides of prisoners' interrogation sheets!)[16]

Paradoxically, while some Soviet translators were being arrested, others who lived under a political cloud sought refuge in this activity. Even translation, however, was a privilege that could be restricted or withdrawn altogether. Boris Pasternak, who viewed translation as a long prison sentence of sorts ("Mayakovsky shot himself while I translate"), discovered that the right to translate could be abridged or taken away. In 1958 he came under attack for the publication abroad of *Doctor Zhivago*. After he was awarded the Nobel Prize, the campaign of vilification against him became especially shrill. His rendition of Schiller's *Maria Stuart*, then being staged by the Moscow Art Theater, was removed from the repertory. After a time it was reinstated, but with no mention of the errant poet as its translator. In fact, the only commission to translate that Pasternak was

---

16. The Gnedich rendering of *Don Juan* was published in 1959. See E. G. Etkind, *Poeziia i perevod* (Moscow and Leningrad: Sovetskii pisatel', 1963), pp. 179–80.

allowed to keep at that time was for another *Maria Stuart*, this one by the Polish poet Juliusz Słowacki.[17]

This was not the first use of such sanctions by the Soviet authorities. In 1946 the lyric poet Anna Akhmatova and the brilliant humorist Mikhail Zoshchenko, both of whom had an immense following, were expelled from the Writers' Union for the sin of *avoiding* ideological problems in their work. This act effectively deprived them of their livelihoods. Lidiia Chukovskaia, daughter of the famous translator and children's writer Kornei Chukovsky and a writer herself, recalled that "henceforth, Zoshchenko and Akhmatova were to remain hungry, awaiting, as an act of supreme mercy, permission to engage in translation."[18] Chukovskaia described her personal reaction to Akhmatova's weariness of translating under duress: "My hatred of translation has grown stronger. Now here is a real instance of waste, of squandering national property: Akhmatova's and Pasternak's time spent on translation instead of on original work."[19] Pasternak's resentment of his role as translator probably contributed to his tendency to treat other writers' work as he saw fit, sometimes with little regard for the author's intent. Nonetheless two other poets of Pasternak's stature, Anna Akhmatova and (in some measure) Marina Tsvetaeva, demonstrated considerable respect for the poets they rendered into Russian. Like him, they were translators not by free choice but out of dire need.

When Marina Tsvetaeva returned from emigration in 1939, Pasternak introduced her to Viktor Gol'tsev, "an influential entrepreneur [*delets*] in the field of minority literatures." Gol'tsev commissioned her to translate "two ballads about Robin Hood," some Bulgarian verse, and two thousand lines of the Georgian poet Vazha Pshavela. The result was some excellent Russian verse. The émigré critic Viktoriia Shveitser wrote: "Even though she worked for the money, Tsvetaeva remained firmly committed to the principle of doing her best, and would not relax it in order to ease her task." The Georgian scholar Alexander Tsybulevsky claimed that Tsvetaeva's renderings of Pshavela were as good as her original verse, while Viacheslav Ivanov said much the same thing about her translations of Western European poetry.[20]

17. Lidiia Chukovskaia, *Zapiski ob Anne Akhmatovoi*, vol. 2, *1952–62* (Paris: YMCA Press, 1980), p. 582.
18. Ibid., p. xiii.
19. Ibid., pp. 276–77.
20. Viktoriia Shveitser, "Vozvrashchenie domoi," *Sintaksis* (Paris), no. 11 (1963): 191–93. Another émigré scholar, Simon Markish, disagreed with Ivanov's estimate.

Akhmatova displayed considerable ambivalence toward her translating activity. Anatoly Naiman, a Russian poet strongly influenced by her, offered important information about her attitude:

> Akhmatova considered translation arduous but necessary work . . . . However important the poet she translated, or whatever her affection for him, to her he was a tormentor because he demanded, in effect, that she compose Russian verse for him, and large quantities of it at that, because she earned her livelihood primarily by translating. She wrote her own poetry whenever she was so disposed, sometimes a lot within a short time, at other times nothing at all in half a year. But she translated every single day from morning until lunchtime.

Though conventional wisdom suggests that a poet should translate only works for which he or she feels an affinity,[21] Akhmatova apparently thought otherwise, according to Naiman:

> *For some reason or other, she preferred to translate poets toward whose work she was indifferent, and was even more eager to translate mediocre poets.* [On the other hand], she turned down an offer to be a co-translator of a volume of Baudelaire and declined to translate Verlaine. *For all that, one cannot say that she disliked translation.* After all, it was poetry, and she was Akhmatova. *She called herself, somewhat defiantly, a professional translator, a pupil of Lozinsky.* She seemed proudest of her renditions of the Serbian heroic epics ("In that, I followed Pushkin"), some samples of classical Korean poetry, Alexander Toma's Rumanian "Wanderer," and Peretz Markish's [Yiddish] "Autumn."[22]

Clearly Akhmatova and Tsvetaeva, Mandelshtam and Pasternak were not *typical* Soviet literary translators. What about the ordinary, reasonably competent practitioners of the craft, who were neither great writers nor disreputable hacks? What were their working conditions in the Soviet state? The following composite picture emerges from my own voluminous read-

---

21. On this point see Chapter 2.
22. Anatolii Naiman, "Rasskazy ob Anne Akhmatovoi," *Novyi mir*, no. 3 (1989): 99; emphasis added.

ing and many hours of conversation with several scores of translators who exercised this profession in the former Soviet Union:

I. *Just as in the West, translators were often simply ignored or not given due credit for their work.* For example, Evgeniia Kalashnikova's name did not appear at all on a 200,000-copy printing of her rendition of Jack London's *Martin Eden.* She was a reputable translator, and I know from a personal conversation with her that she resented it greatly. Nikolai Liubimov translated Molière's *Le Bourgeois Gentilhomme,* but the Vakhtangov Theater somehow forgot to mention this fact when it staged the play, although Liubimov was a famous translator.[23] The Georgian translator Elizbar Ananiashvili declared:

> If the translator is to work better he needs attention, much more attention than he has been getting up to now. Reviewers of translated books, if they mention the translation and the translator at all, do so only in passing. At times they forget him altogether, as if he did not exist. On the radio and on television translators are not mentioned at all, even though this [situation] evoked indignation years ago. In many publishing houses the names of the translators of bulky novels appear only on the inside of the title page, just before the name of the proofreader, but sometimes after that of the artist [who did the volume's cover].[24]

II. *Soviet translation suffered from a lack of quality control over the work of mediocre craftsmen.*[25] *Shturmovshchina* (literally: "storm-itis"), a concept that closely paralleled the Soviet phenomenon of Stakhanovism in industry (that is, the pressure for over-rapid work), could be found in the unlikely realm of translating foreign verse. Occasionally a Western poet's entire collected works were brought out within a single year. All that the publishers cared about was the number of lines and meeting the deadlines (*stroki i sroki*). Prospective translators were recruited on the telephone: "We are bringing out X. Can you take on 500 lines?" Another variant was, "How do you feel about N? Free verse, no need to rhyme. Have it ready within three months." Repeating an observation made earlier by Samuil

---

23. Lev Ginzburg, *Nad strokoi perevoda: Stat'i raznykh let* (Moscow: Sovetskaia Rossiia, 1981), pp. 45–46.
24. *Khudozhestvennyi perevod: Vzaimodeistvie i vzaimoobogashchenie literatur* (Erevan: Izdatel'stvo Erevanskogo universiteta, 1973), p. 74.
25. Andrei Fedorov, in *Teoriia i praktyka perekladu* (Kiev), no. 7 (1982): 4.

Marshak à propos of the publication of Byron, Heine, Shakespeare, and Blake, Lev Ginzburg proposed that translations of foreign verse be allowed to *slowly accumulate,* and only then be published, rather than be produced in haste to accommodate publishers.[26]

III. *Soviet translators (both the good ones and the hacks) paid little attention to translation theory and criticism.* This was attested by Andrei Fedorov, one of the foremost theoreticians and practitioners of the Soviet school of translation, who in many ways ranks (with Kornei Chukovsky) as its co-founder.[27] The same point was made by Nikolai Liubimov, who gratefully recalled that his teacher of literary translation, Boris Griftsov, spent as little time as possible discussing the theory of the craft.[28] This indifference is also borne out by the nearly total absence of references to Soviet translation theory in the hundreds of monographs by working Soviet translators I consulted prior to writing this study. Of course, lip service to the reigning antiliteralist creed might be required. But the theoretical battles bore relatively little relationship to actual translation *practice.*

IV. *Because so many Soviet translators were themselves frustrated poets or prose writers who, moreover, were denied adequate credit for their work, they frequently viewed themselves as coauthors rather than translators.* Literary translation in the USSR often provided authors in political disfavor with the means to sublimate their own creative drive. True, this inclination toward coauthorship did not meet with universal approval. The Soviet scholar V. S. Vinogradov declared that "this constant striving to become the author's equal (and on occasion, his superior) does the cause of translation no good. The translator should not strive to gain laurels for himself, but to preserve the laurels of the author of the original."[29] Of course, analogous tendencies could be found in some other parts of the world as well. In the 1960s dictatorial regimes in Latin America prompted local authors to use translation as a camouflage. As Victor Alba (Pedro Pages) pointed out: "In many of the countries, translating has helped a lot of people to go on writing and keeping their [own] manuscripts in the desk drawer."[30]

---

26. Ginzburg, *Nad strokoi perevoda,* pp. 19–20, 122.
27. Andrei Fedorov, in *Teoriia i praktyka perekladu* (Kiev), no. 7 (1982): 4.
28. Nikolai Liubimov, *Perevod-iskusstvo* (Moscow: Sovetskaia Rossiia, 1977), pp. 33–34.
29. V. S. Vinogradov, *Leksicheskie voprosy perevoda khudozhestvennoi prozy* (Moscow: Izdatel'stvo Moskovskogo universiteta, 1978), p. 7.
30. *World of Translation,* p. 116.

V. *Like their colleagues in the West, Soviet translators complained of inadequate earnings.* Among the most underpaid were those who prepared interlinear trots. They received only a fifth or even a tenth of what "real" translators earned.[31] Editors of translations were paid only a third of what translators received.[32]

VI. *Soviet literary translation was unfavorably affected by chaotic Soviet publishing practices and occasionally by underemployment.* One Soviet commentator in 1976 depicted a typical situation as follows:

> A businessman [*delets*] in translating matters arrives at the offices of a publishing house and pleads for "anything" to translate. He doesn't care what that might be—Ukrainian folk songs, modern Georgian verse, or a Moldavian classic of the last century. And the rendering will be of a corresponding quality. This kind of mass literary production keeps gushing forth.[33]

Lev Ginzburg, a prominent translator of German poetry into Russian, lamented in 1981:

> At a time when many of the most experienced masters and heroes of translation are, to put it mildly, not swamped with work, newspapers, magazines, the radio and the stage are inundated with literary con men and smooth operators, businessmen and sharpies who have zeroed in on literary translation as an easy and dependable source of income.[34]

Sometimes the choice of translator for a Western European or American literary work was simplicity itself: the contract was awarded to whoever happened to own a copy of the original. Nora Gal' commented: "And translate it he did, for the most part, miserably."[35]

VII. *Soviet translators had to contend with two serious handicaps: severe restrictions on foreign travel (to say nothing of residence abroad), as*

---

31. Rafael' Mustafin, "Kak nam pokonchit' s prokliatym voprosom?" *Druzhba narodov*, no. 12 (1976), pp. 229–32; Gerol'd Bel'ger, "Literaturnyi podenshchik ili soavtor?" *Druzhba narodov*, no. 12 (1976): 233–36.
32. M. Armen, "O voprosakh khudozhestvennogo perevoda," *Druzhba narodov*, no. 10 (1956): 157.
33. Iurii Pokal'chuk, in *Druzhba narodov*, no. 12 (1976): 236.
34. Ginzburg, *Nad strokoi perevoda*, p. 36; emphasis added.
35. Nora Gal', *Slovo zhivoe i mertvoe*, 2d ed. (Moscow: Kniga, 1975), p. 180.

well as the shortage of such basic tools of the trade as dictionaries and other reference works. The first limitation is self-evident. Lev Ginzburg attested that as a translator of German poetry, he had benefited immensely from visits to Germany.[36] Ginzburg was lucky. Under the Brezhnev regime, a prominent Soviet translator like himself could visit *East* Germany easily enough. West Germany was another matter, while lengthy and frequent visits to the United States were practically out of the question.

Even ordinary reference works were hard to come by. Ginzburg grumbled: "We translators need help. Things are very bad in our country when it comes to dictionaries. Even Ushakov is now a rarity, to say nothing of Dal'. There are no dictionaries on sale—not only Russian-German ones, but also no Russian-Armenian, Armenian-Russian, Russian-Uzbek, etc."[37] The prerevolutionary four-volume dictionary of Dal' and the Soviet four-volume one of Ushakov are to Russian speakers roughly equivalent to Webster's in the United States. Neither is quite adequate for a professional translator. For instance, they do not include common obscenities or the many varieties of slang.[38]

Over the years, the line separating translations (especially free translations and adaptations) from original writing became increasingly blurred in the USSR. This situation was analogous to the one prevailing in eighteenth-century Europe, where translated plays were routinely misrepresented as original works. Prosper Mérimée's *La Guzla, ou Choix de Poésies Illiriques, recueillés dans la Dalmatie, la Bosnie, la Croatie et l'Herzégovine* so captivated Alexander Pushkin that he translated it into Russian.[39] Millions of Russian readers are oblivious of the fact that a famous work by their national poet, *Pesni zapadnykh slavian (Songs of the Western Slavs)*, is merely the translation of Mérimée's literary mystification, akin to the writings of Russia's own Koz'ma Prutkov."

A similarly disdainful attitude toward literary property finds expression in Feliks Roziner's novel *Nekto Finkel'maer (A Certain Finkelmaer)*, published in Russian in London in 1981. Here a master translator encourages

---

36. Ginzburg, *Nad strokoi perevoda*, p. 22.
37. Lev Ginzburg, in *Druzhba narodov*, no. 12 (1976): 228.
38. *Beyond the Confines of Russian Dictionaries*, published in England in 1973, attempted, not very successfully, to fill the dictionary gap (A. Flegon, *Za predelami russkikh slovarei* [London, Flegon Press, 1973]). The émigré linguist Kirill Uspensky at the time of his death was working at Harvard on a multivolume dictionary of unconventional Russian.
39. Levyi, *Iskusstvo perevoda*, p. 105.

his young disciple to misrepresent his blatantly un-Soviet original poetry as the translation of a Siberian tribesman's verse:

> Your [Siberian aborigine] Manikin is providing you with a splendid opportunity. Neither you, Finkel'maer, nor anybody else for that matter, could get this poetry published, try as you may. They [Soviet editors and publishers] would tell you that these poems are isolated from reality, from society, that they are filled with philosophical heresy, with religious overtones, and moreover, are lacking in any ties to the Russian poetic tradition as well as to the innovationist spirit of Soviet verse. Any editor will tell you that. Fortunately, newly discovered poets of the ethnic minorities are judged by other criteria. We [in the USSR] encourage the cultures of small ethnic groups and will spare no effort to demonstrate that fact. Hence— long live the [Siberian] poet Danil Manikin![40]

However, Finkel'maer's original poetry will not solve his financial problems, even if published ostensibly as a translation. He will still have to earn his living as before. The master translator continues:

> One cannot, to begin with, live on one's income from the writing of verse. Therefore, one must prostitute oneself—honorably, if at all possible. And it is translation that is considered the most honorable kind of literary prostitution. At the very least, one can try to avoid commissions to translate all types of propaganda doggerel. Still, translation is hard work, and if one engages in it all the time, draining work at that. It happens that one completely loses the ability to write original verse.

The conclusion is partly logical as well as unexpected:

> Isn't it simpler, then, to prostitute oneself openly? I mean writing, with some degree of sincerity, whatever is politically required at that particular time? I mean writing about construction sites, about industry, tractors, about our homeland, and pretty little birch trees,

---

40. Feliks Roziner, *Nekto Finkel'maer, Roman* (London: Overseas Publications Exchange, 1981), p. 122.

and workers' calloused hands, and memories of our hallowed past, about our daily labor tasks, and our pursuit of glory.[41]

The influence of translations on a nation's literature can be discerned most readily in the new works produced in a target language, indeed on the language itself. To be sure, Soviet school curricula usually differentiated between domestic and imported writings, subdividing them further by date and by genre. That policy was doubtless prompted by considerations of a pedagogical nature, or even by patriotic sentiments. However, outside the educational establishment such distinctions mean very little. Once published, translations enter the bloodstream of the host nation's literature, culture, and ultimately society itself, leaving their imprint on everyone. As Martin Luther grumbled in 1530: "It is clear for all to see that they [the Roman Catholics] are learning how to speak and write German from my translation [of the Bible] and my German; they are taking my language away from me, and they knew little about it before."[42] Luther's observation was reiterated in a more positive sense three centuries later by Wilhelm von Humboldt. This illustrious German statesman and man of letters wrote in 1816 in the introduction to his translation of Aeschylus's *Agamemnon* that "by translating we increase the effectiveness and the expressive capacities *of our own language.*"[43]

The fact that literary translations help reshape the totality of the host nation's culture has long been known. Cicero was aware of the fact over two thousand years ago.[44] Countless readers owe to translations (and more recently, to foreign films) much of their information (and misinformation) about life outside their own country. Renderings of foreign writing have helped set in motion important processes in the life of nations. Thus F. O. Mathiessen may have exaggerated only slightly when he claimed:

> A study of Elizabethan translation is a study of the means by which the Renaissance came to England. The nation had grown conscious of its cultural inferiority to the Continent, and suddenly burned with the desire to excel its rivals in letters, as well as in ships and

---

41. Ibid., p. 287.
42. Lefevere, *Translating Literature*, p. 8.
43. Cited by Joseph Tusiani, "The Translating of Poetry," *Thought* 38 (August, 1963): 389–90; emphasis added.
44. L. G. Kelly, *The True Interpreter: A History of Translation Theory and Practice in the West* (New York: St. Martin's Press, 1979), p. 213.

gold. The translator's work was an act of patriotism. He, too, as well as the voyager and merchant, could do some good for his country: he believed that foreign books were just as important for England's destiny as the discoveries of her seamen, and he brought them into his native speech with all the enthusiasm of a conquest. And when you set his result beside the original, you find out a great deal about the Elizabethan mind.[45]

Readers do not ordinarily differentiate between original and translated writing. In that respect they bear out the sentiments of eighteenth-century commentators like Lessing in Germany or his contemporary Vasily Tred'iakovsky in Russia, who insisted that the translator is the equal of the author of the original. Lessing drew attention to the translator's responsibility for shaping the canon of world literature, and also warned against the damage that a bad rendition can cause.[46] A similar point was made more recently by Horst Frenz, who concluded that Sir Thomas Urquhart's unfortunate rendering of Rabelais in "a difficult seventeenth-century style" had "helped to obscure the real Rabelais." Frenz also charged Urquhart with "implying erotic undertones where there were none in the original." His conclusion was that Urquhart's translation was responsible for making Rabelais the object of a narrow cult in the English-speaking world, rather than a writer of mass appeal.[47]

On the other hand, a classic example of a very successful translation is the Schlegel-Tieck German rendition of Shakespeare. A. W. Schlegel alone translated seventeen Shakespearean plays (published between 1797 and 1810); the rest were done by Count von Bandissin and Dorothea Tieck with the assistance of her father, the well-known romantic writer Ludwig Tieck. Their translation preserved Shakespeare's own mixture of prose and verse elements and his shifts between rhetorical and conversational prose. In consequence, "the Schlegel-Tieck version transformed Shakespeare into a German classic poet who was read, played, and quoted as widely as the German masters themselves."[48] This German Shakespeare was not an

---

45. F. O. Matthiesen, *Translation: An Elizabethan Art* (Cambridge, Mass.: Harvard University Press, 1931), p. 3.
46. Gotthold Ephraim Lessing's pronouncement is cited in Lefevere, *Translating Literature*, p. 27. On Tred'iakovskii, see above, Chapter 1.
47. Newton P. Stallknecht and Horst Frenz, eds., *Comparative Literature: Method and Perspective* (Carbondale: Southern Illinois University Press, 1961), p. 80. Samuel Putnam agreed that Urquhart created "a false or grossly distorted conception of Rabelais."
48. Ibid., p. 73; emphasis added.

isolated instance of such success. The novels of Cooper, Scott, and Dickens were more popular abroad than at home. Conversely, in a number of European countries foreign writers became more popular than the homegrown variety. For example, the novels of Balzac and Zola became a byword for modern cosmopolitan fiction. Turgenev, Tolstoy, and Dostoevsky outranked native novelists even in some countries with a well-developed native literary tradition. As for writers in Scandinavian languages, Horst Frenz asserted: "Ibsen's fame in Germany and Europe had to silence the opposition at home; *and the world-wide popularity of other Scandinavians such as Strindberg, Jacobsen, Lagerlöf, Undset, Hamsun, to what else can it be attributed than to the potency of translations?*"[49]

I do not share Frenz's view that the popularity of these Scandinavian authors abroad necessarily attests to "the potency of translations." Their appeal may perhaps be ascribed to the fact that their works raised a number of social and ethical questions not yet tackled in local literatures, such as the position of women in Europe at the turn of the century, a subject treated sympathetically by Ibsen though much less so by Strindberg. The fact that most of Zola's novels appeared in Russia within months of their publication in France, and at least one, *Germinal,* actually came out in Russian translation *before* the appearance of the original, tends to support this belief.[50] Be that as it may, translations once published acquire a life of their own. Some become classics in their adopted homelands, like the King James Bible; even now one can find Americans who believe that the Bible was actually *written* in English. James Fenimore Cooper, Jack London, and Mayne Reid continue to be far more widely read in Russia and East Central Europe than in their homelands. Another example is the 1897 novel *The Gadfly* by Ethel Voynich, who is all but forgotten in her native England but famous in Russia. The book's tale of the heroes' noble revolutionary struggle against villainous clerics in nineteenth-century Italy held generations of adolescents spellbound, both in prerevolutionary and Soviet Russia. I remember Soviet visitors in New York in the late 1950s insisting on visiting Ethel Voynich, then in her nineties and living in obscurity in Greenwich Village. Scores of similar examples could readily be found. As Ezra Pound wrote in 1920: "Foreign opinion has at times been a corrective. England has never accepted the [very high] continental opinion of Byron; the right estimate lies perhaps between the two. Heine is, I have heard, better read outside Germany than

---

49. Ibid., pp. 78–79; emphasis added.
50. *Kratkaia literaturnaia entsiklopediia,* vol. 2 (1964), p. 1038.

within. The continent has never accepted the idiotic British adulation of Milton; on the other hand, the idiotic neglect of Landor has never been rectified by the continent."[51]

Translation most often has compensated for the paucity and inferior quality of domestically produced literature. In Russia and East Central Europe, where native authors have produced comparatively few good books of adventure and travel, mystery novels, thrillers, and light comedy for the theater, translation has traditionally filled this gap. It also has introduced foreign readers to new genres. Thus in the first half of the nineteenth century, French readers were treated to such literary imports as tales of the supernatural, Gothic novels, "women's novels," and (prior to 1820) popular fiction as well.[52] Between 1800 and 1850, translations into French paved the way for the eventual victory of Romanticism in France. The "new" and unorthodox alexandrine verse cultivated by the Romantics in their translations of Shakespeare, Schiller, and the Spanish playwrights bore the same innovative features as original works by French Romantic authors. Thus even Shakespeare in alexandrine guise became a "revolutionary" author in France; and translations of foreign drama became the most daring plays on the French stage. In the debate on Romanticism, translated foreign drama and prose played a crucial role even though in many cases the translators themselves worked in complete obscurity.[53] In view of the importance of Shakespeare to French literature, it is interesting to note that the French version of Plutarch by Jacques Amyot, translated into English in 1579 by Sir Thomas North, apparently provided Shakespeare with the material for several of his historical dramas: *Coriolanus, Julius Caesar,* and *Antony and Cleopatra*.[54]

The impact of translations on the shaping of German literature was probably even stronger. Acquaintance with foreign works greatly expanded the potential of German poetry. In fact, the history of translation in Germany provides a rough guide to the sequence of literary genres and artistic devices used by German writers as a whole.[55] As for non-European

---

51. Ezra Pound, *Investigation of Ezra Pound, together with An Essay on the Chinese Written Character, by Ernest Fenollosa* (New York: Boni & Liveright, 1920), p. 5.

52. Theo Hermans, ed., *The Manipulation of Literature: Studies in Literary Translation* (London: Croom Helm, 1985), p. 159.

53. Ibid., pp. 153–54 and 162.

54. Theodore Savory, *The Art of Translation* (London: Jonathan Cape, 1957), p. 39.

55. "Eine Geschichte der Übersetzung könnte durchaus einmal als der Abriss einer Formengeschichte der deutschen Literatur selbst betrachten werden" (Ralph-Rainer Wuthenow, *Das fremde Kunstwerk: Aspekte der literarischen Übersetzung* [Göttingen: Vandenhoeck & Ruprecht, 1969], p. 7).

literary traditions, the imprint of translations has plainly been decisive. In Japan, according to one American translator of Japanese verse, "the whole modern poetry world has begun through translations from the West."[56]

An interesting dialectic may be observed in the long-range global impact of literary translation. While promoting greater diversity in the form and content of the various national literatures, these same translations willy-nilly have contributed to an erosion of their individual uniqueness. The result is a literary *Gleichschaltung*. This is because translations tend to encourage worldwide dissemination of the dominant styles of writing. As Jiří Levý noted, "From the vantage point of *world literature*, they play the role of a unifying factor, an *infectious* factor." At the same time, since several translations of the same literary work may exist in a single language, translation promotes *both* unity and diversity.[57]

The role that translation has played in the literary process of the many nations of the former Soviet Union conforms in part to the patterns made familiar outside its frontiers. Particularly in the case of peoples with relatively recent traditions of written literature, the effect of translations has been enormous. This holds true even for a land like Uzbekistan, with its ancient legacy of Islamic culture that any foreign tourist may observe in the architecture of the centuries-old cities of Bokhara and Samarkand. Owing to translations from foreign literatures, Uzbek writers began to work in nontraditional genres such as the novel, civic and political poetry, lyric verse, and drama. Foreign plays in translation also influenced the development of the Uzbek theater. According to Rano Faizullaeva, "translating was a school that trained [Uzbek writers] to become first-rate writers" in their own right.[58]

To be sure, great novels and important ones are often not the same thing. *Moby Dick* and *Anna Karenina* are great; but *Uncle Tom's Cabin* (1852) and Chernyshevsky's clumsy didactic radical tract *What Is To Be Done?* (1863) have been far more influential. The same is true of translations. While most of Russia's artistically impressive renderings of foreign writing

---

56. Harold P. Wright, cited in Allen Tate, *The Translation of Poetry* (Washington, D.C.: The Gertrude Clarke Whittall Poetry and Literature Fund, 1972), p. 28.
57. Levyi, *Iskusstvo perevoda*, pp. 234–35; original emphasis.
58. Rano Faizullaeva, *Natsional'nyi kolorit i khudozhestvennyi perevod* (Tashkent: Izdatel'stvo "FAN," 1979), pp. 3–4. For information on the impact of translations on Kirgiz literature, see K. Dzhideeva, *Poeticheskii perevod i istoriko-literaturnyi protsess: Iz istorii poeticheskogo perevoda russkoi klassiki v Kirgizii* (Frunze: Kyrgyzstan, 1980), p. 113; also S. Eraliev, in *Voprosy literatury*, no. 5 (1979): 35.

were produced in the nineteenth and twentieth centuries, in my view the most *important* period in Russian literary translation was the eighteenth century. V. M. Zhirmunsky, one of modern Russia's leading scholars, correctly observed that translations and other literary imports are of particular significance in overcoming cultural backwardness.[59]

Russia's backwardness on many levels, the result of centuries of isolation from the rest of Europe, had to be overcome quickly if the country was to survive and prosper. This was the object of Peter the Great's reforms. In the field of literature, translations were more numerous than original works in the eighteenth century. Admittedly, most of the so-called translations were adaptations, sometimes described as "adaptations to conform to our customs." But owing in part to these free renditions, as Vladimir Rossel's noted, "new genres sprang up on Russian soil, the language was honed, and artistic devices perfected. . . . By the beginning of the nineteenth century, translated literature had become an organic part of Russia's original writing."[60]

Vissarion Belinsky wrote in 1835 that the educated elite in Russia "demands [books] that are intelligent and graceful. Finding neither in domestic books, *it reads foreign books alone.*"[61] Many of the elite could read such books in the original language, particularly French or German. At that time, and until the Bolshevik Revolution of 1917, Russia was a major importer of books from Western Europe, though the imports were quite expensive. However, many Russians of the emerging middle class did not know foreign languages at all, or not well enough to read the originals. Therefore, as Belinsky pointed out, literary translations offered educational advantages as well as aesthetic enjoyment:

> They develop artistic taste and disseminate true notions of beauty. Whoever reads and understands a single word by Walter Scott or [James Fenimore] Cooper will be in a position to see the real worth of, say, [such trash as] *Dimitrii Samozvanets* ["False Demetrius"] or *Black Woman*. . . . Besides, translations are indispensable for the formation of our language, which so far is not fully established.[62]

59. V. M. Zhirmunskii, *Gete v russkoi literature* (Leningrad: Nauka, 1981), p. 12.
60. Vl. M. Rossel's, *Skol'ko vesit slovo: Stat'i raznykh let* (Moscow: Sovetskii pisatel', 1984), p. 11.
61. *Perevod—sredstvo vzaimnogo sblizheniia narodov: Khudozhestvennaia publitsistika* (Moscow: Progress, 1987), p. 38; emphasis added.
62. Ibid.

While Belinsky valued foreign books as aesthetically more satisfying than the domestic product, the radical critic N. G. Chernyshevsky preferred them for ideological reasons:

> Objectively speaking, there is no escaping the conclusion that prior to Pushkin [who died in 1837] *the only part of Russian literature that could lay legitimate claim to the title of true provider of ideas to Russian thought was the literary translations.*[63]

This "imported literary legacy" played an important role in Russian literary and ideological battles, as Zhirmunsky pointed out, citing the examples of Samuel Richardson's *Clarissa*, Rousseau's *La Nouvelle Heloise*, Goethe's *Werther*, and the enormous impact of Byron.[64] Indeed, in the 1790s there were more than a few Russian imitations of *Werther*.[65] Nonetheless, I tend to agree with Valery Briusov, who emphasized in the introduction to his 1924 translation of Poe's collected works that "foreign authors influence literature in a real sense through translations alone."[66] Thus it was not the original *Hamlet*, but its translations that gave birth to Russian Hamletism and inspired such works as Turgenev's *Hamlet of the Shchigrov District* and the now forgotten *Hamlets, Two for a Penny* by the Populist writer Iakov Abramov.[67]

Translations enrich the literature of the target language "with new elements which will subsequently become familiar" in that literature, as Chukovsky and Fedorov wrote in 1930.[68] Here they made another important point. While agreeing that "the value of a translation may be correctly gauged only *if viewed from the vantage point of a reader unfamiliar with the original*," they insisted that *only a person who can read the original can do the judging*. This is very different from the self-serving position of those translators who cling to the view that persons able to read the original have

---

63. Zhirmunskii, *Gete v russkoi literature*, p. 13; emphasis added.
64. Ibid., pp. 10–11.
65. Ibid., p. 49.
66. Edgar Po, *Polnoe sobranie poem i stikhotvorenii, perevod i predislovie Valeriia Briusova* (Moscow & Leningrad: GIZ, 1924), p. 7; cited in Iu. D. Levin, "Ob istoricheskoi evoliutsii printsipov perevoda (K istorii perevodcheskoi mysli v Rossii)," in *Mezhdunarodnye sviazi russkoi literatury*, ed. M. P. Alekseev (Moscow and Leningrad: Akademiia Nauk SSSR, 1963), p. 56.
67. *Khudozhestvennyi perevod: Voprosy teorii i praktiki* (Erevan: Izdatel'stvo Erevanskogo universiteta, 1982), p. 30.
68. Kornei Chukovskii and Andrei Fedorov, *Iskusstvo perevoda* (Leningrad: Academia, 1930), p. 225.

no business evaluating renditions that were not written *with them in mind*.[69]

Some of the ways in which translations have enriched Russian literature can be pinpointed with considerable precision. For example, Zhukovsky's renditions of Schiller undoubtedly did much to strengthen the position of the ballad as a literary form.[70] A. Kh. Vostokov's rendering of Goethe's *Iphigenie* in 1812 "represented the first attempt at introducing into Russian verse the five-foot iambic, the so-called blank verse of drama. This meter was used later by Pushkin in *Boris Godunov* and the 'little tragedies.' "[71] Symbolist translations enriched Russian verse with hitherto unknown forms. Thus Alexander Blok's renderings of Heine introduced the *dol'nik*, a type of accentual verse that previously had been found most often in folk poetry.[72] Kornei Chukovsky's translations of Walt Whitman are credited with paving the way for Russian Futurism.[73] As Lev Ginzburg summarized the situation: "Thanks to translations, Russian poetry of the eighteenth and nineteenth century assimilated the hexameter, the alexandrine, the *Knittelvers* [of fifteenth- and sixteenth-century German poetry], Heinrich Heine's accentual verse, as well as the sonnet, the *rondeau*, the *terza rima*. In Soviet times, leading practitioners of translation introduced into Russian poetry such Middle Eastern poetic meters as the *rubai* and the *ghazel*."[74]

The Pushkin specialist V. V. Vinogradov pointed out that exposure to foreign literature enabled that great poet to expand the range of his stylistic choices. In addition to Russian folklore and older Russian authors, Pushkin diligently studied the style of the Bible and the Koran, as well as the artistic manner of Byron, Chenier, Horace, Ovid, Wordsworth, Shakespeare, Musset, Béranger, Dante, Petrarch, Hafiz, and other authors. Vinogradov did not specify which of these the poet read in the original and which in translation (Pushkin knew no Hebrew, Arabic, or Persian). According to another expert, B. V. Tomashevsky, Pushkin's own translations from the French actually had as their specific purpose "not precise reproduction of

---

69. Ibid., p. 227, emphasis added.

70. A. A. Mishustina, in *Teoriia i praktyka perekladu*, no. 1 (1979): pp. 66–67.

71. Zhirmunskii, *Gete v russkoi literature*, pp. 97–98. Pushkin himself mistakenly thought that the meter was first used by the poet Küchelbecker. He had overlooked not only Vostokov, but also its more recent use by Zhukovskii in his rendering of Schiller's *Die Jungfrau von Orleans*.

72. German Ritz, *150 Jahre russischer Heine-Übersetzung* (Bern, Frankfurt am Main, and Las Vegas: Peter Lang, 1981), pp. 13–14.

73. Mishustina, in *Teoriia i praktyka perekladu*, pp. 66–67.

74. Ginzburg, *Nad strokoi perevoda*, p. 6.

the original, but enrichment of Russian verse with [poetic] forms which existed in the alien tongue."[75] Yuri Levin added, "This observation is applicable *to all of Pushkin's translations and adaptations.*"[76] Pushkin made use of formal borrowings in original works with foreign settings, such as *A Scene from Faust, Egyptian Nights,* and *Maria Schoning,* as well as his "little tragedies" (such as *Mozart and Salieri* and *A Stone Guest*) and the poem "The Pilgrim" (*Strannik*), which was inspired by John Bunyan's *Pilgrim's Progress.*[77] He even misrepresented another "little tragedy," *The Covetous Knight* (*Skupoi rytsar'*), as a translation from a nonexistent foreign author named Chanston![78]

Literary translations contributed even to Russia's musical repertory. No fewer than five Russian composers (Nikolai Rimsky-Korsakov, Peter Tchaikovsky, César Cui, M. A. Balakirev, and A. K. Liadov) wrote musical scores to poems by Heinrich Heine, as translated by Mikhailov.[79] Finally, the study of literary translation gave birth to two subfields of literary scholarship in Russia: comparative stylistics and comparative poetics.[80]

In sum: literary translation in eighteenth-century Russia established bridges to Western European writing, thus ensuring that the country's emerging secular literature and culture would have a Western orientation. The rapid expansion of translating activity in the century that followed was inseparable from the expanding volume and growing aesthetic sophistication of Russia's own writing. Impressive strides in combating illiteracy brought both domestic and translated Western foreign literary production to new audiences of lower-class and even peasant readers.[81] The Communist coup d'état of November 1917, with its slogan "Workers of the world, unite!" and the "Internationale" as its anthem, at first viewed literary translation favorably. Translation was regarded as bringing to the masses the cultural legacy of all nations, and as contributing to a sense of kinship

---

75. Levin, *Russkie perevodchiki,* pp. 21–22.
76. Ibid.; emphasis added.
77. Ibid., pp. 22–23.
78. *Rannie romanticheskie veianiia: Iz istorii mezhdunarodnykh sviazei russkoi literatury* (Leningrad: Nauka, 1972), pp. 242–43. *The Covetous Knight,* therefore, belongs to the same "reverse-plagiaristic" works of Pushkin's as his original verse falsely attributed to the French poet Parny.
79. Levin, *Russkie perevodchiki,* p. 200.
80. Levyi, *Iskusstvo perevoda,* p. 6. E. G. Etkind's *Poeziia i perevod* is a classic work of comparative stylistics.
81. For a fascinating account of the expansion of literacy in Russia see Jeffrey Brooks, *When Russia Learned to Read* (Princeton: Princeton University Press, 1985).

with workers and peasants of other lands. The mammoth *World Literature* project, inaugurated while the Civil War still raged, is a case in point.

A gradual reversal of this attitude began with Stalin's accession to power in the late 1920s. The Trotskyite call for world revolution was supplanted with Stalin's slogan of "socialism in one country"; and isolationist moods grew steadily stronger. In the early 1930s the volume and variety of literary translation fell off sharply. After a temporary upsurge during World War II, this decline was resumed following the Soviet victory. Stalin's last years were marked by a pathological xenophobia and a massive witch hunt against everyone, Jews in particular, who allegedly denigrated Russian achievements while simultaneously "kowtowing to the West." Not surprisingly, these moods resulted in considerable damage to the enterprise of literary translation. The repercussions of the anti-foreign campaign transcended cultural affairs. Travel to and from the Soviet Union ground to an almost complete halt. Postal contacts with friends and relatives abroad became suspect. Condemnation of things Western became virtually obligatory. This state of affairs even prompted an American student of the Soviet Union to inquire, in a 1950 issue of *Foreign Affairs,* whether the Soviet Union intended to withdraw from world civilization altogether.[82]

It did not, though it might have tried if Stalin had lived longer. In retrospect, it seems obvious that during the dictator's declining years (he died in 1953), translations of Western writing and Russia's own legacy of nineteenth-century literature constituted one of the Soviet Union's very few repositories of non-Stalinist values. Pushkin and Chekhov, Balzac and Flaubert, Mark Twain and O. Henry, Dostoevsky, Turgenev and Tolstoy, Goethe and Schiller and Thomas Mann helped ordinary Soviet citizens to withstand the propagandistic onslaughts of Soviet Socialist Realism. Books by non-Soviet (Russian or foreign) authors refuted the totalitarian morality contained in the strictly conformist Soviet writing. In Soviet novels, poems, and plays, personal considerations were *always* to be subordinated to the Soviet cause (and unlike in the old Neoclassical writing, enthusiastically so!). Any action, however cruel or immoral, was cheerfully justified by the needs of the Soviet state. Obedience to the Communist leaders was to be both devoted and absolute. Translated works as well as the Russian classics (implicitly, and at times explicitly), condemned such views.

---

82. W. W. Kulski, "Can Russia Withdraw from Civilization?" *Foreign Affairs,* July 1950, pp. 623–43.

Prerevolutionary Russian books and transplanted Western European and American writing enabled Soviet citizens to continue professing, if only secretly, those human values that bind together the heirs of the Judeo-Christian tradition. For that reason the literary translation of the Stalin era, next to that of the eighteenth century, may well have been Russia's most important work of translation to date.

Index

Ablancourt, Pierre d', 81
Abramov, Fyodor, 34n.41
Abramov, Iakov, 206
Académie Française, 46
Academy of Science, Russian, 30
actors, acting, 69, 74, 78, 102, 107–8, 163–64, 168, 181
Adamovich, Georgy, 137
adaptation, 20, 24, 29, 32, 43, 49, 51, 85, 86, 114, 144, 198, 205. *See also* free translation
Ado, Uluro, 183–84
Aeneid, 25, 63, 93, 96, 136, 146
Aeschylus, 44, 200
  Agamemnon, 55, 159, 200
Aesop, 34
Aimatov, Chingiz, 5
Akhmadulina, Bella, 182
Akhmatova, Anna, 7, 60, 79, 114, 116, 135, 163, 178, 193, 194

Aksenov, I. A., 136
Alba, Victor, 196
Aleichem, Sholom, 114
Alekseev, M. P., 88, 89, 108, 111, 113
Alexander I, Tsar, 23
Alice in Wonderland, 41, 42, 43–44, 86, 124–25, 131, 152, 154
American literature
  translations, 3, 4, 5, 10, 14, 24, 45, 55, 65–66, 103, 129–30, 139–40, 145, 147, 155–58, 171, 188, 197, 210
  translators, 84, 101, 116, 117, 178–79, 189, 190, 204
Amfiteatrov, A. V., 48
Amyot, Jacques, 46, 203
Anacreon, 50–51
Ananiashvili, Elizbar, 176, 182, 195
Andersen, Hans Christian, 1, 14n.35
Anderson, Sherwood, 56
Angry Young Men, 18

Annensky, Innokenty, 64, 65
anti-Semitism, 83, 183. *See also* Jews
Antokol'sky, Pavel, 102
Apukhtin, Aleksei, 60
Arabic translation, 24, 82, 207
Aristotle, 24
Armenian translation, 9, 20–21, 167, 172–73, 176, 182, 187, 198
Arnold, Matthew, 94
Asim, Mirkarim, 174
Association for the Advancement of Translation, 34
Astaf'ev, V. P., 131
Aue, Hartmann von, 121
Auezov, Mukhtar, 177, 185
Avar translation, 173, 183
Azeri translation, 168, 180

Babel (journal), 4
Babel, Isaak, 89n.58, 114, 128, 157
Balakirev, M. A., 208
Baldwin, James, 140
Balkar language, 183
Bal'mont, Konstantin, 65–66
Baltic republics, 185
Balzac, Honoré de, 62, 97, 202, 209
  Eugénie Grandet, 35, 38
Bandissin, Count von, 201
Baratashvili, N. M., 150
Baratynsky, E. A., 37, 147
Barbier, A. A., 55
Barkhudarov, Leonid (L. S.), 96–97, 133
Barrett-Browning, Elizabeth, 55
Batiushkov, K. N., 37, 147
Baudelaire, Charles-Pierre, 36, 53, 64, 136, 194
Bazhan, Mykola, 15
Beaugrande, Robert de, 125
Bel'ger, Herold, 175, 176–77, 180–81
Belarus. *See* Belorussian
Belinsky, Vissarion, 38, 39, 40, 41, 44, 46, 49, 51, 52, 59–60, 63, 76, 90–91, 92–93, 94, 99, 130, 140–41, 205–6
"belles infidèles," 81
Bellow, Saul, 139, 157, 188
Belorussian
  language, 20, 158, 168
  translation, 101, 113, 125, 159, 168, 169n.176
Belov, V. I., 131

Ben, George, 120n.27
Benét, Stephen Vincent, 155, 156
Benjamin, Walter, 77, 83
Bentley, Eric, 120
Beowulf, 9
Béranger, Pierre-Jean de, 38, 144, 207
Berg, Nikolai, 38, 59, 60
Berne Convention, 188
Bestuzhev-Marlinsky, A. A., 37
Betaki, Vasily, 120
Bible
  Church Slavonic, 22, 23
  English, 21–22, 23, 34, 202
  German, 21, 25, 75, 82, 200
  Hebrew, 19, 81n.34, 82
  literary references to, 131, 144–45, 145nn.107–8, 157, 207
  Russian, 22–24
  translation of, 8, 16, 19, 21–23, 25, 34, 75, 81n.34, 82, 200
Bible Society, 23, 24
bibliography, bibliographers, 14, 62, 190
bilingualism, 93, 94n.73, 107, 180
Blake, William, 114, 196
Blok, Alexander, 6, 97, 207
Boccaccio, 93, 161
Bodmer, Johann Jakob, 74
Bogdanovich, Ippolit F., 34, 161
Bolshevik (Communist) Revolution (coup d'état), 3, 111, 137, 146, 155, 191, 205, 208
Borowy, Wacław, 46
Boy-Żeleński, Tadeusz, 98–99
Brandl, Alois, 11
Brezhnev, Leonid, 183, 185, 198
Briusov, Valery, 55, 57, 63–64, 65, 89n.58, 136, 146, 166n.167, 206
Brontë, Charlotte, 45, 51
Brower, Reuben A., 159
Brown, Clarence, 115
Brown, Edward J., 154
Browning, Robert, 44
Buber, Martin, 83
Buddha, 20
Bulgarian
  empire, 20
  language, 20n., 22
  translation, 94n.73, 124, 193
Bunin, Ivan, 53, 132, 133, 155
Bunyan, John, 208

Burenin, Viktor, 61
Bürger, Gottfried August, 41, 42, 43
Burns, Robert, 55, 114, 128
Burnshaw, Stanley, 88
Byron, Lord George Gordon, 13, 37, 39, 41, 49, 50, 52, 54, 56, 59, 61, 114, 115, 136, 138, 196, 202, 206, 207
  "The Chain I Gave," 133
  Don Juan, 55, 136, 192
  The Prisoner of Chillon, 40, 42, 44

Calderón de la Barca, Pedro, 37
calques, 3, 30, 63, 95
Camus, Albert, 13, 139
Canada, translation in, 190
Capote, Truman, 139
Carroll, Lewis, 86, 152. See also *Alice in Wonderland*
Castiglione, Count Baldassare, 24
Catholicism, Roman, 24, 93, 200
Catullus, Gaius, 19
Caucasus, languages of, 118, 175, 183, 184
censorship
  Soviet, 7, 13, 16, 33, 42, 79, 105, 136, 139–40, 148, 168, 181
  tsarist (Imperial Russian), 13, 34, 35, 49, 62, 140–43
Central Asia, languages of, 118, 175. See also specific languages
Čermak, Josef, 79–80
Cervantes Saavedra, Miguel de, 42–43, 122. See also *Don Quixote*
Chamisso, Adelbert, 50, 55
Charles V, Holy Roman Emperor, 3n.2
Chateaubriand, F. R., 36, 37, 90
Chaucer, Geoffrey, 26, 103
Chekhov, Anton, 1, 2, 103, 123, 131, 160, 209
Chenier, André, 207
Chernyshevsky, Nikolai (N. G.), 2, 39, 50, 50n.99, 51, 143, 143n.101, 204, 206
Chesterton, G. K., 103
children's literature, 2, 34, 86, 114
Chinese translation, 168, 173
Christianity, conversion to, 20, 22
Chukovskaia, Lidiia, 135, 193
Chukovsky, Kornei, 42, 46, 47–48, 51–52, 62, 65–66, 71, 71n.6, 72, 73–74, 95, 98, 110–11, 113, 117, 128, 130, 132, 143n.101, 156, 196, 206–7
Chukovsky, Nikolai, 117
Chulkov, Mikhail, 31, 33
Church Slavonic, 20, 20n., 22–23, 22n., 28, 172
Churchill, Winston, 122–23
Chuvash language, 173
Cicero, 3, 8, 19, 45, 122–23, 200
Civil War, 4, 139, 209
classicism. See Neoclassicism
classics, Greek and Roman (Latin), 24, 30, 32, 36, 85, 96
Cohen, J. M., 163n.153
Coleridge, Samuel Taylor, 99
collective translation, 50, 111, 137–38, 138n.87, 144n.105
Collins, Wilkie, 14,n.35
comedy, 2, 29, 35, 55, 56, 61, 158, 203
commedia dell'arte, 162
Communism, Communists, 7, 16, 33, 83, 103, 104–5, 106, 111, 112, 113, 139, 182, 188, 209. See also Bolshevik Revolution
  Party, 17, 33, 104, 114, 116, 174
comparative method, 72, 120, 125, 127–28, 208
Conrad, Joseph, 36n.49
Contemporary (journal), 143
Cooper, James Fenimore, 1, 45, 202, 205
Coppola, Francis Ford, 145
Corneille, Pierre, 25–26
Corrigan, Robert W., 163
"cosmopolitans," 83–84
courtly love, 3
Cowley, Abraham, 24
Crabbe, George, 51, 55
cribs (trots, ponies), interlinear, 54, 78, 92, 100n.90, 101, 114, 115, 116, 149–50, 172–81, 183
critics, criticism, literary, 38, 39, 46, 50, 51, 59, 109, 116–18, 124, 151, 157, 189, 193, 196
Croce, Benedetto, 7, 70
Cui, César, 208
Cyprian. See Kiprian
Cyril (missionary), 20
Czech
  language, 10, 73, 132, 168
  translation, 115, 134, 171, 173

Dacier, Madame, 26, 72
Dal' (Dahl), Vladimir, 64, 159, 198
Daniels, Guy, 101, 179
Danish language, 10, 168
Dante Alighieri, 2, 55, 93, 108, 207
Decembrists, 49
Defoe, Daniel, 137
Del'vig, A. A., 37
Demurova, N. M., 125
Denham, John, 25,
Derzhavin, G. R., 34, 37, 126
dialects, 131, 156, 158, 161–62, 165
Dickens, Charles, 12, 13, 17, 45, 47–48, 61–62, 96, 136–37, 159, 202
  David Copperfield, 45, 46, 47–48, 13
  Dombey and Son, 45, 46, 150
  The Pickwick Papers, 45, 48, 61, 62n.125, 136–37
Dickinson, Emily, 192
dictionaries, 20, 161, 198
Dillon, Wenworth. *See* Roscommon
Dmitrenko, V. A., 127
Dmitriev, I. I., 161
Dmitriev, Valentin, 144n.105
Dobroliubov, N. A., 39
Don Quixote, 1, 42–43, 90, 96, 122, 160, 161
Dos Passos, John, 114, 192
Dostoevsky, Fedor, 12, 13, 17, 35, 38, 61, 89n.58, 160, 172, 191, 202, 209
  The Brothers Karamazov, 160, 172
Dovlatov, Sergei, 174
Doyle, Arthur Conan, 14n.35
drama, translation of, 3, 19, 30, 56, 61, 76, 163–64, 203, 204, 207
Dreiser, Theodore, 17
Druskin, Lev, 182–83
Druzhinin, Alexander, 51–52, 55, 143, 143n.101, 148
Dryden, John, 26, 74, 93, 94, 101
Dumas, Alexandre, 14n.35, 55
Dzhideeva, Klara, 184

Eastman, Max, 138n.87
Egyptian language, 116
Elagin, Ivan, 147, 155–56
elitism, 54, 70, 76, 78, 92, 152
émigrés, Soviet, 6, 60, 136, 137, 139, 147, 154–55, 174, 193
England, travel to, 45, 50

English
  language, 131–33, 155, 156–57, 158
  translation, 99, 101, 107, 120, 122, 130, 177–80, 189; from French, 107, 169, 203; from German, 66, 169; from Greek, 36, 44, 66, 94, 188; from Latin, 36, 188; from Japanese, 178, 204; from Russian, 6, 12, 101, 123, 130, 178; from Spanish, 122. *See also specific authors*
"ennoblement" of texts, 42–43
Estonian language, 113
Etkind, Efim (E. G.), 60–61, 72, 102, 105, 169, 192
Euclid, 99, 120, 125, 127, 128, 138
Eugene Onegin, 79, 85–86, 92, 101, 121n.32, 123, 149, 151–52, 154
Euripides, 32
Exner, Richard, 107

fables, 33–34
fairy tales, 1, 14n.35, 134
Faizullaeva, Rano, 174, 204
Fathers of the Church, 81
Faulkner, William, 157
Faust, 11, 37, 49, 53, 56–57, 58, 65, 102, 115, 174, 174n.192
Fedorov, Andrei (A. V.) 64, 72, 98, 100, 112, 121, 129, 130, 138, 196, 206
Fet, Afanasy, 37, 38, 45, 53–54, 57, 63, 85, 135, 152
fiction, translated, 2, 3, 174, 203
Fielding, Henry, 137
Filip, Metropolitan, 22
films, 2, 18, 69, 200
  translation of, 2, 69, 145–46, 167–68
Finkel', A. M., 170
Finnish language, 114
Fiterman, A., 148
Fitts, Dudley, 11, 36, 153
Flaubert, Gustave, 38, 62, 209
  Madame Bovary, 90, 161
Flemish language, 10
Florian, 43
folk literature
  folklore, 59, 106, 174
  poetry, 129, 207
  songs, 78, 197
Fonvisin, D. I., 34
Formalism, Formalists, 5, 16, 83, 113

Fosty, Vera, 130–31
France, Anatole, 136
France, travel to, 45, 50
Frankfurt school, 83
Frankovsky, Adrian, 79, 87, 137
Fraser, G. S., 154
free translation, 16, 26, 35, 37, 40, 43, 47, 49, 51, 53, 58, 60, 72, 74, 76–81, 84, 85, 87, 88, 90, 92, 93, 95, 100–102, 105, 107–8, 110, 113, 115, 123, 126, 137, 147, 150, 152, 154, 181, 198
Freiligrath, Ferdinand, 55
French
  language, 3n.2, 21, 98, 121, 128, 129, 131–32, 134, 136, 136n.82, 205
  translation, 2, 36, 37, 53, 61, 64, 75, 81, 97–98, 99, 118, 129, 158, 175; from English, 36, 36n.49, 37, 64, 70, 90, 121, 188, 203; from German, 11, 13, 64; from Greek, 75, 96, 98–99; from Latin, 36n.49, 70, 96; from Russian, 6, 66, 127, 131; from Spanish, 203
Frenz, Horst, 201–2
Friedberg, Maurice, 121n.32
  A Bilingual Collection, 89n.58
  A Decade of Euphoria, 15
  Russian Classics in Soviet Jackets, 15, 33
  review of Nabokov's *Eugene Onegin*, 121n.32
Frost, Robert, 8, 103
Futurism, 17, 207

Gachechiladze, Givi, 105, 106
Gal', Nora, 130, 145, 145n.108, 162, 197
Galsworthy, John, 157
Gamzatov, Rasul, 183
Garnett, Constance, 178
Garshin, Vsevolod, 89n.58
Gasparov, M. L., 146
Gédoyn, Abbé, 24
gender, grammatical, 134–36
Georgian
  language, 167
  translation, 20, 115, 150, 176, 182, 193, 197
Gerbel', Nikolai, 49–50
German language, 3, 3n.2, 121, 134, 136n.82, 205

German
  language, 134
  translation, 21, 154, 165, 169, 175, 203; from English, 11, 21, 27, 66, 69, 76–77, 99, 109, 116, 164; from French, 70, 190; from Greek, 75, 76–77, 98–99; from Russian, 39; from Uzbek, 174; from Yiddish, 169
Ghose, Zulfikar, 9
Gide, André, 36n.49, 116, 139
Ginzburg, Lev, 6, 10, 12, 90, 114, 121, 123, 172–73, 196, 197, 198, 207
Gippius, Zinaida, 135
glasnost', 7, 17, 136
Glatstein, Jacob, 180
Glück, Ernst, 23
Gnedich, Nikolai (N. I.), 41, 49, 51, 52, 53, 124, 143
Gnedich, Tat'iana, 192
Goethe, Johann Wolfgang von, 30, 37, 38, 41, 50, 55, 56–60, 64, 75–76, 80, 102, 115, 130, 138, 147, 149, 191, 207, 209
  "The Bride of Corinth," 59
  Clavigo, 30
  Faust, 11, 37, 49, 53, 56–57, 58, 65, 102, 115, 174, 174n.192
  Götz von Berlichingen, 130
  Hermann und Dorothea, 11, 37
  Iphigenie, 207
  "Mignon," 14
  Werther, 130, 206
  West-östlichen Diwan, 148
Gogol, Nikolai, 12, 39, 48, 64, 91
  The Inspector General, 69, 103, 191
  "The Overcoat," 129
Gol'tsev, Viktor, 193
Goldsmith, Oliver, 41, 45, 51
Golitsyn, A. N., 23
Golitsyn, Prince Boris, 27
Golyshev, Viktor, 124, 157–58, 159–60
Gorbachev, Mikhail, 5, 17, 105, 136
Gorkina, I., 174
Gorky, Maxim, 4, 95, 165
Górnicki, Łukasz, 24
Grass, Günter, 188
Gray, Thomas, 39, 43
Grebnev, 183
Greek
  language, 3, 151

Greek *(continued)*
  translation, 10, 19, 22, 23, 24, 30, 32, 36, 54, 94
Greene, Graham, 147
Griboedov, A. S., 37, 41
  Woe from Wit, 2, 61, 131
Griftsov, Boris, 196
Grigor'ev, Apollon, 37, 38, 57
Guber, Edward, 57
Gumilev, Nikolai, 12, 137
Gutzkow, Karl, 55, 142

Hafiz, 207
Hamlet, 34, 47, 49, 51, 52, 55, 90, 99, 102, 115, 123–24, 136, 140, 150, 163, 206
Hamsun, Knut, 202
Hardy, Thomas, 70
Harte, Bret, 56, 62
Harvard Interview Project, 6
Havrysh, F., 172
Hayward, Max, 178
Hebrew
  Bible, 10, 16, 19, 22, 23, 81n.34, 82, 92, 207
  translation, 19, 22, 23, 92, 207
Heine, Heinrich, 14, 17, 42, 51, 55, 56, 64, 93, 142, 144, 196, 202, 207, 208
  "Ein Fichtenbaum steht einsam," 135
  "Die Lotesblume ängstigt," 134
Heller, Joseph, 145, 145n.107
Hemingway, Ernest, 7, 17, 103, 129, 139, 179, 179n.206
Henry, O., 209
Herder, Johann Gottfried, 43, 75
Hertz, Paweł, 37n.50
Herwegh, G., 55, 115
Herzen, Alexander, 50
hexameter verse, 19, 53, 75, 151, 207
Highet, Gilbert, 108
Hill, D. E., 88
Hindi translation, 116, 173
Hoffmann, E. T. A., 55
Holmes, J. S., 91
Homer, 10, 16, 26, 32, 54, 72, 75, 94, 108, 123
  Iliad, 26, 53, 72, 124
  Odyssey, 19, 26, 72, 148–49, 176
homonyms, interlingual, 170–71
Hood, Thomas, 52
Hora, Josef, 134

Horace, 126, 151, 207
Howard, Richard, 107, 189
Howe, Irving, 101
Hugo, Victor, 17, 73
Humboldt, Wilhelm von, 26, 80, 137, 170, 200
Hume, David, 7
Hungarian translation, 115
Huxley, Aldous, 13, 139

Iakimov, V. A., 51
Iazykov, N. M., 37, 49
Ibragimbekov, Maksud and Rustam, 180
Ibsen, Henrik, 10, 56, 173, 202
Icelandic language, 10
Il'f and Petrov, 14n.35
imitation, poetic, 29, 33, 34, 41, 44, 74, 78, 79, 87, 100–101, 127, 206. *See also* free translation
Indian languages, 92
"Internationale," 208
Ionesco, Eugene, 139
Iranian languages, 118
Italian
  language, 3, 3n.2
  translation, 36n.47, 66, 161, 164, 188
Ivanov, Georgy, 137
Ivanov, Viacheslav, 193
Ivanov, Vsevolod, 65, 89n.58

Jacobsen, Jens Peter, 202
Jakobson, Roman, 72, 95, 134, 202
Japanese translation, 168, 173, 178, 204
Jastrun, Mieczysław, 168
Jews, Judaism, 16, 17, 19, 22, 81–83, 93, 142, 157, 157n.136, 192, 209
John the Baptist, 145, 145n.108
Johnson, Samuel, 51
Josephus, Flavius, 20
Joyce, James, 13

Kafka, Franz, 13
Kalashnikova, Evgeniia, 195
Kalmyk language, 173, 174
Kan, Maria, 157n.136
Kantemir, A. D., 34
Kapnist, Count P. I., 141
Kapnist, V. V., 34, 161
Karamzin, N. M., 28, 30, 34, 161
Karatygin, V. A., 51

Index

Kashkin, Ivan, 32–33, 71, 83–84, 95, 103–5, 106, 113, 140, 148
Katenin, Pavel, 41, 86
Katkov, N. M., 51
Kaverin, Venyamin, 89n.58
Kazakh translation, 106, 168, 172, 173, 175, 176–77, 185
Keats, John, 114
Keene, Donald, 178
Kelly, L. G., 176
Ketcher, Nikolai, 55
Keupler, Henry, 164
key words (*kliuchevye*), 165
Kharitonov, Vladimir, 157–58, 159–60
Khelemsky, Ia. A., 133
Kheraskov, M. M., 34, 161
Kholodovsky, Nikolai, 57
Khrushchev, Nikita, 139
Kievan Rus', 20, 86
Kim, Anatoly, 123
kindred languages, translation of, 168–71
Kipling, Rudyard, 114, 128
Kiprian (Cyprian), 22
Kirgiz translation, 106, 184, 204n.58
Klemensiewicz, Zenon, 95
Kniazhnin, Iakov, 31, 161
Knittelverse, 57, 207
Koestler, Arthur, 139
Kopanev, P. I., 103, 105
Koptilov, Viktor (V. V.), 120, 125, 172
Koran, 207
Korean translation, 5n.5, 116, 194
Korolenko, Vladimir, 170
Kostomarov, N. I., 38
Kozlov, Pavel, 55
Krivtsova, Alexandra (A. V.), 48, 84, 136
Kroneberg, Andrei (A. I.), 51, 55
Krylov, Ivan, 33–34, 33n., 86n.49, 131
Kuchak, Naapet, 176
Küchelbecker, Wilhelm, 49, 207n.71
Kukharenko, V. A., 179n.206
Kuliev, Kaisyn, 183
Kundera, Milan, 10
Kunitz, Stanley, 178, 179
Kuprin, Alexander, 191
Kuputikian, Silva, 182
Kurilov, Gania, 183
Kurochkin, Vasily, 38, 60, 144
Kvitko-Osnov'ianenko, G. F., 170

La Fontaine, 29, 34
La Rochefoucauld, 27
Lagerlöf, Selma, 202
Landor, Walter S., 203
languages. *See also specific languages*
 age of, 121, 122
 ethnic flavor of, 162, 171
Lann, Evgeny, 48, 79, 84, 87, 136–37
Lassila, Maiju, 114
Latin. *See also* classics
 language, 3, 35
 literature in translation, 11, 19, 21, 24, 30, 45, 169
Latouche, Henri de, 36
Lavrov, P. L., 50
Lay of the Host of Igor, 9
Le Carré, John, 7
Leech, G., 72
Lefevere, André, 13, 72, 73, 88–89, 91–92, 99, 100n.90, 107, 153, 159
Leighton, Lauren, 71n.6, 106, 116, 128
Lenau, Nikolaus, 50, 55
Lenin, Vladimir: 3n.2, 138n.87, 192
Lenore, Lenora, 41, 42, 43–44, 86
Lermontov, Mikhail, 6, 37, 38, 57, 86n.49, 101, 135, 136, 147, 160, 179
Leskov, Nikolai, 89n.58, 127, 131
Lessing, Gotthold, 55, 99, 141, 201
Levik, Vil'gel'm, 133
Levin, Yuri D., 11, 15, 40, 45, 48, 56, 76, 95, 137, 143n.101, 208
Levitov, Alexander (A. I.), 48, 48n.97
Levitskaia, T. R., 130
Levý, Jiří, 14, 73, 81, 85, 106, 119, 122, 130, 162–63, 165, 171, 204
Lewis, Sinclair, 11
Liadov, A. K., 208
Libedinsky, Yuri, 182
Library for Reading, 61, 62, 62n.125
Liedloff, Helmut, 71
Likhachev, Ivan, 192
Lille, Jacques Abbé de, 98
Lipkin, Semen, 118
Lisle, Leconte de, 98–99
literalism, 5, 8, 16–17, 28, 37, 44, 47, 49, 51, 52, 53–54, 57, 63, 74, 76–93, 101, 102, 108, 110–11, 113, 119, 123, 136–37, 146, 147, 150, 152–53, 170, 181, 183, 184–86, 196
Literaturnaia gazeta, 83

Litfond, 55
liturgical language, 20, 172
Liubenov, Liuben, 124
Liubimov, Nikolai, 90, 147, 160, 162, 195, 196
Liudmila. See *Lenore*
Livius Andronicus, 19
Locke, John, 7
Lomonosov, Mikhail, 3, 3n.2, 34, 126
London, Jack, 1, 11, 69, 195, 202
Longfellow, Henry W., 36n.47, 55
  The Song of Hiawatha, 52, 132, 133
Lor'e, Maria, 129, 145, 157–58, 160
Lowell, Robert, 101
Lozinsky, Mikhail (M. L.), 55, 87–88, 102, 119, 136, 137, 163, 194
Lukin, Vladimir, 35
Lunacharsky, Anatoly, 4
Luther, Martin, 21, 75, 82, 200
  "Circular Letter," 25, 187

Machlis, Joseph, 166
Maiakovskii, Vladimir, 3n.2
Maikov, A. N., 37, 135, 161
Maimonides, 82
Maksim the Greek, 22
Malamud, Bernard, 157
Mamin-Sibiryak, Dmitri, 89n.58
Mandelshtam, Nadezhda, 114–15, 178
Mandelshtam, Osip, 79, 114–15, 116, 194
Manikin, Danil, 199
Mann, Heinrich, 174
Mann, Thomas, 209
Markish, Esther, 115n.14
Markish, Peretz, 115n.14, 194
Markish, Simon, 84
Marlowe, Christopher, 50
Marshak, Samuil, 10, 114, 124, 128, 133, 135, 138, 143–44, 196
Marxism (Marxism-Leninism), 33, 71, 73, 104, 106, 111, 113, 126, 137
Masterstvo perevoda, 117
Mathesius, Vilém, 94
Mathiessen, F. O., 200
Maupassant, Guy de, 39, 62, 160
maxims. *See* proverbs
May, Karl, 1
Mayakovsky, Vladimir, 111, 115, 192
Mei, L. A., 37, 38, 161
Melville, Hermann, 192, 204

Mérimée, Prosper, 198
Merkureva, V. D., 136
meter, poetic, 17, 50, 57, 65, 123, 125, 129, 133, 176, 178, 207n.71
Methodius, 20
Meyerhold, Vsevolod, 78, 103
Mezhelaitis, Eduardas, 126, 127
Mickiewicz, Adam, 37, 49
  Forefather's Eve, 49
  Konrad Wallenrod, 37–38, 49
Middle Ages, 24, 82
Mikhailov, Mikhail (M. L.), 38, 50–51, 50n.99, 55, 60, 134, 141, 144, 174, 208
Mikhailovsky, Dmitry, 52–53, 141
Miller, Arthur, 18, 139
Miller, Henry, 7
Miller, Orest F., 38
Milton, John, 26, 203
  Paradise Lost, 37, 49, 90
Min, Dmitry, 38, 54, 55, 60
Minaev, Dmitry, 38, 60
Mineralov, Yuri, 126–27
Minnesänger, 57, 121
minority languages (Soviet), translation of, 4–5, 28, 106, 167, 172–75, 178, 184–86, 199
Minsky, Nikolai, 124, 158–59
Mitin, Genrikh, 62
Mkrtchian, Levon, 9, 137, 176
Modernists, 146
Moiseyev ensemble, 78
Molière, 29, 123, 158–59, 195
Monomakh, Vladimir, 86
Montaigne, Michel de, 25
More, Thomas, 49
Morits, Iunna, 133, 182
Morozov, Mikhail, 150
Mounin, Georges, 25,n.14
Murav'ëv-Apostol, S. I., 49
music (in poetry), 64–65, 74, 123
music, musicians, 84, 103, 107, 113, 116, 149, 163, 166–67, 208
Musset, Alfred de, 53, 55, 207

Nabokov, Vladimir, 79, 85–86, 92, 93–94, 101, 119, 121n.32, 123, 125, 139, 147, 149, 151–55
  Alice in Wonderland (trans.), 86
  Eugene Onegin (trans.), 79, 85–86, 92, 101, 121n.32, 123, 149, 151–52, 154

Otchaianie, 93–94
Pnin, 55, 128
Naiman, Anatoly, 194
"native informants," 178
Nedelin, V., 151n.120
Nekrasov, Nikolai, 37, 38, 52, 143, 161, 170
Neoclassicism, 3, 16, 17, 26–27, 28, 32, 37, 41, 46, 75, 78, 86, 113, 116, 162
Nerval, Gérard de, 11, 36, 64
New Testament, 10, 21, 22, 23, 24
Nobel Prize, 132, 155, 180, 192
North, Thomas, 203
Northern Bee (journal), 144
Norton, Caroline, 45
Norwegian translation, 10, 116, 168, 173
Nosov, E. I., 131
Notes of the Fatherland, 61
Novalis, 21, 74
nursery rhymes, 114, 124

O'Brien, Justin, 73–74, 149, 189
Odoevsky, S. I., 49, 159
Ogarev, Nikolai, 37, 50
Old Belief, 22
Old Church Slavonic. *See* Church Slavonic
Old Slavonic. *See* Church Slavonic
Old Testament, 10, 16, 21, 22, 23, 81
Olesha, Yurii, 89n.58
opera, translation of, 54, 166–67
Oriental literature, 4
Orthodoxy, Russian, 20n, 93, 144. *See also* Bible; Church Slavonic
Orwell, George, 7, 13, 136, 139
Ostrovsky, Alexander, 39
otsebiatina (arbitrary insertions), 45, 46, 47, 48, 49, 51, 151
Ovid, 3, 74, 207
Ozerov, Lev, 115, 116, 124
Ozick, Cynthia, 180

P. E. N., 190
painting (art), 113, 134, 161
Paley, Grace, 157n.136
Pannwitz, Rudolph, 76–77
Parandowski, Jan, 116
paraphrase, 126–27, 131, 146, 147, 170, 183. *See also* free translation
Paris, Jean, 168

Parny, Evariste, 61
Pasternak, Boris, 7, 8, 16, 36, 56, 57, 60, 79, 102–3, 105, 114, 115, 115n.14, 150, 154, 163, 174, 174n., 181, 192–93, 194
  Doctor Zhivago, 115n.14, 178, 192
  My Sister Life, 134
Paustovsky, Konstantin, 131
Pavlov, N. F., 159
Pavsky, Gerasim Petrovich, 23
perestroika, 17
Perrault, Charles, 1
Perret, Jacques, 96
Persian translation, 118, 173, 207
Pervomaisky, L. S., 135
Peter the Great, Tsar, 13, 20, 22–23, 28, 41, 205
Petrarch, 59, 70, 207
Philips, Katherine F., 25
Pilnyak, Boris, 89n.58
Pindar, 25, 126
Pisemsky, A. F., 159
Pleshcheev, A. N., 37, 38, 142
Plisetsky, German, 183
Plutarch, 46, 51, 203
podstrochniki. *See* cribs, interlinear
Poe, Edgar Allan, 11, 36, 64, 70
  "The Raven," 119–20
poetics, comparative. *See* comparative method
poetry, translation of. *See* verse translation
Pogodin, M. P., 130, 140
Polevoi, Nikolai (N. A.), 41, 47, 52, 99
Polish translation, 1, 2, 24, 37n.50, 98, 115, 125, 169, 170, 173
  from English, 37
  from French, 98–99, 169
  from German, 169
  from Greek, 148–49
  from Russian, 99
  from Spanish, 37
politicized translation, 38, 42, 51–52, 61, 102, 105, 110, 112–13, 140, 143–45
ponies. *See* cribs
Pope, Alexander, 9, 99, 187–88
Poulenc, Francis, 166
Pound, Ezra, 36n.47, 202
Priestley, John B., 7
Prokofiev, Sergei, 166–67, 166n.167

prose translation, 34, 36, 40, 61, 62, 70, 75, 98–100, 110, 113, 126, 157, 178, 201, 203
Protestantism, 23
Proust, Marcel, 13, 130, 161, 162
proverbs, 63, 131, 151, 161, 164
"Prutkov, Koz'ma," 59, 198
Psalms, 22, 23, 126
Pshavela, Vazha, 193
publishing
  Imperial Russian, 38, 49–50, 63, 141, 150
  Soviet, 4–5, 113–14, 144, 153, 154, 173 197
publishing, Western, 145, 188–89
Puccini, Giacomo, 167
Pulatov, Timur, 180
Pushkin, Alexander, 2–3, 6, 12, 14, 24, 37–38, 39, 49, 53, 61, 63, 78, 86n.49, 90, 92–93, 97, 123, 129, 152, 191, 194, 198, 206, 207–8, 207n.71, 209
  Boris Godunov, 207
  The Bronze Horseman, 99
  Eugene Onegin, 6, 79, 85, 92, 101, 121n.32, 123, 149, 151, 152, 154, 191
  "The Gypsies," 10
  "The Queen of Spades," 2
  Songs of the Western Slavs, 198
  Tales of Belkin, 131
Pushkin, Vasily, 161
Putnam, Samuel, 201n.47

Rabelais, François, 2, 8, 93, 161–62, 201, 201n.47
  Gargantua and Pantagruel, 90, 161
Racine, Jean, 29
Radchuk, V. D., 59
Radcliffe, Anne, 51
radicalism, 12, 35, 50, 51, 55, 60, 140, 141–42, 144, 204, 206
Radischev, Alexander, 34–35
Radlova, Anna, 132
Raffel, Burton, 84, 189
Ragoisha, V., 101, 125
Rait-Kovaleva, Rita, 157
Rajagopalachari, C., 169
RAPP, 112
Realism, 52, 55. *See also* Socialist Realism
Reformation (Protestant) 24

regional speech. *See* dialects
Reid, Mayne, 1, 202
Remarque, Erich, 17
Remizov, Aleksei, 89n.58
Renaissance, 24, 81, 200
Repin, Il'ia, 134
reviewers. *See* critics
Revolution, Bolshevik, 3, 111, 137, 146, 155, 191, 205, 208
rhyme, 123, 156, 170, 183
rhythm (in poetry) 152, 155, 179
Richardson, Samuel, 51, 206
Rilke, Rainer-Maria, 93, 115, 190
Rimbaud, Arthur, 138
Rimsky-Korsakov, Nikolai, 208
Robert, Marthe, 118
Romanian translation, 116, 194
Romanticism, Romantics, 17, 27, 37, 39, 43, 44, 46, 53, 57, 58, 59, 63, 74, 75, 78, 86, 146, 201, 203
Roscommon, Earl of, 73, 74
Rosenzweig, Franz, 83
Rossel's, Vladimir, 42, 62, 65, 95–96, 130, 136–37, 171, 205
Roth, Philip, 157
Rousseau, Jean Jacques, 206
Rozanov, Vasilii, 89n.58
Roziner, Feliks, 184, 198–99
Rubakin, N. A., 62
Rückert, Friedrich, 50
Rus', Kievan, 20
Ruskin, John, 121
Russian
  language, 3n.2, 31, 98, 121, 131–32, 133, 136n.82, 158, 168, 171
  translation, 2–7, 13, 15–18, 20, 21, 23, 28–30, 62–63, 77, 93, 97–98, 100–107, 110–15, 130, 133, 136–42, 144–47, 155, 158, 174, 193, 195, 197; from Armenian, 167, 172–73, 176, 182, 198; from Bulgarian, 193; from Czech, 115, 171, 173; from English, 3–6, 10, 24, 27, 34, 45–48, 69, 86, 90, 102, 114–17, 119–21, 120n.27, 124, 128–37, 145, 147, 150–59, 161, 172, 176, 177, 179, 202, 203; from French, 6, 10–11, 27, 28, 30, 34, 37, 43, 45, 48, 63, 64, 90, 102, 130, 131, 133, 136, 137, 144, 147, 148, 158, 160, 161–62,

172, 176, 195, 198, 202; from
  German, 6, 13, 14, 37, 41, 45, 51,
  53, 55, 56–59, 90, 102, 115, 121,
  130, 133, 135, 173, 176, 177, 198,
  207, 208; from Greek, 45, 176; from
  Hungarian, 115; from Italian, 161;
  from Japanese, 168, 173; from
  Kazakh, 168, 172, 173, 175,
  176–77; from Korean, 5n.5, 116,
  194; from Latin, 30, 32, 45, 136;
  from minority [Soviet] languages,
  172–75, 184; from Norwegian, 116,
  173; from Persian, 118; from Polish,
  125, 170, 173, 193; from Romanian,
  116, 194; from Spanish, 90, 129,
  130, 147, 160–61, 176; from
  Swedish, 173; from Tatar, 168, 172;
  from Ukrainian, 170–71; from
  Uzbek, 172, 175
Ryl'sky, Maksim, 170–71
Ryleev, K. F., 49

Sachs, Hans, 115
Salinger, J. D., 18, 157
Sand, George, 62
Sandburg, Carl, 103
Sanskrit language, 92
Sappho, 50
Sardou, Victorien, 55
Satin, N. M., 51
Savory, Theodore, 122–23, 169
Scandinavian languages, 202
Schakovskoy, Zinaida, 93
Schiller, J. C. F., 13, 39, 41, 50, 54, 55, 56,
  58, 111, 115–16, 147, 172, 174, 203,
  207, 207n.71, 209
  Kabale und Liebe, 160
  Maria Stuart, 192
  Ode to Joy, 42
Schlegel, August Wilhelm (A. W.), 27, 109,
  154, 201
Schlegel, Friedrich, 8, 11
Schleiermacher, Friedrich, 80
Schopenhauer, Arthur, 53
Schubart, C. F. D., 55
Scott, Walter, 13, 39, 51, 202, 205
secular literature, 17, 23, 67, 208
Seidler, H., 169
self-translation, 93, 152, 170, 180
Seneca, 151

Senger, Anneliese, 82–83
Senkovsky, Osip, 62
Sentimentalism, Sentimentalists, 27, 34, 41,
  43, 58
Septuagint, 19, 23
Serbo-Croatian language, 168, 194
sex, literary portrayals of, 7, 33, 96, 105,
  135–36, 140, 168, 201
Shakespeare, William, 2, 11, 13, 16, 26, 27,
  29, 36n.49, 51–53, 55, 56, 97, 102,
  109, 111, 115, 116, 131, 132, 136,
  140–41, 143, 164, 196, 203, 207
  Antony and Cleopatra, 53, 115, 203
  Coriolanus, 51, 52, 143, 143n.101, 203
  Hamlet, 34, 47, 49, 51, 52, 55, 90, 99,
    102, 115, 123, 124, 136, 140, 150,
    163, 206
  Julius Caesar, 34, 53, 203
  King Lear, 51, 52, 115, 143
  Macbeth, 49, 51, 55, 115, 116
  Othello, 56, 115
  Romeo and Juliet, 51, 53, 115, 150
  sonnets, 49, 135
  Twelfth Night, 51, 55
Shelgunov, N. V., 50, 50n.99
Shelley, Percy B., 55, 66, 115, 136, 142
Shengeli, Georgi, 63, 79, 87, 136
Sheridan, Richard, 51, 55
Sholokhov, Mikhail, 131
Shukshin, Vasili M., 131
Shveitser, Viktoriia, 193
Siberia, 50, 175, 199
Sillitoe, Alan, 7
Simenon, Georges, 14n.35
Singer, Isaac Bashevis, 8, 10, 139, 180
Sinyavsky, Andrei, 181
Slavic languages, 20, 20n., 22, 22n., 92,
  125, 158, 168, 169–70, 173
Slavonic language. *See* Church Slavonic
Slavonicisms, 42, 65, 128
Słowacki, Juliusz, 37, 193
Slutsky, Boris, 118
Socialist Realism, 33, 71, 83, 102–6, 113,
  148, 209
Sologub, Fedor, 64, 89n.58
Solov'ëv, Sergey, 59
Solzhenitsyn, Alexander, 139, 178
Somov, Orest, 41
Sophocles, 10, 98, 123
Soviet languages. *See* minority languages

Spanish
  language, 3, 3n.2, 43, 129, 130
  translation, 36n.47, 66, 90, 129, 130, 147, 160–61, 176, 178, 203
Spielhagen, Friedrich von, 62
Stakhanovism, 195
Stalin, Stalinism, 3, 4, 32–33, 83, 105, 110, 112, 113, 115, 116, 126, 136, 138, 185, 209, 210
Stanevich, V., 97
Stanislavsky, Konstantin, 78, 103
Stankevich, N. V., 37
Stashenko, Irina, 172
Steinbeck, John, 139
Steiner, George, 8
Stenich, Valentin, 114, 192
Stevenson, Robert Louis, 1, 117
Strand, Mark, 178
Strindberg, August, 10, 202
Strugovshchikov, Alexander, 57–58, 60
Strutinsky, V., 172
Sturm und Drang, 30
Sue, Eugène, 62
Suleimenov, Olzhas, 180
Sully Prudhomme, René, 53
Sumarokov, Alexander, 28–29, 33, 34, 126, 161
Suvorin, Aleksei, 64
Swedish translation, 10, 173
Swift, Jonathan, 137
Swinburne, Algernon, 115
Symbolism, Symbolists, 17, 54, 55, 63–65, 111, 146, 167, 207
Syriac translation, 24

Tabidze, Titsian, 150
Tadzhik translation, 175
Tarkovsky, Arseny, 137, 181
Tarlinskaja, Marina, 126
Tasso, Torquato, 26, 55
Tatar translation, 168, 172
Tate, Allen, 9, 112
Tchaikovsky, Peter, 208
team translation, 177–79
Teif, Moishe, 182–83
Tennyson, Alfred Lord, 114
Thackeray, William, 45, 47, 48, 51, 61, 96, 159, 160
  Vanity Fair, 45, 45n.86, 47, 142, 147, 150, 151

theater, 26, 56, 67, 78
  translation for, 163–66
theology, theologians, 16, 22, 81–83, 187
theories of translation. *See* translation, theories of
thrillers, 2, 5, 6, 203
Tibbon, Samuel ibn, 82
Tieck, Dorothea, 201
Tieck, Ludwig, 11, 27, 109, 201
Tikhonov, Nikolai, 173–74
Tindale, William, 21
Tiutchev, Fedor, 37, 38, 135, 147
Todorov, Tzvetan, 94n.73
Tolstoy, Aleksei (A. K.), 14n.35, 37, 59, 60
Tolstoy, Leo, 10, 35, 56, 66, 89n.58, 97, 111, 191, 202, 209
  Anna Karenina, 78, 128, 204
  "Françoise," 38–39
  War and Peace, 128, 161
Toma, Alexander, 194
Tomashevsky, B. V., 207
Toper, Pavel, 171
translation. *See also under specific languages*
  age of, 123–24
  audience for, 126
  by important authors, 36–38
  collective, 50, 111, 137–38, 138n.87, 144n.105
  commercial, 54, 62
  effect (impact) of, 94–97, 100, 101
  importance of, 2–3, 16–18, 204–7
  originality of, 146–47
  pitfalls of, 118–19, 156, 171, 177, 190
  practice of, 15, 24, 28, 31, 33, 35, 37, 53, 54, 56, 58, 64, 73, 84, 92, 93, 95, 96, 98, 100, 102–7, 109–86, 196
  professional, 36, 38, 48, 60, 61, 115, 173, 180, 189
  theories, theoreticians, 15, 24, 32, 42, 47, 56, 69–108, 109–10, 113, 117, 120, 148, 180, 196
translation in Russia
  eighteenth century, 2, 17, 21, 28–36, 77, 176, 191, 205, 207
  nineteenth century, 2, 3, 17, 31, 36, 51, 58, 61, 64, 67, 87, 90, 93, 142, 144, 147, 158, 176, 191, 205, 207
  twentieth century, 17, 36, 144, 147, 158
"translationese," 27, 27n.25, 127, 128
translators, status of, 188–91, 195, 197

travel, foreign, 45, 50, 117, 148–49, 198, 209
Tred'iakovsky, Vasily, 30, 34, 40, 126, 201
Triolet, Elsa, 93
Trollope, Anthony, 62
trots. *See* cribs, interlinear
Trotsky, Leon, 138n.87, 209
Trouffaut, Louis, 83
Tsoffka, V. V., 42
Tsvetaeva, Marina, 154–55, 155n.129, 193, 194
Tsybulevsky, Alexander, 193
Turgenev, Ivan, 12, 37, 38, 191, 202, 209
  Fathers and Sons, 12
  Hamlet of the Shchigrov District, 206
  A Nest of Gentlefolk, 185
  Sportsman's Sketches, 66
Turkic languages, 27, 106, 118
Tuwim, Julian, 99
Twain, Mark, 1, 26, 117, 157, 172, 209
  "The Awful German Language," 134
  Huckleberry Finn, 1, 26
Tynyanov, Yurii, 89n.58
Tytler, Alexander Fraser, 71

Uhland, Ludwig, 39, 42, 50, 55
Ukrainian
  language, 20, 158–59, 168, 171, 174
  translation, 120, 125, 169–72, 185–86
Uncle Tom's Cabin, 204
Undset, Sigrid, 202
Union of Soviet Writers. *See* Writers' Union
Updike, John, 140
Ural-Altaic languages, 168
Urquhart, Thomas, 201, 201n.47
Uzbek
  language, 167, 168, 172, 174, 180, 198
  translation, 172, 174, 174n.192, 175, 204

Vakhidov, E., 174
Valéry, Paul, 8, 36n.49, 70, 190
Veinberg, Petr, 44, 55–56, 57, 94–95, 134–35, 141–42
Vek (magazine), 55
Veltman, A. F., 159
Venevitinov, Dimitri V., 37
Veresaev, Vikenty, 124
Verhaeren, Emile, 63, 136
Verlaine, Paul, 63, 64, 194

vernacular translation, 24, 25, 28, 157
Verne, Jules, 1
verse translation (of poetry), 6, 40, 42, 50, 52, 53, 55, 56, 60–61, 92, 97–100, 100n.90, 110, 123, 125, 129, 152, 154, 155–56, 201, 207
Viazemsky, Petr, (P. A.), 49, 53
Vidal, Gore, 7, 139
Vil'mont, N. N., 148
Villon, François, 10
Vinogradov, V. S., 196
Vinogradov, V. V., 207
Virgil, 3, 10, 26, 36n.49, 70, 88, 93, 96
  Aeneid, 25, 63, 93, 96, 136, 146
Vladimir (Kievan prince), 20
Voloshin, Maksimilian, 63
Voltaire, 16, 26, 26n.21, 137, 191
Volzhina, N., 129
Vonnegut, Kurt, 139, 140, 157
Voprosy literatury, 101, 173
Vostokov, A. Kh., 207
Voynich, Ethel, 202
Voznesensky, Andrei, 102, 178–79
Vronchenko, Mikhail, 48–49, 53, 57
Vsemirnaia literatura. See *World Literature*
Vvedensky, Irinarkh, 44–48, 50, 51, 61, 96, 142, 147, 150–51, 151n.120, 152, 191

Warren, Robert Penn, 124, 157
Weinreich, Uriel, 91
Western Europe, influence of, 28–29, 33–34, 35, 45, 67
Westerns, American, 69
Whitman, Walt, 65–66, 128, 207
Wilamowitz-Moellendorff, Ulrich von, 98
Wilbur, Richard, 178
Wilder, Thornton, 157
Williams, Tennessee, 18, 123, 151n.120
Wilson, Edmund, 153
Wittlin, Józef, 148
Wolfe, Thomas, 157
Wolff, Helen, 145, 189
Wordsworth, William, 114, 207
World Literature, 4, 111, 191–92, 209
Writers' Union, 112, 113, 114, 117, 193

Yashvili, Paolo, 150
Yiddish
  language-flavor, 128, 157, 158

Yiddish (*continued*)
  translation, 8, 10, 114, 115n.14, 169, 180, 182–83, 194
Yukagir language, 183

Zagar'ian, G., 167, 168
Zagul', D. Iu., 135
Zakhoder, Boris, 124
Zamiatin, Evgeny, 4n.3
Zawieyski, Jerzy, 163

Zhdanov, Andrei, 116
Zhirmunsky, Victor (V. M.), 30, 37, 56, 64, 205, 206
Zhukovsky, Vasily, 13, 17, 37, 39–44, 49, 58, 86, 114, 129, 147–48, 149, 151, 161, 172, 176, 207
Zola, Émile, 73, 202
Zoshchenko, Mikhail, 79, 114, 116, 131, 193

www.ingramcontent.com/pod-product-compliance
Lightning Source LLC
Chambersburg PA
CBHW031549300426
44111CB00006BA/240